INDIA
POLICY FORUM
VOLUME 17
2020

W0227943

EDITED BY
Shekhar Shah
Barry Bosworth
Karthik Muralidharan

NATIONAL COUNCIL OF APPLIED
ECONOMIC RESEARCH
New Delhi

Los Angeles | London | New Delhi
Singapore | Washington DC | Melbourne

First published in 2021 by

 SAGE Publications India Pvt Ltd
B1/I-1 Mohan Cooperative Industrial Area
Mathura Road, New Delhi 110 044, India
www.sagepub.in

SAGE Publications Inc
2455 Teller Road
Thousand Oaks, California 91320, USA

SAGE Publications Ltd
1 Oliver's Yard, 55 City Road
London EC1Y 1SP, United Kingdom

SAGE Publications Asia-Pacific Pte Ltd
18 Cross Street #10-10/11/12
China Square Central
Singapore 048423

Library of Congress Control Number: 2021944299

ISSN: 0972-9755
ISBN: 978-93-5479-049-2 (PB)

Published by Vivek Mehra for SAGE Publications India Pvt Ltd and typeset in 10.5/13 pt Times by AG Infographics, Delhi.

INDIA POLICY FORUM 2020

VOLUME 17

PURPOSE AND ORGANIZATION

This 17th *India Policy Forum 2020 Volume* comprises papers and highlights of the discussions at the India Policy Forum (IPF) held virtually on July 13–16, 2020, the year of the Coronavirus pandemic. The IPF is organized by NCAER, the National Council of Applied Economic Research, India's oldest and largest, independent, non-profit, economic think-tank.

The IPF promotes original economic policy and empirical research on India. The IPF Editors commission both empirical research papers and policy-focused expert reviews, the latter also based on robust, original research. It provides a unique combination of intense scholarship and policymaker engagement at the annual IPF Conference, which reviews this research, leading to its eventual publication in this international journal.

An international Research Panel of India-based and overseas scholars with an abiding interest in India supports this initiative through advice, active participation at the IPF Conference, and the search for innovative papers that promise fresh insights, especially from younger scholars. An international Advisory Panel provides overall guidance. Members of the two IPF panels are listed below.

Papers appear in this annual *IPF Volume* after revisions based on IPF discussants' comments, a lively floor discussion, and editorial guidance provided by the IPF Editors. To allow readers to get a sense of the richness of the conversations that happen at the IPF, discussants' edited comments as presented at the IPF are included here. In a break from the past, when the *IPF Volume* also included a summary of the floor discussion for each paper, the 2020 volume now provides hyperlinks to the video of each IPF session, including the floor discussion with IPF participants. This is both in keeping with the ubiquitous use of digital devices, indeed driven by the pandemic itself, and the greater presence and richness of discussion that videos can afford. Consistent with the editorial independence of the IPF, the papers and associated comments represent the views of the individual authors and do not imply agreement by the IPF Editors, the Governing Body, management, and staff of NCAER, or the IPF Panels.

The 2nd *T. N. Srinivasan Memorial Lecture* for 2020, "Data in Coronavirus Times," was delivered virtually on July 13 by Professor Pronab Sen, Director of IGC India and former Chief Statistician of India. The video of the full lecture is available at the hyperlink at the end of the Editors' Summary. The IPF 2020 timing, 6:30 pm to 9:30 pm IST every day, designed to allow participants to join virtually from multiple time zones, limited the overall time available and led to an early decision by the editors to forego the IPF Lecture for 2020.

In recent years, the IPF has also featured one or more IPF Policy Roundtables, which allow a timely discussion of policy issues around topics of current policy relevance, but where no paper is presented. The 2020 IPF featured two roundtables focused on the pandemic: "What Do the Pandemic and India's Economic Shutdowns Teach Us about Meeting India's Safety Net Challenges?" and "What Do the Pandemic and India's Economic Shutdowns Teach Us about Meeting India's Economic Growth and Jobs Challenges?" In lieu of the usual fifth paper the IPF has so far hosted, this *Volume* carries summaries of the two Roundtables and hyperlinks to their videos.

ADVISORY PANEL*

Shankar N. Acharya *Indian Council for Research on International Economic Relations*

Viral V. Acharya *New York University Stern School of Business*

Montek S. Ahluwalia *CSEP* and *former Planning Commission of India*

Pranab Bardhan *University of California, Berkeley*

Suman Bery *Bruegel*

Jagdish Bhagwati *Columbia University* and *NCAER*

Barry Bosworth *Brookings Institution*

Willem H. Buiter *SIPA, Columbia University*

Stanley Fischer *Former Board of Governors of the US Federal Reserve System*

Vijay Kelkar *India Development Foundation* and *Indian School of Public Policy*

Mohsin S. Khan *Atlantic Council*

Anne O. Krueger *SAIS, Johns Hopkins University*

Ashok Lahiri *Former 15th Finance Commission*

Rakesh Mohan *Centre for Social and Economic Progress*

Arvind Panagariya *Columbia University* and *NCAER*

Raghuram Rajan *University of Chicago Booth School of Business* and *NCAER*

Urjit R. Patel *NIPFP and former Reserve Bank of India*

Shekhar Shah *NCAER*

Nicholas Stern *London School of Economics and Political Science*

Lawrence H. Summers *Harvard University*

RESEARCH PANEL*

Abhijit Banerjee   *Massachusetts Institute of Technology*
Kaushik Basu   *Cornell University* and *NCAER*
Surjit S. Bhalla   *IMF* and *NCAER*
Sajjid Z. Chinoy   *J. P. Morgan Chase* and *Economic Advisory Council to the Prime Minister*
Mihir Desai   *Harvard Business School*
Shantayanan Devarajan   *Georgetown University* and *NCAER*
Esther Duflo   *Massachusetts Institute of Technology*
Maitreesh Ghatak   *London School of Economics*
Jeffrey S. Hammer   *Princeton University* and *NCAER*
Vijay Joshi   *Merton College, Oxford*
Devesh Kapur   *SAIS, Johns Hopkins University*
Kenneth M. Kletzer   *University of California, Santa Cruz*
K. P. Krishnan   *NCAER*
Robert Z. Lawrence   *Harvard Kennedy School of Government*
Rajnish Mehra   *Arizona State University* and *NCAER*
Dilip Mookherjee   *Boston University*
Sudipto Mundle   *NCAER*
Karthik Muralidharan   *University of California, San Diego* and *NCAER*
Ila Patnaik   *NIPFP*
Lant Pritchett   *Blavatnik School of Government, Oxford*
Indira Rajaraman   *Former 13th Finance Commission*
Tarun Ramadorai   *Imperial College, London* and *NCAER*
M. Govinda Rao   *Former 14th Finance Commission* and *NCAER*
Pronab Sen   *International Growth Centre India*
Ajay Shah   *xKDR Forum*
Nirvikar Singh   *University of California, Santa Cruz*
Rohini Somanathan   *Delhi School of Economics*
Arvind Subramanian   *Ashoka University*
Arvind Virmani   *Foundation for Economic Growth and Welfare*

*All affiliations are as of April 2021.

CORRESPONDENCE

Correspondence about papers in this *IPF Volume* should be addressed directly to the authors (each paper contains the email address(es) of the corresponding author(s)). All author affiliations in the papers are as of the IPF Conference. Unsolicited manuscripts are not accepted for review because the *IPF Volume* is devoted to invited contributions. Feedback on the *IPF Volume* itself may be sent to: The Editors, India Policy Forum, NCAER, 11 Indraprastha Estate, New Delhi 110002, or by email to ipf@ncaer.org. More information on the IPF is available on www.ncaer.org, including links to downloadable previous *IPF Volumes* and videos of individual IPF sessions for the past several years.

THE IPF TEAM

NCAER is responsible for the development, planning, organization, editing, and publication of the India Policy Forum. Holding the IPF virtually in 2020 for the first time in 17 years posed new challenges. A dedicated team of professionals at NCAER rose to the occasion. The Editors are deeply grateful to the following NCAER staff for their major contributions to the 2020 IPF Conference and this *Volume*:

Sudesh Bala	*Team Lead and overall coordination*
Anupma Mehta	*Editing*
Jagbir Singh Punia	*Publication*
Ritwik Kinra	*Technical editing and research assistance*
Shilpi Tripathi	*Media relations*
Khushvinder Kaur	*Team assistance and logistics*
Sangita Chaudhary	*Team assistance*
Eman Rahman	*Digital communication and video editing*
Praveen Sachdeva	*Paper production and digital services*

Additional thanks to those who helped with this first virtual IPF, including Sukriti Chauhan, Rakesh Srivastava, Anika Kapoor, Rajender Lenka, and Ritesh Tripathi.

Editors' Summary

The India Policy Forum (IPF) marked its 17th year in 2020 with its first virtual conference held on Zoom during July 13–16, 2020. With the world in the grips of the Coronavirus, the rapid rise of daily infections (about 215,540 worldwide on the IPF 2020 opening day, with India reporting some 553 deaths that day), and grave uncertainty about therapies or vaccines, the IPF Editors had decided in early March that the IPF 2020 would continue as a virtual conference. There was broad support from the IPF Advisory and Research Panels for this—everyone saw the need and relevance of the IPF in these troubled times—and postponing the conference was not an option. To accommodate our overseas participants, especially in the US, the IPF was held daily from 6:30 pm IST onwards.

The primary goal of the India Policy Forum continues to be the promotion of original policy and empirical research on India. The annual IPF Conference provides a unique combination of intense scholarship and commentary on the IPF research papers with a sharp focus on their policy implications. The revised papers are published in this journal and benefit from a wide international readership. RePEc rankings suggest that the IPF *Volume* is the highest ranked economics journal out of India by a wide margin.

As we have noted in the past, over the past 17 years since the IPF was started, interest in India has grown to the point where there is now much more original research on India appearing in international economic journals. The IPF's original goals have also changed, making room for more policy-focused review articles that seek to define the best policy advice based on robust, empirical research. The IPF has also added one or more topical roundtable discussions on issues dominating current Indian policymaking.

Not surprisingly, the focus of the 2020 IPF was squarely on the Coronavirus pandemic, with two papers and two roundtables devoted to it. This annual journal volume of the India Policy Forum contains the 2020 IPF Conference papers, the discussants' comments on each paper, and, for the first time, for the IPF *Volume* summaries of the two IPF Policy Roundtables. Also, in a break from the past, we are not featuring the written summary of the floor discussion for each IPF paper, but instead inviting readers to view the video of that session to get a much richer and immediate sense of the intense discussion around each paper that is the hallmark of every IPF session.

Our Editors' Summary ends with hyperlinks to the IPF 2020 program with onward links to video recordings and all slide presentations made in each

IPF 2020 session, including the 2nd T. N. Srinivasan Memorial Lecture, the two IPF Policy Roundtables, and a special celebration of our 2019 Nobel Prize-winning IPF panel members, Abhijit Banerjee and Esther Duflo. We also end by bidding farewell to one of us, Shekhar Shah, Director General of NCAER, who has been principally responsible for steering the IPF during the past 10 years to its present premier position.

Whither India's Economy Post-COVID-19?

Despite grave uncertainty in July 2020 about the impact the Coronavirus pandemic would have on the Indian economy, Prachi Mishra, then Chief India Economist for Goldman Sachs, gamely took on the assignment to prepare an IPF paper on this topic. The resulting paper was most timely when presented and discussed at the IPF, as emphasized by the session chair, Duvvuri Subbarao, former Reserve Bank of India (RBI) Governor. As carried here without major updating, it also provides a unique snapshot five months into the pandemic of the way analysts were assessing the depth and breadth of the harm the pandemic and its associated lockdowns would impose on the Indian economy.

The author notes that India's economy, already weak since 2016, appeared to be bottoming out by the end of 2019. The RBI had eased monetary policy and had committed to stabilize the financial sector. The government had introduced a large corporate tax cut. Although these did not add up to a vigorous cyclical stimulus that could produce a sharp rebound, as judged by the author, she had thought that combined with better external conditions, India's growth would be back to its long-term trend by late 2020 or early 2021. Then the COVID-19 crisis hit, turning out to be the biggest shock to the Indian economy in a long time. Against this backdrop, the paper presents a synthesis of the author's analysis on the macroeconomic and fiscal implications of the crisis for India as seen in mid-July 2020 and lays out the policy design and implementation challenges India faced for a recovery.

The paper notes the unprecedented post-World War II shock that the global economy was facing. But comparing it with the Global Financial Crisis of 2008–09 was misplaced. A key difference was that the pandemic's fear factor among citizens was not present during previous recessions. The COVID-19 shock was also unique in that the response to the shock, for example, social distancing, was in itself imposing physical constraints on economic activity that were unprecedented in postwar history.

The paper projected global GDP to contract by around –3.5 percent in 2020, almost certainly the deepest recession since World War II, but hopefully also the shortest, as global recovery had already begun. The key risk to global recovery was that the US in July 2020 had not brought the virus under control, as had not several emerging market economies. Compared to the rest of Asia, the situation was worse in India, where new cases had accelerated, especially since the reopenings had started. The situation in India and the US, along with localized outbreaks in several parts of the world, raised the risk of increasing infections as economies opened up further, which might trigger renewed government restrictions, or voluntary changes in behavior, that could weigh on growth.

The pandemic lockdowns, starting in March 2020, led to a sharp deterioration in economic activity in India. After a deep contraction in the April–June 2020 quarter, the author expected the economy to rebound sharply, albeit mechanically, moving gradually thereafter to a lower growth path. The paper discusses how different parts of the economy were likely to recover at different speeds. Industrial activity might recover faster, especially in manufacturing, where virus control might be easier. Sectors where virus control was harder—for example, travel or entertainment—would normalize more gradually and would probably not rebound fully until vaccines were administered to a large segment of the population or effective medical therapies became widely available. The paper's quarterly GDP estimates suggested that real Indian GDP would contract by –4.4 percent, year-on-year, in FY 2020–21, 10 percentage points below the author's pre-pandemic projections and the deepest recession India had witnessed since 1980.

The paper suggests that with several high-frequency economic indicators already showing steady improvement in July 2020, there was a tug of war between improving economic data and the still escalating pandemic situation. The paper notes that this improvement was more likely just the normalization of activity from extremely low levels and not strong evidence of firm improvements in domestic macroeconomic fundamentals. The author feared, rather presciently given the devastation India went through in the pandemic's second wave some eight months later, that the improvements were making policymakers, citizens, and market participants complacent.

The paper points out that the central, medium-term question facing India in July 2020 was about what the key macroeconomic drivers of growth going forward would be. Discretionary fiscal support—defined as targeted support to households and businesses that could revive an economy quickly in times of an unprecedented shock—was tepid in the author's view. Monetary policy had been the key driver thus far, but the transmission of conventional monetary policy continued to be a challenge. The exchange rate had remained remarkably stable in the crisis: the RBI's real effective exchange rate had actually strengthened and would be a drag on export growth. Therefore, while pent-up demand, favorable base effects, and massive policy support in advanced economies driving the global recovery could lift India's economy in FY 2020–21 and beyond, the author was not convinced at the time of IPF 2020 that there were strong fundamental domestic forces that could drive India's growth in the medium run.

Mishra's paper ends with three key risks to India's medium-term outlook and rapid recovery. *First*, India faced the risk of the pandemic not being brought under control over the next few months in India and globally, leading to another round of shutdowns, a large human toll, and further scarring of labor and other markets. *Second*, there was a risk to the domestic financial sector arising out of the government announcing a series of credit guarantee schemes and several moratoriums of principal and interest payments. These posed implementation challenges in India, as was true elsewhere. The key risk was lackluster credit offtake from these programs, while at the same time their building up medium-term risks with regulatory forbearance, leading to moral hazard, higher nonperforming loans in the future, and fraud.

Third, the paper highlights the fiscal risk. With nominal GDP and therefore revenues contracting, the government's fiscal and debt positions could come under sharp pressure. With the interest-growth differential turning positive, debt dynamics would turn adverse. However, the paper notes that market participants and credit-rating agencies appeared to be less worried about the worsening fiscal and debt positions in the short term—in fact, quite the opposite. They appeared to be concerned more about India not possessing the administrative and fiscal capacity to implement substantial fiscal support, which would be a headwind to growth. The author felt that what would reassure markets and avoid further credit rating downgrades was not lower fiscal spending in the short run as many perceived, but a strategy to revive growth combined with a credible fiscal plan and framework for the medium term.

Indian Health Policy in Light of COVID-19: The Puzzle of State Capacity and Institutional Design

There have been many concerns about India's public health and health care systems even before the Coronavirus pandemic hit. The pandemic has tested both severely, raising questions about what a revamped health policy and a public and private health sector should be that can make a difference going forward. In his paper, Ajay Shah pulls together pandemic-related developments in India in public health and health care as of July 2020, evaluates strengths and weaknesses, and provides a public and private goods framework for what needs to be done to strengthen state capacity and improve institutional design to rebuild a better functioning health sector in India. Underscoring the importance of this paper, this IPF session was most appropriately chaired by Rajesh Bhushan, Secretary in the Ministry of Health and Family Welfare in the Union Government.

Like Prachi Mishra's IPF 2020 paper, Shah's paper was not updated significantly so as to serve as a snapshot and a benchmark for thinking about the future of health care in India from the perspective of four months into the pandemic. Remarkably, when seen against the devastation that India suffered in the pandemic's second wave eight months later, the paper's conclusions and recommendations ring even more true.

The paper sketches key elements of how India's health system had fared in the months leading up to July 2020 to gain insights into four questions:

- What difficulties did India face after the pandemic arrived?
- What were the pluses and minuses of the resulting health sector response and of health outcomes?
- What can we learn from the difficulties India faced to be able to inform a revamped and integrated health policy in India covering both public health and private-sector led health care?
- What insights can be drawn from the experience so far for prioritizing health policy in the short, medium and longer term?

Starting with **public health**, the paper notes that in a pandemic, the goal has to be disrupting the spread of the disease. This can be done by testing, tracing, social distancing, and isolating until a population is adequately vaccinated.

On testing, though government-run testing facilities ramped up their work early on, the majority of Indian diagnostic laboratories are private. The government's engagement strategy with the private laboratory sector was weak and halting. The paper notes that there are three distinct testing elements: clinical testing as part of the conversation between a doctor and a patient, testing special groups (e.g., among workers in a factory, which can be used to improve safety protocols), and testing in a neighborhood or a city in order to shape individual and public health responses in that area. All three testing types needed to be ramped up in a pandemic. Simultaneously, aggregate testing data must be released in real time for the purposes of epidemiological monitoring and research, which was also a problem. Overall, Shah sees significant gaps in testing and in using the testing data to drive decisions by public and private decision-makers.

The paper notes that contact tracing requires institutional capabilities, including the management capacity to rapidly increase the tracing work-force at short notice. Tracing is not a particularly difficult problem in public administration. While there are multiple transactions, there is low discretion, low stakes, and low opacity. Contact tracing worked well in some parts of India, but not everywhere.

Enhanced social distancing can help slow the epidemic. The government ran a large-scale communication campaign for informing people about the disease and safety measures, which helped modify behavior. This should be supplemented by good behavior choices by individuals, families, and firms based on fine-grained data about infection rates at the PIN code level. Unfortunately, this data is not publicly released in India. The state can use its coercive power to force reduced social interaction through varying degrees of lockdowns, which is what India did. These are best done in a decentralized way, responding to infection rates in a locality and balancing the trade-offs between public health and social and economic objectives for that locality. The early lockdowns in India were led by the Union Government.

The paper places its observations about India's public health experience during the early months of the pandemic against known principles of public economics. A renewed focus on public health in India and a more decentral-ized approach are needed. Contact tracing as a key pillar of public health needs organizational capability, including the option of surge capacity in an epidemic. Recognizing that the major part of testing in India is in the private sector, and recognizing the market failure here due to asymmetric information, there is a need for multiple mechanisms through which this market failure can be addressed in productive ways.

The essence of public health is a health data system that accurately measures births, deaths, causes of death, and testing results, and ensures that these datasets are shared in near real time with the research community while also fully protecting individual privacy. On research, while there is a case for public funding of scientific research, the paper notes that value for money is maximized when the government contracts with private and public researchers through a system of grant-making and research review. Such an approach would work better than the government hiring scientists as civil servants. At the Central Government level, an effective organization, in both form and function roughly like the US Centers for Disease Control and Prevention, is required. This would need work in establishing the mandate, the law, organization design, and accountability mechanisms. The author ends the discussion of public health by noting that the public health reform agenda will centrally involve the construction of state capacity.

Turning to **health care**, Ajay Shah first notes that perhaps the most important problem in fighting a pandemic is possessing the surge capacity for the relatively simple supportive health care required for most infected patients. The pandemic's later arrival in India compared to the US and Europe, the early lockdowns, and India's relatively young demographics, all gave time to prepare the private and public health care systems for surge capacity in multiple locations.

As it so happens, it is the public health care system that had borne the brunt of health care for COVID-19 in the first four months. This is despite preexisting constraints on intensive care unit (ICU) beds, ventilators, or even the number of specialist doctors in government hospitals. When the surge reached cities such as Mumbai, Delhi, and Bengaluru, this created difficulties, much like those seen in cities elsewhere in the developed world that had not prepared themselves. It did not help that India's health care workforce also faced difficulties through a combination of poor safety protocols, the fear of falling ill with COVID-19 and COVID-19-related health worker deaths, and the problems of commuting to work in the middle of lockdowns. To deal with this, governments needed to contract with the private sector in order to augment capacity that could be brought on line when a surge was needed. The bulk of health care in India is of course in the private sector, and this should have been deployed more fully. But there is also an important market failure in private health care in the form of asymmetric information. Mechanisms for addressing this market failure are at early stages of development in India and need to be accelerated and thought through more carefully.

The paper notes that private health care organizations also faced considerable difficulties. The decline of non-COVID-19 health care activity was an adverse shock to their cash flow. Their health care workforce was also stretched. There was legal risk from bans, lawsuits, and price controls, both in handling current events and the uncertainty about future policies and pricing. This uncertainty and lack of predictability adversely impacted the private health care sector's ability to rapidly expand capacity and lost precious time in the early days of the pandemic.

Health care expenditures associated with COVID-19 also interacted with the difficulties of health care financing in India. While employees of large private firms are covered by the Employees' State Insurance (ESI) arrangements, in practice, ESI facilities are not adequately available for many workers. Government-sponsored health insurance schemes have become a significant part of Indian health care financing. But they face constraints in designing and complying with complex contracting arrangements with private health care firms. Looking ahead, the paper draws lessons for health care on finding private and public mechanisms to address market failure and notes that this agenda is a more complex version of the market failure in testing.

The author concludes by noting that the pandemic has created insights and opportunities for health sector reform in India focusing on public health. While devoting adequate resources to public health will remain an issue, the primary problem according to Shah is that of institutional reform and policy design. He maintains that there is considerable knowledge in India on how to build state capacity, on establishing checks and balances and more accountability, and on coming up with organization and mechanism designs that can help construct capable state institutions and sensible regulation of private health care. This considerable knowledge on building state capacity and using sensible institutional design should now be urgently applied to the field of health policy with the focus on public health.

Inflation Targeting in India: An Interim Assessment

Eichengreen, Gupta, and Choudhary present an interim assessment of the RBI's inflation targeting framework adopted in 2016 and scheduled to be formally reviewed in 2021. The authors, writing some four years after 2016, believe that this time frame is not really adequate to judge a major policy shift such as inflation targeting, but they nonetheless use the limited data available to analyze what changed, and to what purpose, with the arrival of inflation targeting in India. They feel that an interim assessment would be useful to gauge what flexibility the RBI has to respond to the economic damage to jobs and incomes that the pandemic and associated lockdowns were causing. Rakesh Mohan, former RBI Deputy Governor and former NCAER Director General, expertly chaired this session.

The paper starts with a detailed discussion of the evolution of India's monetary policy framework. It includes a useful Appendix table built up from RBI sources that summarizes the objectives, targets, operating procedures, and other explanatory comments on India's monetary policy starting right from 1935, when the RBI was established, to current times, with this period usefully divided into six subperiods. The paper then goes into a detailed discussion of inflation measures, including the wholesale price index (WPI) and the consumer price index (CPI), and asks the question about which series the RBI should be using for inflation targeting. It notes that the RBI had used the WPI until 2014 and had then switched to the headline CPI. The authors examine whether it makes sense to use a core (non-fuel, non-food) CPI rather than the headline CPI. They conclude that neglecting or 'looking through' food price inflation (as in the core CPI) that diverges from the target for an extended period of time can have negative consequences.

The authors next ask whether the RBI's policy decisions are influenced more by the output gap or by inflation, whether the reaction function has changed with the adoption of inflation targeting, whether the output gap and inflation carry different weights in the reaction function at high and low values, and whether the reaction function is different for headline and for core inflation. They estimate various reaction functions. They also ask the question whether policy rates react to the inflation series that the RBI tracks formally, or to one or more of the other CPI inflation series. They find that monetary policy responds to headline and core inflation but not to food inflation.

Next, they compare a range of economic and financial variables before and after the adoption of inflation targeting. They conclude that inflation was lower after the adoption of inflation targeting: CPI headline inflation declined by almost 5 percentage points relative to the post Global Financial Crisis period. They find that inflation, and the volatility of the call money rate, was lower post inflation targeting relative to the preceding decade. They also find no change in exchange rate depreciation or appreciation post inflation targeting. In sum, the authors find that the exchange rate, the stock market, and the call money rate all became less volatile following the adoption of inflation targeting.

The authors then ask whether inflation targeting impacted growth and its volatility. They find no impact on the growth rate and find lower volatility. They then look for evidence of whether the transmission of policy impulses to banking and financial markets improved with the adoption of inflation targeting. They find that transmission to government bond yields and bill rates improved somewhat following the adoption of inflation targeting, but transmission to bank lending rates was weak and had not improved with the adoption of inflation targeting.

The paper's empirical analysis finally addresses the question of whether inflation expectations were better anchored under inflation targeting. They find that inflation expectations declined after inflation targeting. To the question of whether current inflation shocks pass through to expectations of future inflation, the authors find that for the professional forecasters that the RBI polls, the pass-through had declined significantly, but for households it had remained the same post inflation targeting. The last question they ask here is whether inflation expectations feed into actual inflation, and they find that the impact of inflation expectations on inflation has decreased under inflation targeting, which is consistent, they feel, with better anchoring.

The paper notes that the RBI has pursued a flexible version of inflation targeting and remains responsive to output fluctuations. They also find a shift in the central bank's response to actual inflation, so that policy rates respond less to movements in inflation post inflation targeting. They do not see this as a decline in policy commitment, but rather as an increase in policy credibility. Smaller policy rate changes are now needed to signal the RBI's intentions.

The authors conclude by asking the question: How should an inflation-targeting central bank respond to an exceptional shock like the COVID-19 pandemic? They argue that the better anchoring of inflation expectations has enhanced the scope for the RBI to respond to an exogenous shock, despite inflation already running at the top of the target range and the negative supply shock likely to raise inflation further.

Structural Change and Economic Growth: Patterns and Heterogeneity among Indian States and Implications for a Post-COVID Recovery

The fourth IPF paper by Sanyal and Singh examines the relationship between economic growth and structural change in India in recent decades, a relationship that they feel has been relatively underexplored. Indeed, N. K. Singh, Chairman of the 15th Finance Commission, who chaired this session, started by emphasizing how important this paper would be for the work of the Finance Commission. Economic reforms helped India become one of the fastest growing economies worldwide, but its growth pattern has not conformed well to traditional models of economic development. Indian manufacturing has not increased much as a share of GDP, even as agriculture's GDP share has declined, though agricultural employment has been much slower to change. Services, including software and information technology-enabled services, have contributed the most to accelerated growth.

One approach to measuring structural change across subsectors is based on productivity improvements, but the authors feel that this biases results in favor of finding a positive impact of structural change on growth. The alternative approach, implemented in their paper, uses a pure distributional measure of structural change, averaging changes in shares across different sectors. The authors' main results are presented using a Norm of Absolute Value Index of structural change. Indian states are a natural unit for disaggregated analysis, with population sizes comparable to those of typical European or Latin American countries and significant governance and economic policymaking responsibilities in India's federal structure. The paper uses data for 20 Indian states and union territories, covering two decades starting in the mid-1990s.

The paper's initial visualization of the data on structural change and growth indicates considerable variation over time and across the states in the authors' sample. However, to relate to previous empirical work, the paper first estimates panel regressions, examining the impact of structural change on growth and vice versa, assuming constant impacts across states and over time. Bidirectional causality is found, which holds across different specifications and estimation methods: each variable positively impacts the other in a positive feedback loop. Factory growth has a significant positive impact on both structural change and state-level growth. Lagged per capita state GDP levels have a positive impact on structural change but a negative impact on growth. Finally, lagged national growth levels have a positive impact on state-level growth but no effect on structural change.

In the second part of their paper, Sanyal and Singh relax the assumption of constant impacts across states and over time, estimating time-varying, auto-regressive models for each state and each pair of variables. The impact of structural change and growth on each other seems to vary across different states, as well as over time, and is differentially affected by state per capita income levels and national growth rates. It is not possible to assign precise statistical properties to the differences, but some of the results are suggestive. For example, in the case of Punjab, its evidently weak interaction between structural change and growth may be a symptom of being locked into a particular pattern of agriculture. In other cases, the results are less obvious and require further investigation: for example, Himachal Pradesh appears to be a positive outlier in its growth-structural change interactions.

Overall, it does seem that structural change was somewhat higher in the late 1990s, which would be consistent with India's national growth experience, namely an acceleration in the early 2000s. The paper also examines productivity decompositions (limited to labor productivity and not including total factor productivity), but finds them to be not very large, and with gains within sectors larger than those associated with structural change between sectors. Delhi, Chandigarh, and Haryana have some of the highest gains associated with structural change, and Uttar Pradesh, Uttarakhand, Bihar, and Chhattisgarh have the lowest.

The authors infer that national economic policy formulation would benefit from closer consideration of the structural differences across Indian states and the resulting differences in growth responses. Their finding of the positive impact of factory growth on both state GDP growth and structural change is a reminder of the most obvious example of India's failure to achieve consistently rapid economic growth—its industrial sector has remained stunted.

Finally, Sanyal and Singh consider some implications of their analysis for India's post-pandemic recovery as seen from July 2020. As an example, they consider Himachal Pradesh and Uttarakhand, both displaying strong feedback effects between growth and structural change and good economic performance, plausibly associated with food processing or high value-added crops, for both of which access to outside markets is crucial. They suggest therefore that the states' policies for economic recovery must focus on protecting and strengthening access to such markets.

The authors then consider Punjab. If one believes that part of the reason for its lackluster economic record is the political economy of its dominant position in supplying wheat and rice for national procurement, then the pandemic crisis could disrupt that equilibrium and spur policies promoting structural change that can yield higher growth. The disruption of migration from states such as Bihar could also be a factor in reshaping Punjab's economy after the pandemic.

The paper's final comparison is between Bihar, Madhya Pradesh, and Uttar Pradesh, all relatively poor states. Despite similar per capita incomes, their experience of structural change and growth over the sample period has been very different. Their post-pandemic recoveries may be tied to new frictions in movements of people and goods, such as migration from Bihar, or movement from UP to Delhi. In conclusion, the authors suggest that Indian states display very different growth sensitivities to national growth performance. The implication is that states may suffer differently as a result of the pandemic, and their recoveries may also be different as the national economy picks up.

The 2020 T. N. Srinivasan Memorial Lecture and IPF Policy Roundtables

The 2020 IPF hosted the 2nd T. N. Srinivasan Memorial Lecture. Professor Srinivasan, who passed away in November 2018, was one of the IPF's most ardent supporters, not missing a single IPF over its first 15 years. His persistent focus on the quality of data and empirical analysis remains a guiding theme for the IPF.

Pronab Sen, former Chief Statistician of India and Secretary, MoSPI, and currently associated with IGC India, delivered the Memorial Lecture entitled "Data in Coronavirus Times." Amitabh Kant, CEO NITI Aayog, chaired the session, flagging the importance of the topic for the government. Sen highlighted issues pertaining to data gaps in Indian metadata and administrative data, and the serious consequences of such gaps in a crisis like the Coronavirus pandemic. He emphasized that people involved in data design and collection should be thoroughly familiar with the theory and conceptual basis of the data they were collecting and its intended use. Stressing the need for better communication between data collectors, curators, and users, Sen suggested that data systems should be configured to provide accurate, timely information in times of crisis, such as the one the country was going through. Sen's T. N. Srinivasan Memorial Lecture is available on video on NCAER's website: Please see the hyperlinks below.

The 2020 IPF also featured two pandemic-related Policy Roundtables that are summarized in this *Volume*. The first Policy Roundtable on "What Do the Pandemic and India's Shutdowns Teach Us about Meeting India's Safety Net Challenges?" was moderated by Ashok Lahiri, Member of the 15th Finance Commission, with panelists Abhijit Banerjee from MIT and JPAL; Karthik Muralidharan at the University of California, San Diego and NCAER; Renana Jhabvala at SEWA; and T. V. Somanathan, Expenditure Secretary in the Ministry of Finance in the Government of India.

Shekhar Shah, NCAER's Director General, moderated the second Policy Roundtable on "What Do the Pandemic and India's Shutdowns Teach Us about Meeting India's Economic Growth and Jobs Challenges?" with panelists B. J. Panda of the Bharatiya Janata Party; Jahangir Aziz at JP Morgan Chase; Rohini Somanathan at the Delhi School of Economics; Junaid Ahmad at the World Bank; and Ananth Narayan at the SP Jain Institute of Management and Research.

The IPF 2020 afforded the joyous opportunity to felicitate IPF Panel members and long-time supporters Abhijit Banerjee and Esther Duflo for their 2019 Nobel Prizes in economics. Karthik Muralidharan traced the work of Banerjee and Duflo, their role in the IPF over the years, and the way his own professional journey had been shaped by their work.

With this 17th edition of the *IPF Volume*, the India Policy Forum also takes leave of Shekhar Shah, who has led the IPF as its principal editor since 2011 when he joined NCAER. Shekhar has borne the brunt of not only planning, organizing, and steering the IPF at NCAER for the past ten years but has also led the intense editorial work each year in producing the *IPF Volume* as one of the highest quality economics journals out of India. As he leaves NCAER and the IPF editorship, having already arranged the papers and the 3rd T. N. Srinivasan Memorial Lecture for IPF 2021, his two co-editors, the IPF Advisory and Research Panels, and the team at NCAER owe him a huge debt of gratitude for all that he has done over the years for the India Policy Forum. We look forward to his continuing association with the IPF as a member of the IPF Advisory Panel.

The 2020 IPF papers, author presentations, and videos of all sessions, including the Banerjee–Duflo felicitation, the T. N. Srinivasan Memorial Lecture, and the IPF 2020 Policy Roundtables, are available on the NCAER website, www.ncaer.org, and can be accessed through individual hyperlinks on the IPF 2020 conference program available by scanning the QR code below. Relevant hyperlinks are also available at the end of each paper in this *Volume*.

To view the IPF program with hyperlinks to all IPF papers, slide presentations, and videos of all sessions, scan this QR code or use the following URL:

https://www.ncaer.org/IPF2020/Agenda/Agenda_IPF_2020.pdf

PRACHI MISHRA[*]
Goldman Sachs India

Whither India's Economy Post-COVID-19?[§]

ABSTRACT   India's economy was weak in 2019 but appeared to be near a trough. A protracted slide in growth had continued since 2016. The continued challenges in implementation of the 2017 national Goods and Services Tax and credit stresses in the domestic financial sector beginning in 2018 weighed on growth and sentiment. Sectors such as construction, housing, and autos reflected extremely low levels of activity. The RBI eased monetary policy and pledged to stabilize the financial sector, and the government introduced a large corporate tax cut to attract manufacturing activity, among other measures. While we did not believe that any of these measures represented a forceful cyclical policy stimulus that would result in a sharp rebound, we thought that, together, they would help put a floor under the deceleration in growth, and combined with better external conditions, we would see India's growth climbing back toward its long-term trend. However, just as the Indian economy was starting to look up in the beginning of 2020, the rising tide gave way to the COVID-19 shock. Against this backdrop, this paper presents a synthesis of our research on the macroeconomic and fiscal implications of the COVID-19 crisis for India and lays out the challenges in setting and implementing policy.

Keywords: Indian Economy, COVID-19, Macroeconomics, Fiscal Policy, Monetary Policy

JEL Classification: E0, E5, E6

1. Introduction

The year 2019 was a difficult year for the Indian economy, which slowed significantly and sharply, with some market participants worried about India being on an inescapable path to a hard landing. Just

[*] *pmishra0513@gmail.com*
[§] I would like to thank Swapnil Agarwal and Suraj Dhunna for their contributions, and Andrew Tilton for his comments and discussions. By agreement with the IPF Editors Shekhar Shah and Barry Bosworth, the paper presents a snapshot and a benchmark for what we knew of the impact of the pandemic by July 2020 but does not seek to bring the paper up to date with subsequent developments.

1

when the Indian economy was starting to look up after a continued and significant slowdown, the rising tide gave way to the COVID-19 shock (Mishra and Tilton 2020a). In India, the spread of the virus, announcements on the shutdown of important sectors, social distancing measures, and fears among consumers and businesses have all escalated sharply since early March 2020.

There were five pillars supporting our relatively optimistic view on growth in late 2019—improvement in global growth, easing of domestic financial conditions, fiscal support, positive sentiment, and high-frequency indicators turning favorable. In fact, all five pillars dramatically turned around after early March 2020. The Goldman Sachs global team sharply downgraded its 2020 global growth forecasts and was forecasting a global recession (Hatzius, Struvyen, and Walker 2020). The softening of domestic financial conditions since early 2018 had reversed by March end 2020. Although policies are clearly evolving, the fiscal impulse so far is at best moderate and has fallen short of market expectations. The uplift in sentiment that was beginning to play out early in 2020 also reversed, driven by both domestic and global factors. Finally, the early signs of economic stabilization that had been evident from late 2019 also turned around.

Against this setting, this paper provides an overview of the evolving macroeconomic situation in India. Section 2 discusses the global backdrop, Section 3 presents facts on the spread of the virus, Section 4 analyzes the economic impact, Section 5 goes over the fiscal implications, and Section 6 discusses some of the challenges with the economy's restart underway. We finally conclude with some policy implications.

2. World in Recession: Global Recovery Has Begun but Risks Remain

Back in March 2020, the Goldman Sachs global team sharply downgraded its growth forecasts across most of the world's major economies. The global team estimated that global real GDP had fallen 16 percent (not annualized) in the three months from mid-January to mid-April 2020, and by July was forecasting global GDP growth to be at −3.4 percent in 2020, with risks remaining on the downside. This is almost certainly the deepest recession since at least World War II.

Global recovery has now begun, and global GDP is rising (Hatzius 2020). The most striking piece of evidence that the global recovery has begun was the 2.5 million US payroll employment gain in May 2020 and the drop in the US unemployment rate from 14.7 percent to 13.3 percent. Europe has seen active virus cases decline consistently since mid-April 2020, despite a gradual loosening of restrictions. The policy support, especially in advanced economies, has been massive, leading to stabilization in disposable incomes.

The key risk to the global sequential recovery is the fact that the virus has not been brought under control in the United States, and several emerging economies. The US has not managed to control the virus as effectively as the Euro area (Figure 1a). Compared to the rest of Asia, the situation is also strikingly worse in India (Figure 1b), where new cases have accelerated, especially since the reopening started, and now stand at 16,000 per day. This compares with less than 1,000 new daily additions on average in the rest of the Asia region (Tilton 2020). The situation in India and the US, along with localized outbreaks in several parts of the world, raises the risk of a rise in infections as economies open up further, which might trigger renewed government restrictions or individual changes in behavior that could weigh on growth.

FIGURE 1a.   US Underperforms in Virus Control

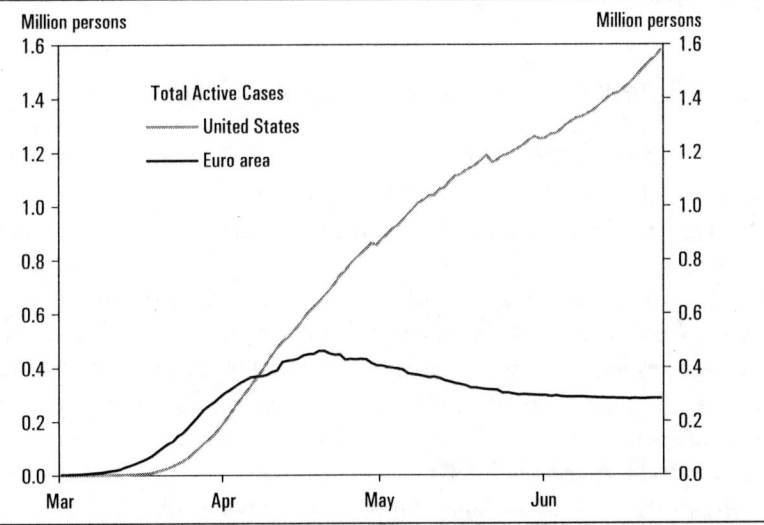

Source: Johns Hopkins University Center for System Science & Engineering, CEIC Data, Goldman Sachs Global Investment Research.

FIGURE 1b.   **India an Exception in Virus Control in Asia**

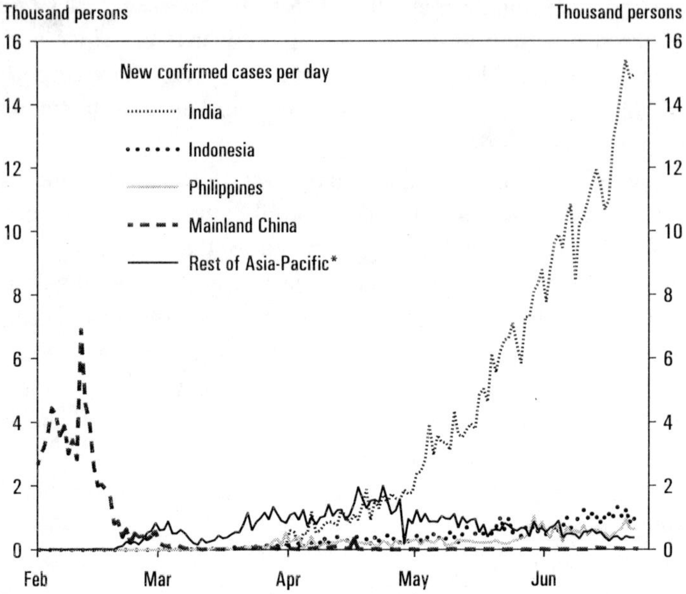

Source: Johns Hopkins University Center for System Science & Engineering, CEIC Data, Goldman Sachs Global Investment Research.
Note: *Economies in Goldman Sachs coverage.

3. The Spread of COVID-19 Has Accelerated in India

The total number of COVID-19 cases in India crossed the 500,000 mark on June 26, 2020. As of June 28, 2020, daily new positive cases also continued to increase, with a record of approximately 20,000 cases added on June 27 (Figure 2).

The silver lining may be that the cases appear to be concentrated in certain states. Maharashtra continues to be the most impacted state, with total confirmed cases above 160,000, followed by Tamil Nadu, Delhi, and Gujarat. Together, these four states still account for nearly 65 percent of the total cases in the country. In total, 80 percent of the cases are concentrated in only eight states (Figure 3).

Next, we look at the total number of "active" cases (i.e., subtracting recoveries and deaths from total positive cases). While these reported a declining trend at the nationwide level in the first week of June 2020, driven by higher recoveries (Figure 4a), they have begun to rise once again. The number of active cases in Maharashtra, particularly in Mumbai, was a key

FIGURE 2. India Added about 20,000 Confirmed Cases on June 27, 2020, with Total Number Nearing the 550,000 Mark

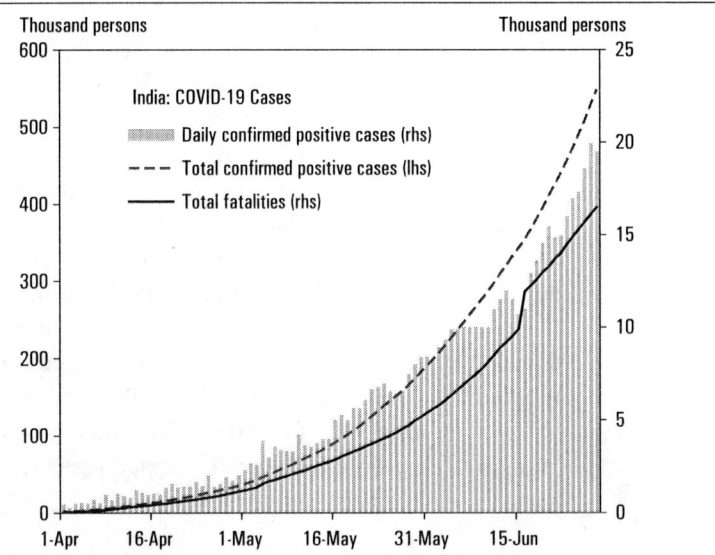

Source: Ministry of Health and Family Welfare.
Note: Data as of June 28, 2020; "lhs" is left-hand-side axis; "rhs" is right-hand-side axis.

FIGURE 3. Eight Indian States Account for 80 percent of Total Cases

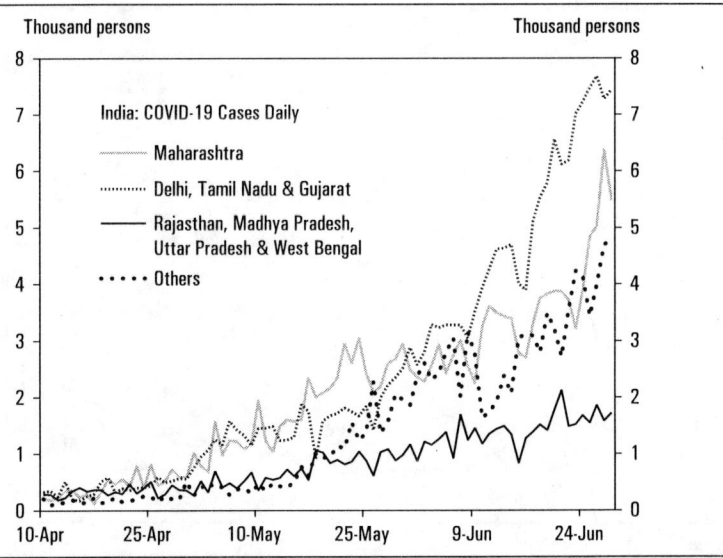

Source: Ministry of Health and Family Welfare.
Note: Data as of June 28, 2020.

driver of nationwide trends until May 2020. Reported cases in Tamil Nadu and Delhi have risen rapidly since then and now appear to be leading India-level trends in active cases.

As the virus spread accelerated, testing for COVID-19 has been ramped up sharply. Therefore, we also look at cases adjusted for testing, that is, the positivity rate, defined as the number of confirmed positive cases as a percentage of total tests. Except for certain states such as Rajasthan, Uttar Pradesh, and Madhya Pradesh, the positivity rate has increased since mid-May 2020. In particular, we note that for Delhi and Tamil Nadu, the positivity rate rose sharply from mid-May to mid-June 2020, even though there was no change in testing strategy during this period (Figure 4b). This could be attributed to the relaxation of lockdown restrictions since May 18, 2020, as also confirmed by the increased mobility in these states measured by Google mobility indices (see more on this below). Testing, on the other hand, was ramped up only after June 17, 2020, after which the positivity rate declined as tests rose at a faster pace than reported cases (the period between May 18 and June 17 is marked by vertical lines in Figure 4b). For

FIGURE 4a. **The Number of Active Cases was Driven by Maharashtra till May 2020, then Led by Delhi and Tamil Nadu**

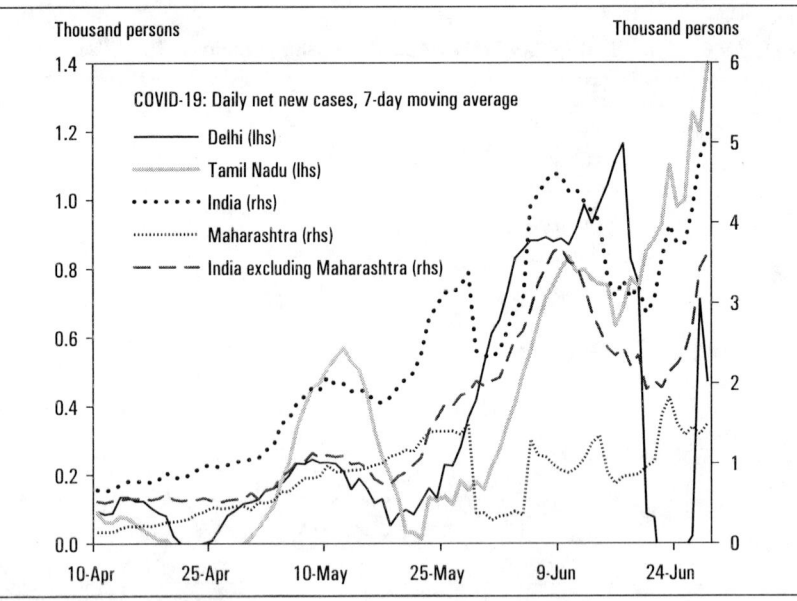

Source: Ministry of Health and Family Welfare, COVID19India.org.
Note: Data as of June 28, 2020; "lhs" is left-hand-side axis; "rhs" is right-hand-side axis.

FIGURE 4b.   The Positivity Rate Rose Sharply in mid-May, though Testing
Numbers Remained Unchanged

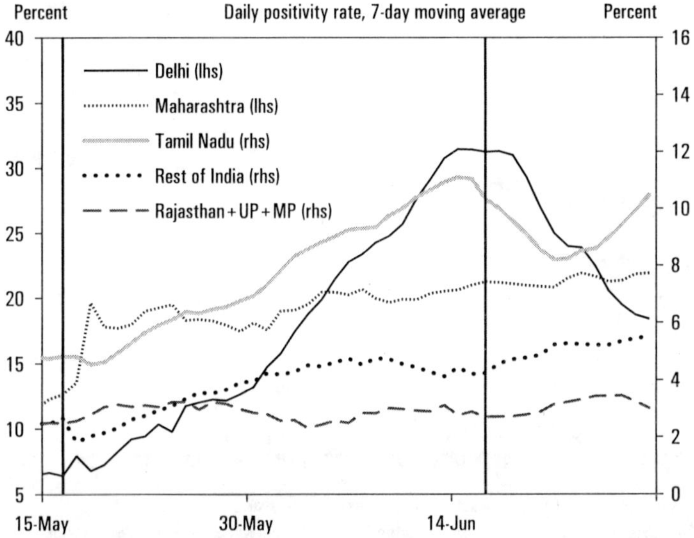

Percent   Daily positivity rate, 7-day moving average   Percent

Source: Ministry of Health and Family Welfare, COVID19India.org.
Note: Daily positivity rate = Daily confirmed cases/Daily number of tests; Data as of June 28, 2020; "lhs" is
left-hand-side axis; "rhs" is right-hand-side axis; the vertical lines indicate the time between when lockdown
restrictions were first relaxed (May 18, 2020) and when testing was ramped up (June 17, 2020).

Tamil Nadu, however, the positivity rate has started to rise once again,
which has been followed by a reimposition of lockdown restrictions in the
four hardest-hit districts, including Chennai.

4. Severe Early Economic Impact of COVID-19 in India:
Expect Sequential Recovery, but Risks Remain

Our baseline assumption is that after the deep contraction in Q2 of calendar
year 2020 (–45 percent QoQ annualized rate), activity will rebound sharply,
and mechanically in Q3. For Q4 of 2020 and Q1 of calendar 2021, we
expect a step-down to a more normal and lower sequential growth pace.
The main reason for this is that different parts of the economy are likely to
recover from the virus hit at different speeds. By the end of Q3, industrial
activity could possibly normalize, especially in manufacturing, where
virus control might be easier, with limited room for big further gains. In
contrast, industries in which virus control is harder—for example, travel

FIGURE 5. Our Forecast of −4.4 percent Growth in FY21 is Very Close to the Deepest Recession between 1972 and 2021 that India Witnessed in 1980

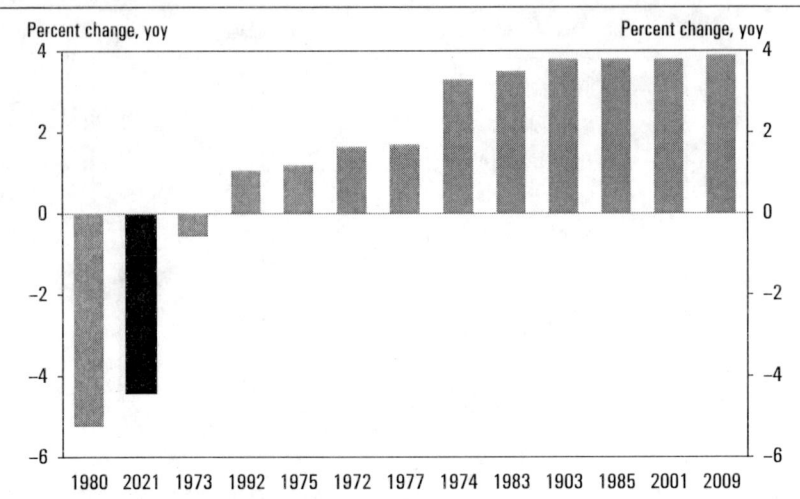

Source: Haver Analytics, Goldman Sachs Global Investment Research.
Note: The *x*-axis shows growth rates for selected fiscal years between 1972 and 2021 for comparison with 2021, shown according to increasing annual GDP growth rates.

or entertainment—will still be in a gradual normalization process, and probably will not rebound fully until a vaccine or another comprehensive medical solution is available.

Our quarterly estimates imply that real GDP would contract by −4.4 percent in FY21. This forecasted −4.4 percent decline in FY21 would be close to the deepest recession India has witnessed, which was in 1980 (Figure 5).

4.1. Comparing Projected FY21 Growth with the Pre-pandemic Baseline

Next, we dig into the components of the sharp drop in growth compared to our pre-pandemic baseline. We expect the impact of the pandemic to work through three channels: decline in India's exports from a slowdown in global demand, and domestic supply chain bottlenecks; a hit to services consumption arising from the shutdowns, virus fears, and social distancing measures; and a slowdown in investment from factory closures, the dip in demand, and supply chain disruptions.

Let us start with our estimates of the effect of the virus on consumption. Figure 6 provides illustrative estimates of how large the GDP impact of these consumption cutbacks could be for India. The bottom of the chart shows

F I G U R E 6 .   Estimated Peak Impact of −30 percent on Monthly GDP through Consumption Spillovers

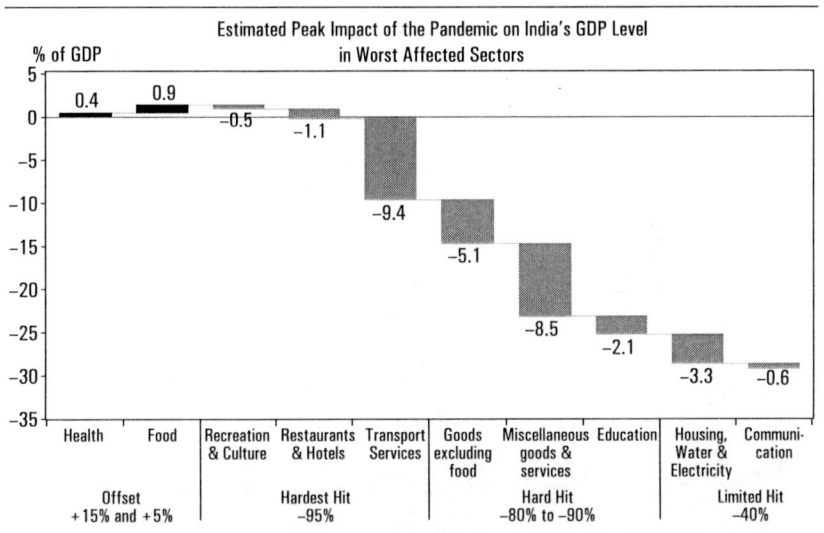

Source: Haver Analytics, Goldman Sachs Global Investment Research.

our assumptions about the peak magnitude of cutbacks—for example, we assume a 95 percent decline in spending on "recreation and culture," and in "restaurants and hotels," and an 80–90 percent decline in "education" services. Overall, consumption contributes 60 percent to Indian GDP. The bars in the chart multiply these assumed cutbacks by the GDP share of each category to estimate the annualized impact on the level of GDP (relative to a no- pandemic counterfactual). In total, our assumptions about consumption cutbacks imply a peak hit of about −30 percent to the monthly GDP level through consumption spillovers.

We assume that these peak consumption effects would last for more than half of Q2. Even if we assume that everything had become fully normalized by mid-May 2020, that would still imply that Q2 GDP would be roughly 15 percent below the norm (half of the quarter would be 30 percent below the norm). Against our pre-COVID-19 trend growth assumption of roughly 6 percent, 15 percent below the norm for the quarter would imply Q2 growth of −9 percent on a year-on-year (YoY) basis. This is with an assumption of immediate and total recovery, which obviously would not happen; therefore, we expect Q2 to report a decline of more than −9 percent in YoY terms.

We assume roughly two months of peak shutdown, and translate the monthly hit to consumption in annualized terms, which would be about −6.0

FIGURE 7. Lower Global Growth, Hit to Consumption from the Lockdown, and Investment Spillovers Explain the Roughly 10.2 Percentage Points Lower GDP Growth at –4.4 percent Compared to the Pre-virus Situation

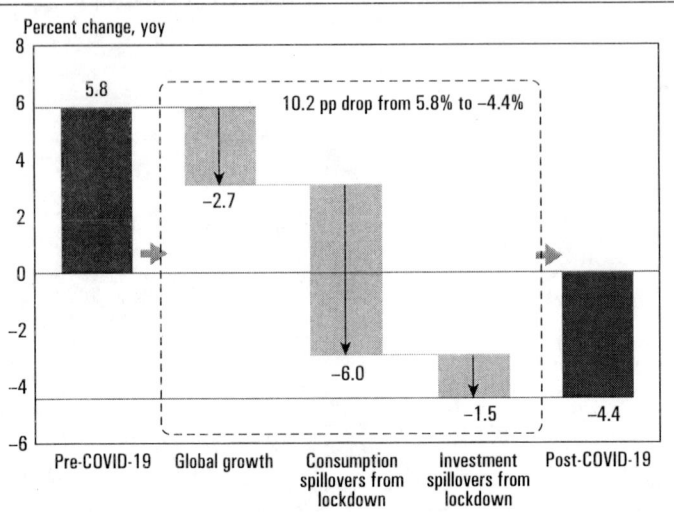

Source: Haver Analytics, Goldman Sachs Global Investment Research.

percent. To the consumption hit, we add the impact on India's exports (–2.7 percent) and investment (–1.5 percent). Figure 7 summarizes the components of the downgrade in growth compared to our pre-pandemic baseline.

4.2. Stronger Mechanical Rebound in Q3, but Gradual Recovery Thereafter

We do not believe that the later half of the fiscal year will see any more rapid sequential growth than we thought previously. While macroeconomic policies have clearly eased, and we expect them to ease further, we believe that policy support, in particular discretionary fiscal policy support (defined as direct support to households and businesses) that can minimize second-round effects of the pandemic and make any economy quickly rebound in times of an unprecedented shock, has been tepid so far. Our calculations suggest that in aggregate, the discretionary component of fiscal support across the seven phases of announcements by the Finance Ministry, including a ₹1.7 trillion package announced in March 2020, five rounds of announcements from May 13–17, and an extension of the free provision of food grains announced on June 30, 2020, stands at 1.8 percent of GDP (₹3.6 trillion; Table 1), which is much smaller than the aggregate figure of 10 percent of GDP (₹20 trillion) costing of the economic package announced by the government.

TABLE 1.   **Total Discretionary Spending Stood at 1.8 percent of GDP during March–June 2020**

Stimulus Package until June 30, 2020	Relief Amount (₹ billion)	Relief Amount (% of GDP)
Revenue loss due to tax concessions since March 22, 2020	78	0.04
Health infrastructure fund announced on March 24, 2020	150	0.07
Stimulus amount announced in:		
Phase 1, March 26, 2020	1,700	0.84
Phase 2, May 13, 2020	5,946	2.95
Phase 3, May 14, 2020	3,100	1.54
Phase 4, May 15, 2020	1,500	0.74
Phase 5, May 16, 2020	81	0.04
Phase 6, May 17, 2020	400	0.20
Phase 7, June 30, 2020	900	0.45
Total fiscal and monetary stimulus announced until June 30, 2020	**13,855**	**6.87**
Amount infused by RBI between February and April 2020	7,985	3.96
Total fiscal and monetary stimulus announced until June 30, 2020	**21,840**	**10.83**
Health infrastructure	150	0.07
Discretionary spending in:		
Phase 1	980	0.49
Phase 2	596	0.30
Phase 3	50	0.02
Phase 4	500	0.25
Phase 5	0	0.00
Phase 6	400	0.20
Phase 7	900	6.45
Total discretionary spending until June 30, 2020	**3,576**	**1.77**

Source: Ministry of Finance, Goldman Sachs Global Investment Research.

Further, our "fiscal impulse" calculation (see Mishra and Tilton 2020b), which captures a complete set of seasonally adjusted quarterly tax and spending flows at the Central and state levels, combined with our assumption on multipliers that vary across different tax and spending items, estimates only a neutral fiscal impulse (of +1.1bp, Figure 8), even after including the Central Government's stimulus package announced so far.

Importantly, the discretionary component of India's fiscal policy support remains small compared with other emerging economies, and far less compared with advanced economies (Figure 9).

FIGURE 8. Discretionary Spending of 1.8 percent GDP Would Lead to a Fiscal Impulse of Only 1.1 bps

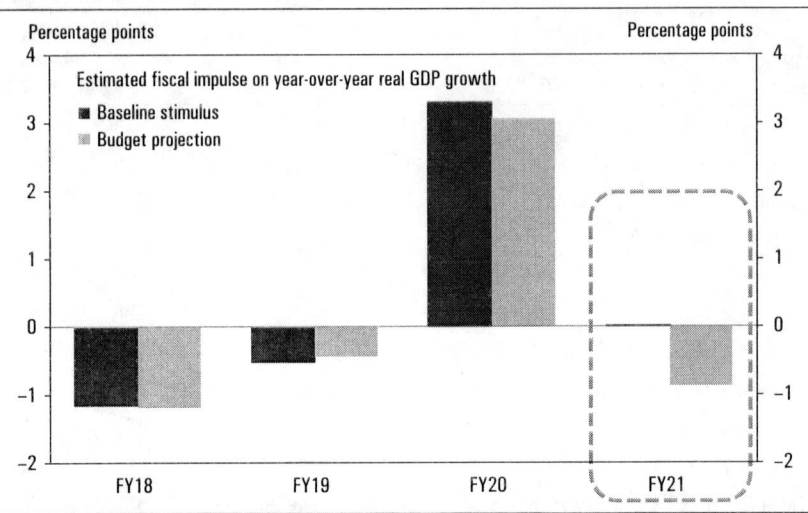

Source: Union Budget FY21, Ministry of Finance, Goldman Sachs Global Investment Research.

FIGURE 9. India's Discretionary Fiscal Stimulus of 1.8 percent GDP is Much Lower as Compared with Other Emerging Market (EM) and Developed Market (DM) Economies

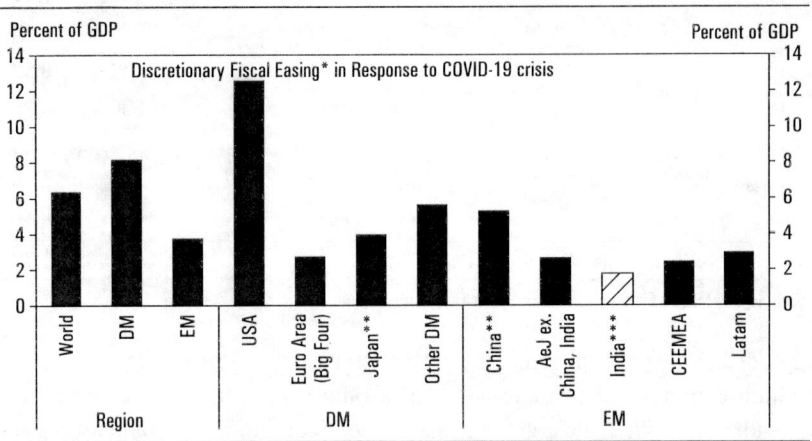

Source: Ministry of Finance, Goldman Sachs Global Investment Research.
Note: *Discretionary policy actions taken since the outbreak that lead to higher government expenditures or lower tax receipts. **Goldman Sachs expected easing. ***Does not include stimulus announced by various states. "AeJ ex. China, India" refers to Asia excluding Japan and China and India; CEEMEA refers to Central and Eastern Europe Middle East and Africa; Latam refers to Latin America.

FIGURE 10.   **RBI has Cut Policy Rate by 115 bps since March 2020**

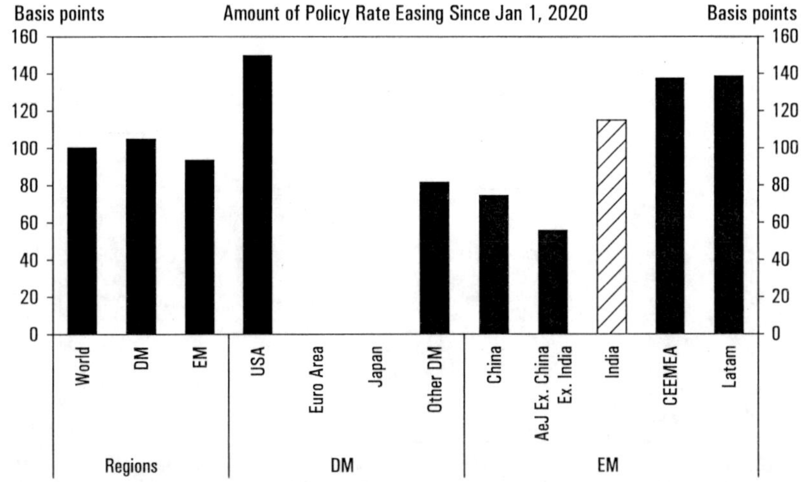

Basis points   Amount of Policy Rate Easing Since Jan 1, 2020   Basis points

Regions   DM   EM

Source: RBI, Goldman Sachs Global Investment Research.
Note: Data as of end-June 2020. RBI cuts are since March 2020. "AeJ ex. China, India" refers to Asia excluding Japan and China and India; CEEMEA refers to Central and Eastern Europe Middle East and Africa; Latam refers to Latin America; DM and EM refer to Developed Market and Emerging Market Economies, respectively. Euro Area and Japan showed negligible cuts as of end-June 2020.

On the monetary side, markets have perceived the Indian central bank as the main game in town. The RBI has reduced policy rates by 115 bps since the COVID-19 crisis hit and combined policy rate changes with other tools such as liquidity injection, long-term repo operations, and regulatory measures. India's policy rate easing, in fact, remains comparable with the average conventional monetary policy support we have seen across emerging and advanced economies (though lower than CEEMEA and Latam; Figure 10).

Transmission of conventional monetary policy, however, remains a challenge. Indian banks have transmitted RBI's prior policy actions, but only to a limited extent (based on RBI data for scheduled commercial banks, since January, the average pass-through of policy rates into bank lending rates and deposit rates is around 40 bps; Figure 11). The transmission of policy rate cuts has been a long-standing issue, and it continues to be delayed and muted in magnitude. Banks have essentially not been willing to cut rates as deposits and household financial savings are at historical lows. Even while policy rates are down, the rates paid by the government on small savings are significantly higher than bank deposit rates. Transmission has continued to be weak, despite the nudges by the RBI in moving from a base rate to a marginal cost of lending rate (MCLR) to more accurately reflect the

FIGURE 11. Bank Lending Rates Declined Only by 40 bps between January 2020 and May 2020

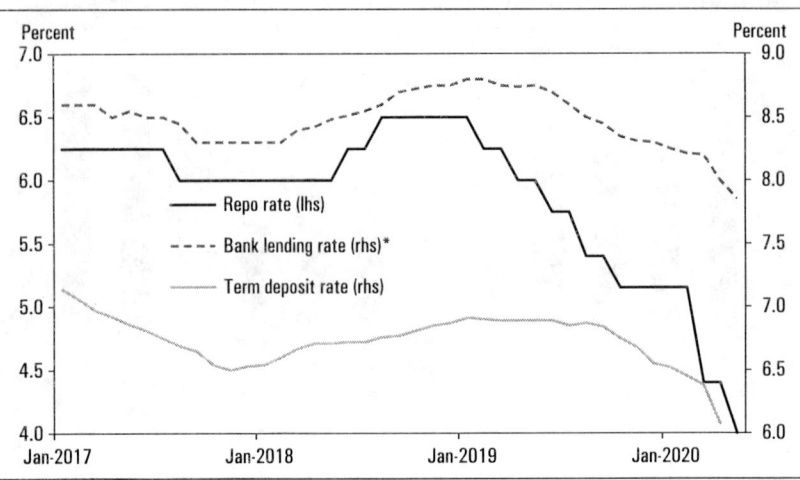

Source: RBI, Goldman Sachs Global Investment Research.
Note: *Marginal cost of funds-based Lending Rate (1-yr) for scheduled banks; "lhs" is left-hand-side axis; "rhs" is right-hand-side axis.

marginal costs of funds, and more recently to the introduction of external benchmarks on the asset side.

Domestic financial conditions have softened considerably following the measures taken by the central bank since the end of March 2020. Figure 12a shows the Goldman Sachs India Financial Conditions Index (FCI), which is a weighted average of short-term and long-term interest rates, equity prices, credit spreads, and the trade-weighted exchange rate. The FCI has eased by roughly 200 bps since early April 2020. The spreads for NBFCs have declined too by about 100 bps from mid-May 2020, but still remain elevated compared to previous years (Figure 12b).

Despite the easing of financial conditions, our overall sense so far is of a less aggressive policy stimulus by Indian policymakers even when compared to 2009, for example, where the shock was different in nature and less severe, but when monetary and discretionary fiscal policies were each eased by more than 400 bps. Despite stronger initial conditions and positive output gaps pre-Global Financial Crisis and a liquid and well-capitalized domestic financial sector, the direct policy support was larger in magnitude. This time around, the initial conditions were weaker in India—a negative output gap and a weak financial sector—when the COVID-19 crisis hit the economy. Yet the direct support from macro policies so far has been strikingly smaller in magnitude (Table 2).

FIGURE 12a.   Financial Conditions have Eased by 200 bps since Early
April 2020

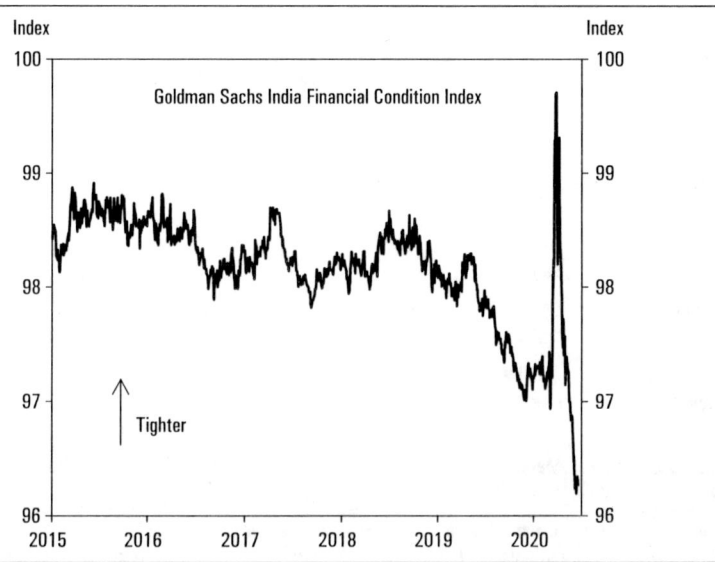

Source: Goldman Sachs Global Investment Research.

FIGURE 12b.   NBFC Spreads have Fallen by 100 bps since Mid-May 2020,
but Remain Historically High

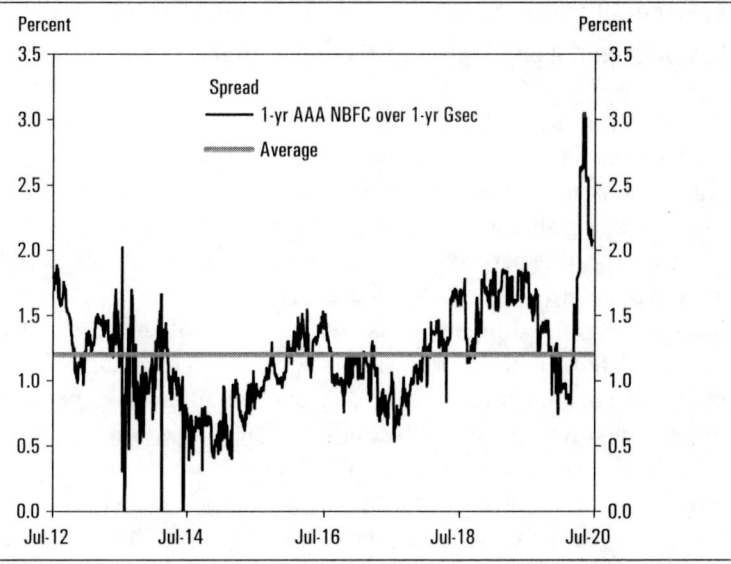

Source: Bloomberg.

TABLE 2. Current Slowdown has been Very Deep, yet the Monetary Response has been Relatively Modest

Recent Episodes of Slowdown	Period	Duration (No. of Months)	Decline in CAI (pp)	Policy Response		
				Monetary	Fiscal	FX
Global Financial Crisis (GFC)	Jun-08 to Jan-09	8	−7.0	−425 bps	+4.3 pp	Unchanged
Post GFC	Feb-11 to Oct-11	9	−3.3	+200 bps	+1 pp	−3.3%
	Feb-12 to Sep-12	8	−2.6	−50 bps	−1 pp	−4.3%
Demonetisation	Oct-16 to Jan-17	4	−2.0	No Action	No Action	−0.7%
Pre-covid slowdown	Jan-18 to Dec-19	24	−2.6	+50 bps followed by −135 bps	No Action	−2.1%
COVID outbreak	Mar-20 onwards	4	−11.7	−115 bps	+1.8pp*	−4.1%

Source: CEIC, Haver Analytics, Goldman Sachs Global Investment Research.
Note: CAI refers to the Goldman Sachs Current Activity Indicator. Monetary policy response is measured by the change in repo rate during the episode; fiscal policy response is measured by the change in general government fiscal deficit (as a percentage of GDP); FX policy response is measured by change in Real Effective Exchange Rate (REER). *Based on our calculation of discretionary fiscal spending.

5. Fiscal Uncertainty at a High; FY21 Budget Framework Loses Relevance in Light of COVID-19 Shock

We expect nominal GDP to contract in FY21 (vis-à-vis government budget expectations of 10 percent growth). This would obviously have dramatic implications for the fiscal outlook for 2020 and 2021. On the tax side, even assuming similar buoyancy in tax collections as originally budgeted for, we expect a sharp shortfall in total receipts. While some shortfall in direct tax collections and Goods and Services Tax would be offset by the recently announced higher excise duties on petrol and diesel, it would at best be partial. On top of the risk to tax revenue collections, the execution of the privatization program—the key linchpin of the government's budget framework—would also pose serious challenges this year. The execution of privatization plans was weak in FY20, as has historically been so, with the government resorting to sales within public sector entities in order to achieve budget targets rather than to private buyers. Asset sales underperformed significantly in FY20 in comparison with what was originally envisaged, yet were pegged at even more ambitious levels for FY21 (0.9 percent of GDP). While the intent to undertake privatization is clear, and we think the plan to sell part of the government's holding in the Life Insurance Corporation is a welcome move, the COVID-19 crisis, as well as weak global and domestic market sentiments, would obviously make it even harder to achieve progress on implementation. On the spending side, the usual strategies to achieve budget targets—lower spending on subsidies, lower transfers to states, and squeezing capital spending—would, and perhaps should, be limited this year, given the contraction in economic activity and the need for fiscal policy support.

We form our baseline scenario where we build in the impact of the COVID-19 shock on tax, non-tax, and privatization receipts, and a discretionary fiscal stimulus of 1.8 percent of GDP. With revenue collections falling short, and the government unable to squeeze spending by as much, we project a Central Government deficit of 7.1 percent of GDP in this scenario (Table 3), 360 bps above the original budget projections.

Assuming that state governments use their enhanced borrowing limits recently allowed by the Central Government, and net borrowing of public sector enterprises follows historical patterns, we forecast that the consolidated deficit for FY21 could reach close to about 15 percent of GDP. This

TABLE 3.   **Fiscal Budget Targets for FY21 Seem Unrealistic Post COVID-19 Outbreak**

% of GDP	FY20	FY21BE	FY21F Fiscal Response Equal to 1.8% of GDP
Fiscal deficit	4.6	3.5	7.1
Expenditure	13.2	13.5	16.1
Capital	1.7	1.8	1.6
Revenue	11.6	11.7	14.5
Revenue	8.3	9.0	8.3
Tax	6.7	10.8	7.2
Non-tax	1.6	1.7	1.0
Recovery of loans	0.1	0.1	0.1
Privatization receipts	0.2	0.9	0.7

Source: Union Budget FY21, Haver Analytics, Goldman Sachs Global Investment Research.
Note: FY21F refers to Goldman Sachs forecasts and FY21BE refers to Budget Estimates for financial year 2020-21; FY20 is actual data from financial year 2019-20; Total discretionary spending, as per our calculations, is 1.8 percent of GDP or ₹3.6 trillion. Assumed ₹600 billion is spent in FY20, rest will be spent in FY21. Nominal GDP levels in FY21BE and FY21F are different.

FIGURE 13.   Debt-to-GDP Ratio Might Increase to 85 percent in FY21

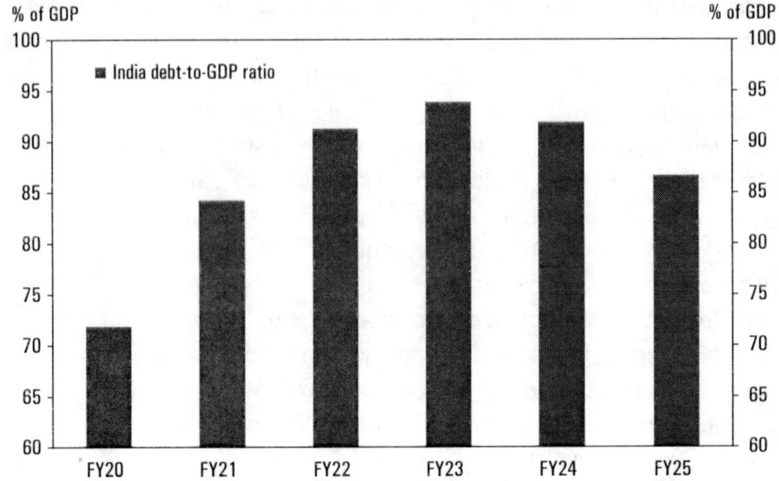

Source: Goldman Sachs Global Investment Research.

would lead to a sharp increase in the government's debt to GDP from an estimated 72 percent of GDP in FY20 to as high as 85 percent of GDP. Going forward, how the debt dynamics evolve will depend on the evolution of real and nominal GDP growth, and the government's fiscal plan. Under a scenario of gradual economic recovery, even with a sharp consolidation in the primary deficit, the interest-growth differential would remain positive, and debt as a share of GDP would continue on an upward path for the next few years. The debt-to-GDP ratio could start to decline from FY24, assuming that the interest-growth differential turns negative, putting downward pressure on debt dynamics, and with continued consolidation of the primary deficit by the government (Figure 13). Moreover, even when debt starts to decline, it would likely be at significantly higher levels than it is currently.

6. The Restart and the Challenges

The restart of the Indian economy is underway. In this section, we explore how mobility is normalizing, how the virus is spreading, and how economic outcomes are evolving across states with different degrees of reopening. Based on Google mobility data, mobility has picked up nationwide since early May 2020, but has remained significantly below normal levels in all states through June 23, 2020 (Figure 14).

FIGURE 14. Mobility has Improved in All Major States since Early May 2020, but Remains Significantly below Normal

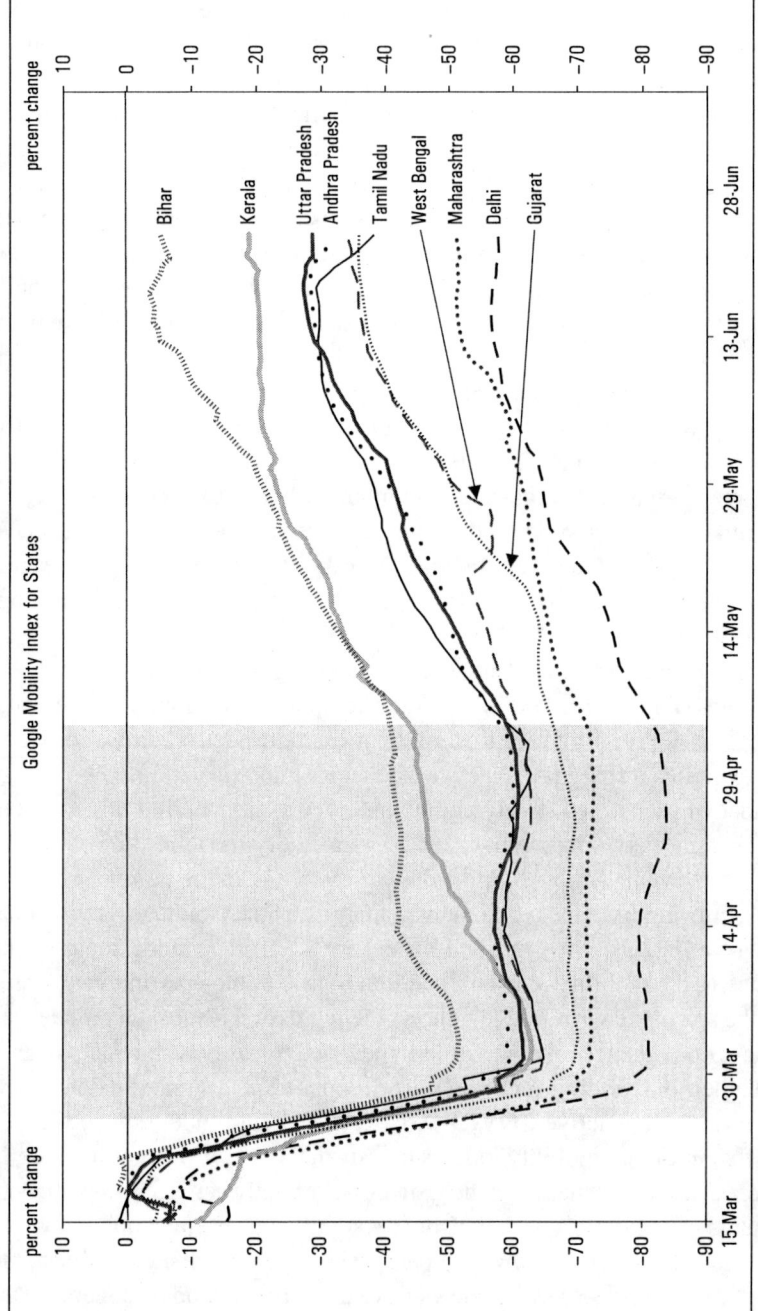

Source: Google LLC "Google COVID-19 Community Mobility Reports."

Note: The Google Mobility Index compares mobility on various days of the week with median day-values from the 5-week period between January 3 and February 6, 2020. The mobility index reported in the figure above is the average of grocery/pharmacy, parks, retail and recreation, transit, and workplace mobility. 7-day moving averages are shown in the figure. The shaded portion highlights the lockdown period (from March 25 to May 4, 2020). Data as of June 23, 2020.

The "de facto" restart of the economy exhibits significant variation across states and also sectors. Across states, Maharashtra reopened the least within a month of relaxation of restrictions since early to mid-May 2020. Mobility, however, plateaued nationwide more recently as cases rose, and in certain states like Tamil Nadu, due to the reimposition of lockdown restrictions. While visits to grocery stores have increased the most, those to parks have risen the least (Google mobility data by activity type not shown here).

But is the increase in mobility causing the virus to spread? In order to explore this, we define the degree of restart (or reopening) at the state-sector level by measuring the change (percentage point difference) in the five mobility sub-indices and the aggregate mobility index between two points in time. These two points are (a) the peak of the lockdown, just before the lockdown rules started to be relaxed: we take a 7-day moving average ending May 3, 2020 (the first wave of lockdown relaxations started on May 4) and (b) mobility data as of June 12, 2020 (the last week before lockdown restrictions were reimposed in several states and mobility began to decrease).

Unlike in several advanced economies, we find net new cases to have risen sharply immediately following the relaxation of restrictions in states that reopened the most (Figure 15). Notably, even after adjusting for testing, the positivity rate rose sharply for Delhi and Tamil Nadu between mid-May and mid-June 2020, coincident with the relaxation of lockdown rules in these two states (Figure 4b). Testing was ramped up only after June 17, 2020, post which we did observe a further spike in cases, especially in Delhi. Delhi also exhibited a sharp fall in active cases after mid-June 2020 due to a large number of recoveries (likely cumulated over a short period of time), but active cases were once again on a rising trajectory in Delhi.

Finally, we fit a model for the daily growth rate in the number of active cases, drawing from the cross-country analysis by the Goldman Sachs global team (see Hatzius, Struyven, and Rosenberg 2020). The model includes the change in the mobility index, in addition to lags in the growth rate of cases and the age of the virus. Table 4 shows the regression results. Our model can explain 66 percent of the variation in new active cases. The results further strengthen our finding that states that reopened to a greater extent show higher growth in active COVID-19 cases. The magnitude of the estimated coefficient on the mobility index suggests that every 1 percent increase in aggregate mobility increases the growth rate of daily active cases by 0.4 pp, which is economically and statistically significant. For example, mobility in Maharashtra increased by 3.84 percent on June 10, which is estimated to have lifted the growth rate of new active cases by 1.45 pp on June 12. This is also evident from the spike in active cases on June 12 for Maharashtra before they declined (Figure 15).

FIGURE 15.   Net New COVID-19 Cases are on a Rising Trend in States That have Reopened the Most

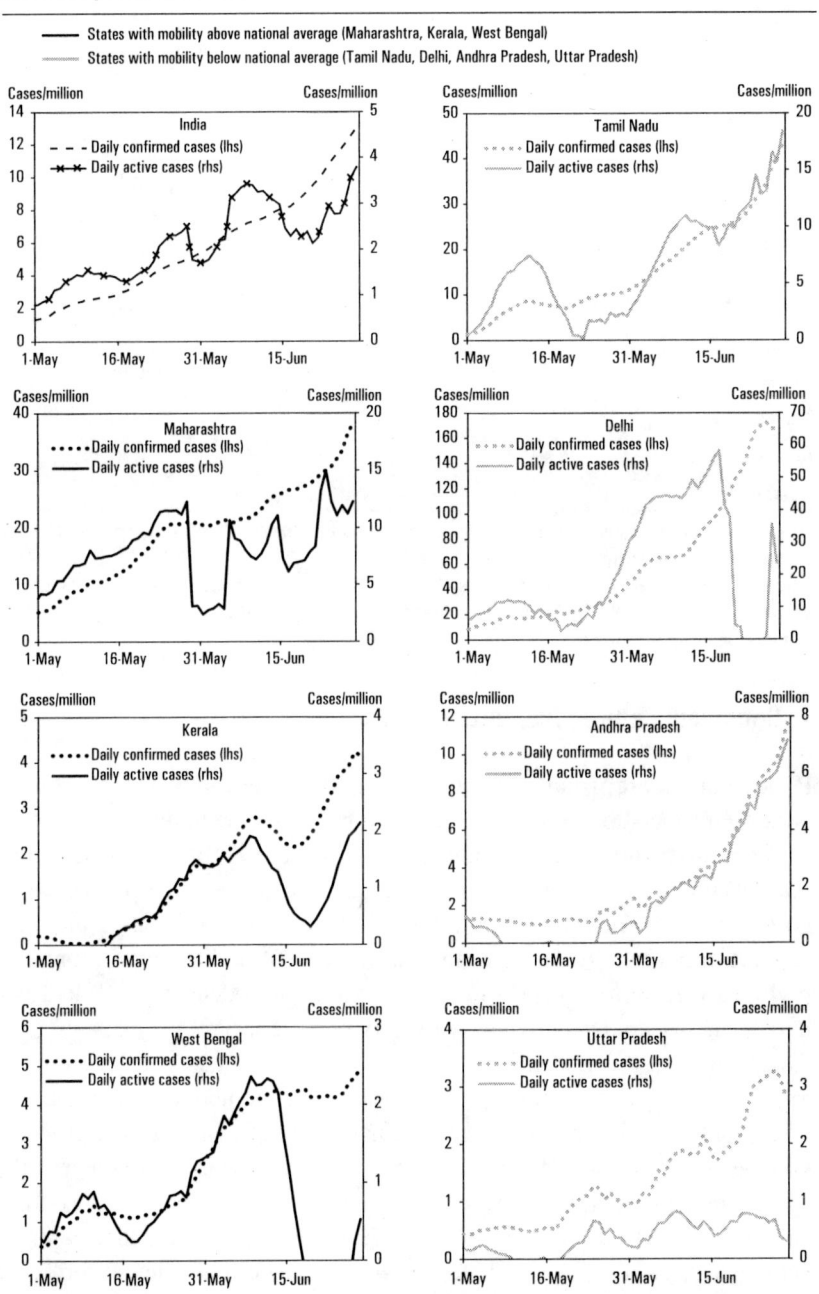

Source: Data as of June 28, 2020. Ministry of Health and Family Welfare, COVID19India.org.
Note: "lhs" is left-hand-side axis; "rhs" is right-hand-side axis.

TABLE 4. Every 1 percent Increase in Aggregate Mobility Increased the Growth Rate of Active COVID-19 Cases by 0.4 Percentage Points

	Daily Growth Rate of Active Cases per Million^
1-day lagged growth rate	0.209*** [3.838]
2-day lagged growth rate	0.182*** [3.321]
Average 3–7-day lagged growth rates	0.187** [2.514]
Days since start of outbreak	−0.061** [−2.194]
2-day lagged growth rate in aggregate mobility (7-day moving average)	0.378*** [2.717]
Number of states	12
Observations	316
R-squared	0.663

Source: Goldman Sachs Global Investment Research, Google LLC "Google COVID-19 Community Mobility Reports," COVID19India.org.
Note: Model built on data from May 17 to June 12, 2020; t-statistics in brackets; ^natural log difference of active cases per million, multiplied by 100; states fixed effects have been included in this regression; $*p < 0.1$, $**p < 0.05$, $***p < 0.01$.

7. Conclusion and Policy Implications

Policymakers are usually focused on short-run economic management issues. But the short-run has to be a bridge to the medium and long run. The central medium-run questions facing India are as follows: Where will growth come from? What will be the key macroeconomic drivers of growth going forward? Discretionary fiscal policy support—defined as targeted support to households and businesses, the kind of policy support that can revive any economy quickly in times of an unprecedented shock like we have seen—is tepid in our view. Monetary policy has been the main game in town; however, the transmission of conventional monetary policy continues to pose challenges; the exchange rate has remained remarkably stable in this crisis, and the RBI's real effective exchange rate has, in fact, strengthened by 4 percent since pre-COVID-19 and would actually be a drag on growth. Therefore, while pent-up demand, favorable base effects, and massive policy support in advanced economies driving the global recovery could lift India's economy in 2021, we struggle to see any domestic fundamental forces to drive India's growth forward in the medium-run.

That said, the uncertainty around the medium-term outlook continues to be very high. There are several unknowns—how the virus will evolve globally and domestically? How successful will government actions be in limiting the spread of the virus? How quickly potential vaccines will develop globally? How strongly and for how long people will choose to cautiously avoid normal activities? And how effective will macroeconomic policies be in supporting the economy?

Overall, we see three key risks to the medium-term outlook. The first key risk to sequential recovery is that of the pandemic not being brought under control over the next few months, leading to another round of shut-downs. The second key risk to watch out for would be domestic financial sector risks. There was a high degree of risk aversion in the financial sector even before the pandemic. State-owned banks, which form 60–70 percent of India's banking system assets, reported no YoY growth in credit pre-COVID-19; nonbanking financial companies were struggling with their own problems after the failure of ILFS in September 2018, and growing loans at low single digits; private banks were supporting credit growth, but ever since the crisis in a domestic Indian bank even private sector bankers went risk averse (see Jain and Verma 2020a, 2020b). Post the COVID-19 outbreak, the government has announced a series of credit guarantee schemes and several regulatory measures with moratoriums around principal and interest payments. All these pose a host of implementation challenges—this is true not only in India but also across the world. The key risk we see is the lack of a significant credit offtake from these programs and, at the same time the building up of a host of medium-term risks in the system with regulatory forbearance, leading to moral hazard, higher non-performing loans in the future, and risks related to fraudulent practices.

Finally, the third risk to watch for is the fiscal risk. As discussed above, with nominal GDP contracting, revenues will likely contract, and that would put sharp upward pressure on the government's fiscal and debt positions. With the interest rate–growth differential turning positive, debt dynamics are likely to turn adverse. Market participants and credit rating agencies appear to be less worried about the worsening of fiscal and debt positions in the short-term—in fact, the opposite. They appear to be more concerned about the fact that India may not have the administrative and fiscal capacity to implement a large fiscal support, and that would be a headwind to growth. What would reassure markets and avoid further credit rating downgrades is not lower fiscal spending in the short-run, as many perceive, but most importantly a strategy to revive growth, combined with a credible fiscal plan for the medium-term.

References

Hatzius, Jan. 2020. *"Global Views: The Deepest and Shortest Recession"*, June 8. New York: Goldman Sachs Global Investment Research.

Hatzius, Jan, Daan Struyven, and Isabella Rosenberg. 2020. "Projecting the Outbreak in the Short Run." *Global Economics Comment*, April 10. New York: Goldman Sachs Global Investment Research.

Hatzius, Jan, Daan Struvyen, and Ronnie Walker. 2020. "The World in Recession." *Global Economics Comment*, March 17. New York: Goldman Sachs Global Investment Research.

Jain, Rahul, and Shagun Verma. 2020a. "Crisis of Confidence to "Crisis of Growth": Navigating a Recessionary Phase", April 1. New York: Goldman Sachs Global Investment Research.

———. 2020b. "Navigating a Recessionary Phase III: Liquidity Stress Scenarios", April 28. New York: Goldman Sachs Global Investment Research.

Mishra, Prachi, and Andrew Tilton. 2020a. "India: Rising Tide Gives Way to Coronavirus Shock." *Asia in Focus*, March 22. New York: Goldman Sachs Global Investment Research.

———. 2020b. "India: Fiscal Policy Budget Points to Drag on Growth in FY21, Likely To Be Mitigated by the Stimulus Package." *Asia Economics Analyst*, March 26. New York: Goldman Sachs Global Investment Research.

Tilton, Andrew. 2020. "A Staggered Rebound." *Asia Views*, June 25. New York: Goldman Sachs Global Investment Research.

To view the entire video of this IPF session and the General Discussion that ended the session, please scan this QR code or use the following URL
https://www.youtube.com/watch?v=XfGmo0TuwIc

Comments and Discussion[*]

Chair: **Duvvuri Subbarao**
Former Governor, RBI

Shankar Acharya
ICRIER

A topic like "Whither the Indian Economy" tempts one to talk for at least an hour, but Subbarao chairing this session has squeezed that down to 10 minutes. So I will make my points in a somewhat more staccato way than perhaps I might have otherwise done. I will not try to cover all the territory that Prachi could because in 30 minutes she could do a lot more. Let me focus on a few points on growth projections in FY 2020–21 (henceforth FY21) and beyond, and some related issues. Let me also say that I think Prachi has been remarkably optimistic. I would not be quite so optimistic.

First, let me say a few words about the evolution of growth projections for the year FY21. Around February 2020 at Budget time, most observers hoped or expected growth to be around 5–6 percent in FY21. After the lockdown began, sometime in April, "institutional" projections from the World Bank, the IMF, various investment banks, credit rating agencies, and others, certainly through April and at least the first half of May 2020, were still looking at GDP expansion, with some positive rate between 0 and 2 percent. I found that quite incredible because, by mid-May, one had seen some awful high-frequency numbers on the economy, and I could see no reason for growth to be in positive territory at all.

So, in mid-May, I published (*Business Standard*, May 14, 2020) a couple of scenarios. I am mentioning them because they are pertinent for comparing Prachi's with mine and those by others. I presented a quarter-by-quarter "guestimation" of what might happen to growth during FY21. In the more optimistic scenario, GDP went down by about 11 percent YoY, and by about 14 percent in the other. By the way, I was not the only one doing this. Pronab Sen expressed similar expectations, as far as I recall, of about 11–12 percent

---

[*] To preserve the sense of the discussions at the India Policy Forum, these discussants' comments reflect the views expressed at the IPF and do not necessarily take into account revisions to the conference version of the paper in response to these and other comments in preparing the final, revised version published in this volume. The original conference version of the paper is available on NCAER's website at the links provided at the end of this section.

negative growth for the full financial year. NCAER, in the first version of its *Quarterly Review of the Economy*, had a number of scenarios, one of which depicted a 12 percent decline and the others were much more optimistic, based on various kinds of assumed policy interventions.

In the subsequent three weeks after May 14, I think we saw a lot of downward revisions in these institutional projections from the IMF, the World Bank, investment banks, credit rating agencies, and others. They came down, broadly speaking, to the –4 to –7 percent range for growth in FY21. I think Prachi and Goldman Sachs came down to –4, but others like the State Bank of India had around –7.

To my mind, what is interesting is that a subset of these projections were actually for Q1 YoY of FY21. That included Prachi and Goldman, of course. She is perhaps the most pessimistic, I think at –45 percent for Q1, if I remember correctly. CRISIL was –25 percent for Q1, NCAER in its revised paper was –26 percent, my mid-May projections were –25 and –33 percent, and Pronab Sen's, as far as I can recall from his paper, was –37 percent. So note that Prachi's was actually the worst, comparing quarter-to-quarter, year-on-year, whereas her full-year projection was much more in the standard, moderate range, not in double digits, as some of us are.

I would be willing to make a bet with Prachi: if Q1 FY21 GDP goes down by 45 percent YoY, as she seems to expect, there is no chance of getting any full-year decline below 10 percent. Basically, my view is that if we get knocked down by the lockdown to the extent of about –25 to –30 percent YoY for Q1, then, scrambling our way up quarter by quarter—and I agree that what is going on is now a sequential improvement each quarter—it will be quite challenging to get down to a single-digit number for GDP decline in the full year FY21.

When we talk about growth during this year and the next, we should be looking not just at growth rates but also at the level of GDP by quarter. This is what I did in my June 11 article in the *Business Standard*. I agree that we will probably see some version of a modified V, and we are already seeing that: a very sharp downturn in Q1, and then a substantial improvement in Q2, which has just begun, of course. But, in level terms, it will be a fairly miserable story. Throughout the year, we may be well below the average quarterly level for 2019–20 in real terms.

The key question is: what will be the point in time when we recover to, say, the average quarterly level of 2019–20? At present, I do not see that happening till the second half of 2021–22, and that is assuming that the un-lockdown proceeds relatively smoothly, for which the current evidence is not wholly reassuring. So I think it is going to be significantly grimmer than the picture that Prachi painted. My expectation is, if we are lucky, that we will get to 2019–20 GDP levels in the second half of 2021–22.

What about beyond 2021–22? This will depend, I think pretty obviously, on what is happening to the global economic environment, what is happening to the pandemic, and our own policies this year and the next. Speculating about post 2021–22 on present trends and policies, it is possible that average growth in the medium term (say five years after 2021–22) in India could be in the 3–5 percent range.

Another point, which arose more from the author's presentation than my initial reading of her paper, is that I disagree with her strongly on the characterization of the fiscal situation. If we use the standard definitions of fiscal deficit and fiscal impulse, FY21 will see a massive fiscal deficit. The combined (Centre plus states) deficit would be, in my view, 12 percent plus, essentially because of huge revenue shortfalls. And as for impulse, comparing to the previous year, we will see perhaps plus 5 percent. Now, the point is that it is not going to matter a whole lot from the GDP point of view since I think the dominant factor is likely to be the supply side during most of the year, that is, the binding constraint is going to be coming from aggregate supply rather than aggregate demand.

When we come to the policies and key concerns, I think we are in much closer agreement. First, I think the key challenge going forward will be how to manage localized lockdowns better than we are doing, because otherwise public policy is hitting supply more than it should. It will not be easy and I do not have any silver bullets because this requires enormous medical knowledge. Second, I agree with the author that the issues of debt sustainability will emerge, with government debt up to 85 percent of GDP in nominal terms by the end of FY21. We will also face major challenges in grappling with the renewed stress on our financial sector, which has been under continuous pressure for quite a few years. Things looked to be improving until COVID-19 hit, and now, of course, because of the lockdowns, there is enormous stress on the financial sector. It will be a huge challenge for whoever is making policy to deal with that.

Finally, let me point out a couple of things that the author did not mention, and which I would emphasize on the policy side as we look to the future. First, I think we need to try to keep a strong commitment to open trade policies. It is not happening; indeed, it has not been happening for the past three years. But it is something that we must try to do because otherwise we gain less from the updraft in the global economy as it recovers. I see all sorts of problems here, particularly now that it is complicated by the unpleasant events on the northern frontier of our country.

We must also seriously try to live by the slogan, "Ease of Doing Business." Business has become difficult as a consequence of COVID-19 and associated policy responses such as lockdowns and continued mini-lockdowns. These have temporarily conferred massive discretionary authority to different layers of government, which is often implemented in an uncoordinated, sometimes unjustified, manner. I am not saying any of this is easy, but as far as economic agents are concerned, particularly producers, the situation is sometimes reminiscent of the bad days of the Licence-Permit Raj. So, we must fight to not let that become a permanent state of affairs.

Vijay Joshi
Merton College, Oxford

This is a very nice, interesting, and valuable paper. My main comment is that it would become even more of a valuable paper if it discussed policy options in greater detail.

I begin with a couple of minor points about the early parts of the paper. I wish that there had been more detail about the employment and unemployment situation because that is important from both a macroeconomic and a welfare point of view. I also think there could have been more detail about the destruction of supply chains since the pandemic is partly a supply shock and partly a demand shock.

I now turn to my main points. The paper contends that (a) the government's discretionary fiscal support is only 1.8 percent of GDP and (b) the fiscal impulse is around zero. These are very important claims. The paper's fiscal impulse figure of approximately zero means that there has been hardly any genuine fiscal expansion at all. However, the concepts of "discretionary fiscal support" and "fiscal impulse" are not very commonly understood by non-macroeconomists, so I think the author should explain them clearly and show with their help why the government's figure of 10 percent of GDP as the fiscal stimulus is highly exaggerated.

The main gap in the paper is that it does not include an extended discussion of policy options at the current juncture. The paper uses the word "tepid" to describe the policy response, and I would certainly agree with that description. But there is a crying need to examine the issues in much greater depth than I am about to do. As I see it, the task before the government is twofold—the first one is the recovery objective, which is to get the economy back to normal working, and the second is the growth objective, which is to correct the drift which has been happening in the last few years and return the economy to rapid and inclusive growth. As the author correctly observes, capital markets are not much concerned right now about overruns in fiscal deficits and debts, rather the reverse. But what they are looking for is a strategy to revive growth that also contains a credible plan for medium-run fiscal consolidation.

On the recovery objective, given the severity of the slump, it is vital to support incomes and consumption across the board. This is so on humanitarian grounds. But, happily, this does not conflict with sensible macroeconomic policy at this point because, with the easing of the lockdown, an expansion of demand is necessary not only to bring about greater capacity utilization but also to encourage the rebuilding of supply chains and, thereby, the return of workers and jobs to cities. Conventional monetary policy has its limits because of transmission problems, so the main action has to be in fiscal policy. In my view, there should be an immediate universal cash transfer of at least 1 percent of GDP, possibly 2 percent of GDP. I say "universal" in order to avoid any problems of identifying beneficiaries, which would massively slow down the process. How would this stimulus be financed? In my view, half of it should be financed in the normal way and half of it should be financed by printing money. You can call the latter helicopter money if you wish, you can call it selling bonds to the RBI if you wish, but basically it is printing money. If the fiscal expansion was 1 percent of GDP and it was monetized to the extent of 0.5 percent of GDP, there would be a one-off increase in money supply of around 2 or 3 percent of GDP.

The usual objection to such a move is that it would be inflationary. But note that oil prices and commodity prices are low, and food stocks are high. Current inflation is running at 6 percent a year because of the destruction of supply chains. However, given the slump, there is a lot of disinflation in the pipeline, and it is important at this point to crank up demand if supply chains are going to be revived. Imports would increase under this scenario, but that is not a worry because we are starting from a current account surplus and the reserves position is very comfortable. The second objection is that printing money could become a habit. But I do not find that plausible, since we now have a credible inflation targeting regime. The third objection is that markets will take fright, but I do not think that is correct. What they are looking for is a revival plan (which also includes a medium-run fiscal consolidation plan).

Now I turn to the inclusive growth objective. We want to have a step-up in growth, and this objective can be pursued either sequentially or simultaneously with the recovery objective. The elements of the unfinished reform agenda are well known. Many people, including myself, have written about it. Of course, any reform program would require not merely greater liberalization but also more public investment, and more social expenditures on health and education, along with fiscal consolidation. How can that be achieved? Note that there is a huge amount of fiscal space that could be available once the economy returns to normal. If we undertake a program for winding up dysfunctional subsidies and tax exemptions, for more extensive privatization, for some taxation of agricultural incomes, and for winding up ineffective social welfare schemes (while retaining the effective ones), all these things put together could potentially yield up to 10 percent of GDP. There is thus no shortage of potential fiscal space. In addition, I would say that it would probably be quite safe to conduct some extra borrowing externally from either official sources or from commercial sources.

In conclusion, there are two paths that the government could take at this point. One path is to play it very safe but that, I think, is actually likely to hinder recovery and continue the drift. The second path is more ambitious: take some risks and use the occasion for some immediate expansion, as well as a complete reset of the economy. My vote is for the ambitious path.

General Discussion

Participants in the General Discussion included **Rajeswari Sengupta, Raghuram Rajan, Sudipto Mundle, Karthik Muralidharan, Govinda Rao**, and **Gunajit Kalita**.

To get a sense of the richness of this discussion, we invite you to view the video of the General Discussion segment of this IPF session. Please use the appropriate hyperlink on the IPF 2020 Program available at the links below.

The session video and all slide presentations for this IPF session are hyperlinked on the IPF Program available by scanning this QR code or going to
https://www.ncaer.org/IPF2020/Agenda/Agenda_IPF_2020.pdf

AJAY SHAH*
xKDR Forum

Indian Health Policy in Light of COVID-19: The Puzzle of State Capacity and Institutional Design§

ABSTRACT   The Coronavirus pandemic has been a severe stress test for the Indian health system. In this paper, we review India's experience with COVID-19 in the first half of 2020. An array of initiatives are required in public health and health care in response to this experience. In testing and health care, the substantial role of the private sector needs to be recognized and integrated into thinking about health policy. There is a need to reform government organizations that wield coercive power or spend public money so as to refocus them on addressing market failures and improving state capacity. There is considerable knowledge in the field of building state capacity in India that can help in this task.

Keywords: India, COVID-19, Health Policy, Public Health, Health Care, Market Failure, State Capacity, Regulation

JEL Classification: H11, H23, H41, H42, H77, I11, I13, I15, I18, K23, K32, O53

1. Introduction

Prior to the pandemic, there were many concerns about the working of public health and health care in India. The pandemic constituted a severe stress test to these systems. In this paper, we pull together knowledge about the events in health and health policy in India in 2020, evaluate strengths and weaknesses, and obtain insights about the grand questions of health policy in India drawing upon these experiences.

* *ajayshah@mayin.org*
§ This paper draws on conversations with Amrita Agarwal, Harleen Kaur, Ila Patnaik, K. P. Krishnan, Nachiket Mor, Naman K. Shah, Renuka Sané, Reuben Abraham, Shubho Roy, and Vijay Kelkar. We thank participants at the India Policy Forum 2020 Conference for insights and ideas for improving the paper. By agreement with the IPF Editors Shekhar Shah and Karthik Muralidharan, the paper presents a snapshot and a benchmark for what we knew of the pandemic by July 2020 and soon thereafter, but does not seek to bring the paper up to date with subsequent developments.

At the time of writing this paper for the IPF 2020, the pandemic had not yet played out fully. There was no single epidemic curve for the entire country; each location was experiencing a curve with different characteristics and a different timeline. When the dust settles, it will become possible to look back and understand these events better. The ideas in this paper are thus necessarily preliminary and incomplete.

1.1. Public Health

Public health is primarily about disrupting the spread of the disease. Examples such as Taiwan, a country of 24 million people that has strong linkages to China and which had recorded a low 449 cases and 7 deaths as of July 5, 2020, hint at the possibilities of what institutional capacity in public health can achieve.

The standard recipe of public health involves testing many people, finding those who test positive, tracing their contacts, and isolating all these persons for a period of time. This requires institutional capabilities for contact tracing, including the management capacity to rapidly increase the contact tracing workforce at short notice. For the country as a whole, perhaps 300,000 contact tracing workers would be required. Contact tracing is not a particularly difficult problem in public administration; while there are multiple transactions, each transaction has low discretion, low stakes, and low opacity. There was significant heterogeneity within the country on how these functions work.

Enhanced social distancing can help slow the epidemic. The first element of this involves better choices by individuals and firms based on fine-grained data about the share of the population that is infected at the PIN code level. The public release of such data is not done in India. Second, the government ran a large-scale communication campaign for informing people about the disease and about measures that will enhance safety, which has helped modify behavior.

The third line of attack in enhanced social distancing is the use of the coercive power of the state to force reduced social interactions through varying degrees of "lockdowns." There is room for greater sophistication in the policy analysis that leads to such decisions. These are best done in a decentralized way, reflecting the infection rate in a city and the trade-offs involved between public health objectives and social and economic objectives. The early lockdowns in India were led by the Union Government. Government-run testing facilities ramped up their work substantially. The bulk of the diagnostic laboratories in India are, however, in the private sector.

There were weaknesses in the engagement strategy of the government with this private industry.

While there is a universal admonition to do more testing, there are actually three distinct elements of testing that need to take place: testing in the context of clinical care (as part of the conversation between a doctor and a patient), testing special groups (e.g., finding out the infection rate among workers in a factory, which can be used to improve safety protocols), and testing in a neighborhood or a city in order to shape public health responses there. When there is considerable variation and shifting in testing protocols and capacity constraints in testing, the interpretation of aggregated data for the purpose of epidemiological research is problematic. Data on excess deaths, causes of death, and hospitalization could be a useful fallback for researchers, but these datasets also have constraints in India. Overall, we see a significant gap between the required systems of measurement and data release when compared with the requirements of private and public decision-makers in India.

There are many scientific questions about COVID-19 that are unique to India. There is a need for a better organized research community that can pursue these questions. In the coming months, one or more research teams worldwide will have efficacious vaccines against COVID-19. The Indian public health community needs to think about the variety of policy questions about how these developments can best be utilized in the Indian context.

These experiences encourage a renewed focus on public health in India. A more decentralized approach, with an emphasis on city governments, will help. Contact tracing is a key pillar of public health; there is a need to build organizational capability, including the option of surging this capacity when faced with an epidemic.

Recognizing the fact that the bulk of testing in India is in the private sector, and recognizing the presence of market failure in this market, there is need for multiple mechanisms to address this market failure. At the level of the Union Government, an organization roughly like the US Centers for Disease Control and Prevention (CDC) is required. This would require corresponding work in establishing the mandate, the law, the design, and the accountability mechanisms for such an organization.

While there is a case for public funding of scientific research, the bang for the buck can be maximized when the government contracts with private and public researchers through a system of grant-making and research review. Such an approach would work better than the conventional path of government hiring scientists as civil servants.

The essence of public health is more robust health statistics. Better measurement of births, deaths, and tests is required, and these datasets need to be connected to the research community while fully protecting the privacy of individuals.

Many elements of this public health reforms agenda involve the construction of state capacity. There is considerable knowledge in the field of state capacity in India—about the establishment of checks and balances, and about organization design—with the help of which capable state institutions can be constructed.

1.2. Health Care

The most important problem in health care, in each country that has faced the pandemic, is about surging health care system capacity for the relatively simple supportive care that is required for most patients. The pandemic came relatively late to India, the lockdowns bought more time, and India has relatively young demographics. This gave greater time to prepare the health care system for the peak surge of cases in most locations.

The public sector health care system has borne the brunt of health care for COVID-19. This is despite limitations in what was possible in the public sector, owing to pre-existing constraints such as the number of ICU beds or the number of specialists.

The bulk of health care in India is in the private sector. There is an important market failure in private health care in the form of asymmetric information between the provider and the patient. Mechanisms for addressing this market failure—private clubs, domestic and overseas accreditation, sophisticated buyers including public sector buyers, and a light layer of law and regulation—are at early stages of development.

When the COVID-19 surge reached cities such as Mumbai, Delhi, and Bengaluru, this generated difficulties much like those seen in cities elsewhere in the world. There is an important possibility that needs to be harnessed, that of contracting with the private sector, in order to augment capacity.

The health care workforce faced difficulties through a combination of poor safety protocols, health care workers succumbing to the disease, the fear of workers about the possibility of getting sick and the consequences of getting sick, and the problems of commuting to workplaces under conditions of lockdown.

Private health care organizations also faced considerable difficulties. The decline of non-COVID-19 health care activity was an adverse shock to their cash flow. Their health care workforce was stretched. There was legal risk in the form of bans, lawsuits, and price controls, both as a flow of events and as uncertainty about future events of this nature. This has adversely impacted their ability to surge health care capacity.

Health care expenditures associated with COVID-19 have also interacted with the difficulties of health care financing in India. While employees of large private firms are covered by the Employees' State Insurance (ESI), in practice, ESI facilities are inadequately present for most workers. Government-sponsored health insurance schemes have become a significant part of Indian health care financing. However, they face constraints concerning the complexities of contracting with private health care firms.

Looking forward, the lessons that we can draw for health care lie in finding private and public mechanisms to address market failure. This agenda is a more complex version of the market failure in testing. The solutions include private clubs, domestic and overseas accreditation, public procurement that has features designed to combat market failure, and a light-touch approach to regulation through law.

2. Questions on Health Policy Raised by the Pandemic

The Indian health system represents a slow evolution from the early beginnings in colonial India. The academic community and the policy community have evolved in their thinking. Health policy has gone through three main phases: from an early focus on public health to an emphasis on government-run health care facilities starting with the Bhore Committee, and then into government-funded health insurance schemes such as the *Rashtriya Swasthya Bima Yojana* (RSBY).[1] Through this period, health outcomes as seen in some standard metrics such as longevity, infant mortality, and maternal mortality have improved considerably, but remain at absolute levels that are inconsistent with a country at the present level of income.

There is a broad consensus on the difficulties in health policy in India. The foundations of public health (i.e., addressing market failure in the form of public goods and externalities) are in poor shape. In health care, the citizenry has begun to exit government-run facilities in a fashion that is similar to the exit from government-run schools that was seen in the field of elementary education. Private health care is now the dominant force in Indian health care. However, the private market for health care suffers from important market failure in the form of asymmetric information. The state

1. A history of ideas in Indian health policy is given in Patnaik et al. (2018).

has retreated into an owner/operator of a network of hospitals with declining salience and has not played an adequate role in addressing market failure.

It was in this context that the novel Coronavirus appeared on Indian shores in early 2020. The following period has proved to be an acid test for the Indian health system. Can health policy make a difference to these outcomes?

In this paper, we sketch the key elements of how the Indian health system fared when faced with this challenge and utilize these experiences to obtain insights into Indian health policy. Thus, we try to address the following questions:

1. What happened in India when the pandemic appeared here?
2. How do these difficulties illuminate the traditional debates about policy questions in health policy?
3. What insights can we draw from these experiences for the priorities of health policy in the coming year and for the long run?

The rest of the paper is organized as a section on public health (Section 3) and a section on health care (Section 4). Finally, Section 5 concludes the paper.

3. Public Health

From the first principles of public economics, market failure in health has a clean split between public health and health care (Kelkar and Shah 2019). Public health is about externalities and public goods. In recent years, the WHO has initiated a "Common Goods for Health" initiative, aiming to bring back the focus in global health policy on these issues (Shah et al. 2019; Soucat 2019).

The field of public health is about state interventions at the *population* level rather than at the level of one individual at a time. This primarily comprises scientific research, the statistical system in health, combating communicable disease (e.g., eradicating some diseases, fighting epidemics and disease vectors, disrupting disease transmission) and creating conditions in which morbidity will be reduced (e.g., improving air quality in North India). Going beyond the narrow confines of health policy, there is an array of fields in public policy that should be viewed as being part of the field of public health, areas such as water, sanitation, air quality, and road safety, among others.

Public health is largely about the prevention of ill health and not about curing people. There is an essential role for the state in public health. It is hard to envision coping mechanisms through which private persons can overcome failures of public health. The puzzles of public health are largely problems of state capacity; the expenditures involved in public health are relatively modest.

There is considerable interest in India in *health care*, including primary health care. Health care is, however, largely a private good, with some kinds of market failure (asymmetric information, when faced with a private producer, and positive externalities when communicable disease transmission is diminished). Health care and primary health care are distinct from public health.

In this section, we focus on public health, the population-scale activities of the state that combat market failures of public goods and externalities. The six big issues that have confronted Indian public health in 2020 are contact tracing, social distancing, testing, the statistical system, medical research, and the coming vaccines.

3.1. Institutional Capacity for Contact Tracing

The machinery of public health when faced with an epidemic consists of testing a large number of persons, finding persons who are infected, tracing their contacts, isolating and testing their contacts, and treating the sick. Through this, the epidemic is contained.

A critical step in this is contact tracing, which requires complex organizational capability. Contact tracing requires a large workforce. A rough estimate suggests that India may require a contact tracing workforce for COVID-19 of about 0.3 million individuals for the entire country, or about 0.1 million individuals if this is done in the dense cities that add up to a third of the population.[2] This correspondingly calls for management capacity to overcome principal–agent problems and get frontline workers to be effective. It involves writing process manuals, training staff, and establishing oversight to monitor their work.

In the class of problems in public policy, contact tracing is not a particularly difficult challenge for achieving state capacity. It is useful to think about this problem from the classification framework of Pritchett and

---

2. The values per 100,000 of population for some countries are as follows: the USA's requirement is 66, Germany's is 25, the UK's is 37, and Iceland's is 14 (Luo et al. 2020; Morris and Beck 2020; Triggle 2020); if we use a value for India of about 25 per 100,000, this scales up to an overall headcount of 337,500.

Woolcock (2004), as extended by Kelkar and Shah (2019), which determines the complexity of building state capacity on a given problem by asking the following four questions:

1. *Are there a lot of transactions?* Contact tracing involves a high number of transactions.
2. *Is there a lot of discretion with frontline workers?* Contact tracing involves low discretion in the hands of frontline workers.
3. *Are the stakes high?* In contact tracing, the stakes are low; the decisions of frontline workers cannot have a large impact on an individual.
4. *Is there opacity?* It is possible to do contact tracing under conditions of high transparency.

By this reasoning, contact tracing meets one test of what creates difficulty in building state capacity: it involves a lot of transactions. As with other transaction-intensive problems in Indian public administration, there is the ever-present danger of frontline workers sinking into apathy or becoming overbearing (Parsheera 2020). Some of the ideas about how this can work, which are well understood elsewhere in the world, do not port readily to most Indian settings; for example, Sané (2020) draws attention to the difficulties of ensuring isolation of infected persons in crowded Indian cities.

The public administration challenge with contact tracing for COVID-19 was accentuated by the fact that in most of India institutional capacity for contact tracing was either fledgling or absent, and there was a need to build or scale this in merely one or two months.[3] This is a unique dimension in the public administration challenge, one that has not been part of the reasoning around the framework of transactions-discretion-stakes-transparency mentioned above.

Contact tracing for COVID-19 seems to have fared better in some states such as Kerala and Tamil Nadu, and it is important to understand how this was achieved (Das et al. 2020; Isaac and Sadanandan 2020; Sadanandan 2020). These states have foundations of public health in terms

---

3. In early February 2020, the first newspaper columns about the concerns about COVID-19 were appearing in India. Sethi and Shrivastava (2020) document two papers by government scientists in the *Indian Journal of Medical Research* which appeared in the last week of February. In early March, some health policy papers started appearing (e.g., Kelkar and Shah 2020; Rajagopalan and Tabarrok 2020; Shah 2020a), and the first nationwide lockdown began on March 25, 2020.

of organizational structures and laws of the kind that are not seen elsewhere in India.[4] At the same time, given the large differences in local conditions all across India, it is not easy to directly transplant the institutional design of public health in Kerala or Tamil Nadu into many other states. This is a problem that requires careful local solutions, one city at a time.

Given the difficulties of building state capacity for public health in the form of organizational capability to do contact tracing, there was some initial attraction to a technology-intensive solution: an application on a mobile phone that would keep track of every person-to-person contact, so that once a positive result is obtained, a central computer database would be able to show all the individuals who have been met in recent weeks. However, such an application is no substitute for the painstaking work of contact tracing by a large field force of trained contact tracing staff. In addition, there are many concerns associated with personal information being visible to the Indian State (Bhandari and Rahman 2020). There is a need to focus on process engineering for contact tracing, where the development of applications is an element of institution-building for contact tracing.

3.2. Social Distancing

Enhanced social distancing is an important mechanism through which human societies modify the dynamics of an epidemic and create incentives for pathogens to evolve towards reduced virulence.

The first element of this is the optimization by each individual (Cochrane 2020). Each individual has an assessment about their own trade-offs and manages the tension between the health hazard and the economic/social imperative. Different persons will face different trade-offs. The first line of attack in public health must be to earn the trust of the populace, deliver accurate knowledge to the people, and obtain gains from non-coerced modification of behavior. These individual decisions will be supported by better knowledge about mechanisms of virus propagation, better estimates of the conditional probability of grave illness or death, and neighborhood-specific updated data about the extent of infection. These three elements of knowledge are a public good, and there is a case for state provision. Alongside this, there is a need for a communication strategy, which can take this knowledge and send accurate and consistent messages on a population scale.

In India, there was fair access to information about virus propagation and the conditional probability of grave illness or death based on international

---

4. For example, there are public health laws in these states in the form of the Tamil Nadu Public Health Act, 1939, and the Travancore Cochin Public Health Act, 1955.

experience. The government ran large-scale information communication programs, and these appear to have been effective. There was relatively little information about India-specific questions, for example, the links between COVID-19 and spitting *paan*. Similarly, an article such as Thomas (2020) utilizes papers done elsewhere in the world to illuminate what might happen under Indian conditions of temperature, humidity, and insolation, but little research was available under Indian conditions that directly informed decision-making in India.

When an individual chooses to engage in economic and social activities, there is a small negative externality that is imposed upon others. The magnitude of this negative externality is proportional to the infection rate prevalent at each point in time. In order to correct for this market failure, there is a case for using the coercive power of the state to force reduced social interactions.

In the limit, this leads to ideas such as lockdowns. While extreme measures might sometimes appear attractive, it is important to bring logic and evidence to analyzing a lockdown (Melnick and Ioannidis 2020). For an analogy with cholera, though cholera is a waterborne disease, closing down the water supply of a city is not a wise path to control cholera.

Some countries have used lockdowns to successfully control the COVID-19 epidemic (Baker et al. 2020), but these were small populations with high state capacity. Asymptomatic transmission poses serious challenges for lockdown policies (Gandhi et al. 2020), which suggests that lockdowns are useful either when they are done very early, or when they are accompanied by very large-scale testing–tracing–isolation. An overall analysis (Islam et al. 2020) suggests that earlier and longer lockdowns were associated with reduced spread of the disease. However, conditions in India (high density housing, low state capacity in testing–tracing–isolating, and the economic imperative for many households to obtain an income) suggest that controlling the epidemic through lockdowns was going to be hard. A second class of arguments in favor of a lockdown is based on the objective of gearing up with increased health care capacity.

There are complex puzzles in addressing the trade-offs faced in such regulation. Using state power to close temples and bars appears reasonable. As an example, the "Ashadh pilgrimage" in Pandharpur, Maharashtra, was closed for the first time after 1944 in 2020. In contrast, the Kumbh Mela in Haridwar, Uttarakhand, which was scheduled for 2022, was moved to March/April 2021. In many other respects, the picture is less clear. There is a case for decentralized action that utilizes local data for the infection rate, weighs trade-offs in a way that is sensitive to local conditions of economic and social life, engages in a cost-benefit analysis, achieves democratic legitimacy through consultation and the display of expertise, and emerges with the cautious use of state coercion to increase social distancing, over and beyond the rational decisions of individuals.

The use of the coercive power of the state in forcing social distancing rules faces pitfalls in India owing to foundational difficulties on civil liberties. These weaknesses in the "invisible infrastructure" shape health policy thinking in India, while they are not a concern in mature liberal democracies. As an example, few health policy experts could have anticipated the episode in Tamil Nadu, where two persons were arrested for allegedly keeping their shop open for 15 minutes more than the time allowed in a lockdown and died in police custody.

In the Indian story, decisions about the design of social distancing regulations were taken at the Union Government level and not in cities; there was insufficient information available about the true infection rate, and a high extent of coercion was applied. It was hard to see a sophisticated analysis of trade-offs. These problems are related to the lack of checks and balances in the Epidemic Diseases Act, 1897, and the Disaster Management Act, 2005 (Kaur 2020; Kumar 2020; Shah 2020c).

The lockdowns in India helped in gearing up the public sector health care system in terms of things such as PPEs, ventilators, and training. Most of the guidelines published by the Ministry of Health and Family Welfare came out after March 23, 2020. Alongside these successful elements, there was slow progress on engaging with the private sector, which holds the key to scaling up health care and testing. Improvements in the measurement of COVID-19, which could have been established during the lockdown, were limited.

3.3. Testing

Government-run testing facilities were significantly enhanced in response to the pandemic. The throughput through these labs went up dramatically once that happened. However, the bulk of testing capacity in India is in the private sector, particularly in the West and the South. The business of testing contains a market failure, asymmetric information, as it is hard for the customer to know the extent to which the test is accurate. There were long-standing gaps in private and public initiatives that could address this market failure. There is an interesting tension between state power and a private health care system. One element of this was seen in diagnostic laboratories, which do testing. This is analyzed in Kaur et al. (2020). There was a process of obtaining approvals through which the government gave approvals to over 200 private laboratories and only thereafter did testing in private laboratories start.

When the pandemic started, the Indian Council of Medical Research (ICMR) was thrust into a regulatory role on testing. ICMR is primarily a research organization, and it did not have the organizational capacity for regulation of a private industry. The laws that were employed for the purpose (the Epidemic Diseases Act, 1897, and the Disaster Management Act, 2005) lacked checks and balances, and were, therefore, not conducive to the development of state capacity (Kaur 2020; Kumar 2020). ICMR and other state organizations drifted into an intrusive command-and-control approach toward private testing, featuring bans, price controls, and interference in the management choices of private persons. These intrusive actions are generally inefficient.

One pathway to utilizing the testing capacity in the private sector is public procurement. The government could become a large-scale purchaser of the services of private diagnostic laboratories. This procurement process can include elements that address market failure, for example, it can ensure minimal quality standards.

3.4. Statistical System in Health

A key function in public health is obtaining high-quality information about the state of health in the country. A statistical system needs to be constructed in health featuring microdata from all across the country, where the information is timely. Statistical analysis of this data would then reveal outbreaks, epidemics, and pockets of unusual morbidity, which can kick off investigative work by public health authorities in order to solve these problems at their root cause.

All over the world, the response to COVID-19 has demanded high quality data. These data (and models based on these) are required at the city and neighborhood levels in order to understand the threat, shape the public health response, optimize the behavioral decisions of each individual, and shape social distancing measures that are adopted at the community level.

There has been a clamor for "more testing" worldwide. Governments have come to compete on achieving more tests per day. There was a dramatic gain in the raw number of tests per day that took place in India over the early months of 2020. ICMR COVID Study Group et al. (2020) show basic facts about the measurement work at the ICMR in early 2020. However, it is important to see the four distinct elements of testing as delineated below (Malani, Mohanan, Balsari et al. 2020; Mukhopadhyay 2020a; Shah 2020b):

1. *Testing in the health care context:* When an individual reports certain symptoms to a doctor, the doctor might prescribe an RT-PCR test. The results of all RT-PCR tests can be aggregated and, as a high-frequency time series, can be a valuable decision-making tool at the neighborhood, village, district, or city level.
2. *Public health objectives in small groups:* Consider an at-risk group such as nurses or railway employees. It would be valuable to obtain a statistical estimate of the infection rate every week. This can guide improvements in processes and improve the morale of these groups.
3. *Public health objectives in a neighborhood:* At a neighborhood level, accurate and timely estimates of incidence are valuable as they feed back into the decisions of each individual about the optimal level of economic and social activities. These estimates can also be used to shape state coercion on social distancing, which can be useful when the probability of getting infected is high.
4. *Restarting the economy:* The scientific community is working on a fuller understanding of immunity, which can ultimately lead to one or more tests generating an "immunity passport," which will tell the individual that the disease is no longer a threat.

Each of these four objectives is important and needs to be pursued. In the present state of the science, the fourth is not yet feasible, so we discuss the first three. A large number of tests can take place in a clinical care context. However, for many reasons there are concerns about the extent to which the aggregate data is useful:

1. There have been fluctuations in the prescribed decision process ("protocol") that a doctor is supposed to use when prescribing a test.
2. When each change in the prescribed protocol takes place, there are vagaries in the communication of these changes to every doctor in India.
3. There have been capacity constraints in testing.
4. The bulk of both health care and testing capacity in India is in the private sector, but state coercion was used to limit the ability of private doctors to prescribe tests and private labs to conduct tests.

In standard epidemiological models such as the Susceptible–Exposed–Infected–Recovered (SEIR) model, the measured I is the fraction of persons who are infected in the population. This should ideally be measured by a statistical sample. It can be approximated by using data from a clinical setting if the protocols are stable, applied consistently, with sound frontline measurement procedures, and are in place on a large scale. These features were not in place in India in early 2020. As a consequence, the conventional data about the number of tests and the fraction that test positive are difficult to interpret (Bajpai 2020; Bansal 2020; Das et al. 2020; Mukhopadhyay 2020b; Rukmini 2020a; Sharma and Premkumar 2020). This limits the usefulness of papers such as Philip et al. (2020), which estimated that the age-adjusted case fatality rate in India was higher than would be expected based on estimates from 14 countries.

Some papers are more effective in estimation. As an example, Malani, Mohanan, Kumar et al. (2020) did antibody testing for a statistical sample of migrants returning to Bihar from many locations across the country and found numerical values that were difficult to reconcile with conventional estimates reported from source locations or for the whole country. While epidemiological modeling is a difficult area even with the best of data, in India, data limitations have particularly hampered the extent to which the analysis of aggregate data could become useful.

One natural fallback for measuring the state of the pandemic would have been to fall back from estimating the number of persons infected to estimating the number of deaths. Here, we encounter the weaknesses of the systems that attribute the cause of death (Barnagarwala 2020; Rukmini 2020b; Sinha 2020). In particular, once officials are evaluated on the number of deaths owing to COVID-19, they have an incentive to understate the number of deaths. Trusted daily statistics for birth and death, and hospitalization data, can also be highly influential for public health work, but they are not available in India. Novel approaches to estimating all-cause mortality using panel household survey data can be brought to bear on the problem (Sané and Shah 2021).

There is thus significant uncertainty surrounding published estimates of the number of infected persons at a point in time, the number of persons who were ever infected, and the number of deaths that can be attributed to COVID-19. Statistical sampling offers a natural path to sidestep these difficulties and obtain sound estimates of the number of persons infected (using the RT-PCR test) and a lower bound of the number of persons ever infected (using data from antibody tests). There was one such episode of measurement through statistical sampling, where the ICMR conducted a study in late April 2020 in 70 districts. A key finding of this appears to be the presence of high heterogeneity within these 70 districts, where some locations, such as the containment zones in Mumbai, had seroprevalence rates as high as 30 percent, while there were other districts with values near zero. There are some newspaper stories that give a sense of these results, but the dataset or paper has thus far not been released. As of this writing in July 2020, this one survey dataset from end-April 2020 was the most recent measurement project of this nature.

There are weaknesses in the information systems through which test data are assembled and released. With all its weaknesses, a substantial amount of testing has taken place in India, and there are many opportunities for utilizing these data in ways that would better inform the actions of citizens, firms, doctors, and various arms of the government. However, there are limitations in the mechanism through which aggregate time-series information is published (Agarwal and Kaur 2020). Unit-level information is not released.

Weaknesses in the statistical system are present in other aspects of COVID-19 also. As an example, assuming that useful forecasts could be obtained of future infections and hospitalizations, these would need to be compared against the health care system capacity in terms of the number of regular beds, ICU beds, and ventilators, among other things. These things are, however, not easily measured. The bulk of health care capacity in India is now in the private sector, and there is no measurement system that is able to obtain and update this information. The Ministry of Health has a National Health Resource Repository (NHRR) that enumerates facilities and their capabilities. The institutional infrastructure for continuous updating of the NHRR is not yet in place; it is updated episodically. It was last updated in 2019, but there was no data release.

Within public sector health care, Roy (2020) points out that when officials are measured on the total number of beds, they have a tendency to portray progress on the total number of beds while sacrificing the ratios that are normally maintained about the number of ICU beds and number of ventilators per unit hospital bed; this hampers the estimation of (say) ICU beds using thumb rules based on the total number of beds.

Overall, it appears that there was a gap between measurement and data dissemination in India when faced with the pandemic, as opposed to information production that would have been influential in improving decisions by many persons across the country. It is important to see these difficulties in the initial conditions in the core public health objectives of the statistical system in health that were in place before the pandemic arrived (Chandra Sharma 2019; Rajan and James 2016; Sharma 2016). From that starting point, the outcomes from the firefighting in a few months when the pandemic arose are not surprising.

3.5. Medical Research

Once the pandemic started, there was remarkable progress worldwide on producing research in real time, which unlocked many of the secrets of the virus and the disease. Knowledge is a global public good, and India has been a great beneficiary of this knowledge.

There is an array of scientific questions, however, that are more specific to India, and for which researchers elsewhere in the world will not ordinarily embark upon research projects. Some examples of these include the following:

1. A significant body of evidence has been obtained from natural history studies in Wuhan (China), Lombardy (Italy), and New York (USA). The temperatures prevailing in the months of rapid growth of the pandemic there were 3–11°C, 4–9°C, and 0–10°C, respectively. How do Indian conditions of temperature, humidity, and insolation change disease transmission?

2. What are the implications of Indian social practices (e.g., spitting *paan*, customs in temples, death rituals) for disease transmission?

3. What statistical techniques of epidemiological research are required to find patterns in Indian unit-level data about who gets infected and who gets adversely affected when infected, so as to create feedback loops that can help alter behavior by individuals?

4. How do the standard results about the probability of serious illness and death, and their variation with age and comorbidities, get modified under Indian conditions? Is there geographical variation? Is there variation by income or other social class?

5. What are effective clinical protocols that are feasible under median conditions in an Indian health care facility? As an example, once we assume that ventilators cannot be used on a large scale in India, how can oxygen therapy be best applied (Sudhir and Mor 2020)?

6. What is the immune system response in India to the Coronavirus? What is the demographic variation seen in India on issues such as cross-reactivity, antibody neutralization, and reinfection?

7. The high prevalence of adult malnutrition in India is unique; could it interact with COVID-19 fatality in some ways?

8. India has the largest pool of persons who are or have been infected with tuberculosis. To what extent is this an important comorbidity?

9. What variants are prevalent, and how effective will mainstream vaccines be against contemporary variants at different points in time?

These are, of course, only examples. A robust process of the exchange of questions and ideas between researchers, persons in health policy, and medical practitioners is required through which questions are identified and answers are rapidly discovered. The ICMR has established teams as part of the COVID-19 "Rapid Response Team," which are doing medical research. There is a need for a strong scientific community that is able to rapidly produce such papers, with large-scale capacity across the public and private sectors. This community will benefit from better linkages into researchers and research institutions outside India.

3.6. The Coming Vaccines

There is an active global race to build vaccines that protect against COVID-19. There are about 30 vaccine research projects in India, including the major work at Bharat Biotech. It is likely that in the coming months, multiple high-quality vaccines will come about. This optimism draws on the remarkable scientific advances in the development of vaccines that has come about in the last 20 years.

Even if good vaccines are invented outside India, India is an important producer of vaccines on a global scale. As an example, Ramu (2015) shows a global vaccine development project that chose to use certain elements of the overall project in India. Some of the prominent vaccine designers worldwide are likely to turn to Indian companies for their manufacturing capabilities. Whether through research or manufacturing, there will be significant movement on vaccines in India in the coming months.

At that point of time in the future, the following important questions will arise:

1. How can the vaccine approval processes of mature market economies be harnessed to make decisions for the approval of vaccines in India?
2. How will Indian economic agents be able to purchase large quantities of vaccines at relatively affordable prices? What can be done to secure supplies of sufficiently high volumes at sufficiently low prices?
3. A vaccine is a private good with a positive externality. What is the optimal combination of private purchase and public financing that can share costs wisely?
4. How can a nationwide program be organized to distribute this vaccine to a large mass of people? The present state-led immunization programs have many flaws. How can the private health care sector be harnessed for this problem?

5. Assuming that there are supply limitations, is there a role for voucher programs from the state in favor of certain persons? Should the vaccine first be given to high-risk populations, health care workers, or front-line workers who could become super-spreaders because they are in contact with many?
6. Herd immunity could be achieved in theory without immunizing the entire population. What is an optimal strategy for India that puts the epidemic to an end, protects those persons who are at risk, and yet minimizes cost?

There is a need for innovative policy research on these questions in the coming months.

3.7. Building a Public Health System in India

The COVID-19 pandemic has brought fresh emphasis on building institutional capacity for public health in the country. Based on these experiences, we have fresh insights on elements of the public health system in India that would help deal with such a situation.

3.7.1. THE GAINS FROM DECENTRALIZATION

A recurring theme is the importance of the Constitutional vision of India as a union of states. The bulk of the work in public health is best performed by cities and states. How to solve the trade-offs between livelihoods and contagion? How to allocate resources in testing? How to mobilize health care? What are the precise tactical details of organizing a response that would work well? This work is best placed at the level of the city or district government. Officials at the local level understand their neighborhoods and economic activities the best and face greater feedback loops of accountability.

Local context is highly important. As an example, in a Kerala setting with significant institutional capacity in contact tracing, there may be a certain optimal pathway for building sound institutional arrangements for contact tracing, and there might be a certain optimal role for contact tracing apps in that context. But this context, and thus the optimal role for a contact tracing app, could be quite different in other states. This emphasizes the need for a decentralized approach.

There is a small negative externality suffered by society when each individual interacts with others in the course of economic and social life. The magnitude of this negative externality is proportional to the infection rate prevalent at a point in time, which varies sharply across cities. The trade-offs about the kinds of economic and social activities that should be sacrificed depend upon local conditions. Hence, the best way to organize state coercion in social distancing is at the city level.

Public health work is best conducted through discussion and persuasion and not the use of coercive power. Officials at the local level are well connected to local human networks. They have the ability to organize meetings with residents of the city, engage in communication, persuasion, and negotiation layered with a small amount of coercion. An example of a feasible mechanism design at the local level, involving a "Social Distancing Committee," is presented in the Appendix. One argument in favor of local control is that in fighting the epidemic, officials at the local level have to "eat their own dog food." Success or failure will directly impact them through the health of their family and friends, and through the respect or criticism that they earn for their efforts. This is one element of the gains from decentralization from the subsidiarity principle, which argues that every government function is best placed at the lowest level of government where it can possibly be done efficiently.

The problems of the entire 3.3 million sq. km of India are dauntingly large. It is difficult for any one mind, or any one team, to envision the correct strategies for health and economic policy on this large a scale. As an example, if a policy team had to think about doing antibody measurement for a random sample of India, this is a difficult project to design and execute. The problem statement, "Establish a random sample of 1,000 people in Pune and run an antibody test on them," is a more tractable one when compared with the statement, "Establish an adequate sample of people all over India and run an antibody test on them."

Large states of India are of the size of countries elsewhere in the world. The decentralization agenda in India is not just about decentralization to the state capital; it is critically about decentralizing all the way to the city. The most important level of government for high-transaction public health functions is the city government. This is another dimension in which states such as Tamil Nadu and Kerala have fared better than mainstream Indian arrangements.

At present, the organization of Union, state, and city governments in India has many problems. There is a fragmentation of authority between the state government and the city government. Officials in the city government or at the district level are often overloaded and find it difficult to meet this challenge. Policy design needs to recognize these capacity constraints and envision commensurate responses to these constraints. The decentralized approach to health policy needs to go hand in hand with capacity enlargement for local government.

As an example, by default many functions are often placed with a chief medical officer (CMO), who easily slips into the role of being the point person for anything connected with health. However, problems of public health, and particularly the problem of COVID-19, are intersectoral and often go beyond the capacity of a CMO. The CMO may often be the point person for the operations of government hospitals, but public health is distinct from hospital management.

In establishing a decentralized approach to health policy for COVID-19, there is a need to precisely articulate the problems that local governments have to solve, and the support that will be available to the leadership of local governments from state and Union governments.

3.7.2. BUILDING STATE CAPACITY FOR CONTACT TRACING

Each state and city needs to address the problem of organization design and developing state capacity for contact tracing. Recent events remind us that this organization design is not like, say, hiring a lot of school-teachers. What is required is a flexible, small organization that is able to rapidly scale up when faced with an epidemic and go back to its original size after the epidemic has ended. The small "standing army" must be primarily about the option value of rapidly achieving large-scale contact tracing when the need arises. As an example, while New York City had world-class public health institutions, once the pandemic arrived, 3,000 additional workers were hired into contact tracing. In this aspect, contact tracing presents a challenge in public administration that is a bit different from mainstream problems in organization design as seen, for example, with police and schoolteachers.

3.7.3. ADDRESSING MARKET FAILURE IN TESTING

The private sector is the dominant force in the Indian diagnostic testing industry. There is a market failure due to asymmetric information in this area. This market failure needs to be addressed through a three-pronged effort with (a) private certification initiatives; (b) mechanisms of public procurement; and (c) a light layer of regulation.

In this, we need to recognize the difficulties associated with more intrusive tools, such as price controls, bans, export bans, and government control of the technology used in testing. As an example, when the prices of PPE rose in India, this was not a cause for concern. In fact, this was the signal that worked its way through the market economy and induced a large supply response to the point where India is now a large exporter of PPE. Every state interference in the prices of PPE served to slow down this supply response.

The construction of state capacity for a light layer of regulation can draw upon modern thinking in India about the difficulties of building state capacity in regulation.

3.7.4. PUBLIC GOODS AT THE LEVEL OF THE UNION GOVERNMENT
There is a need for institutional capacity that is akin to the US CDC. While the ICMR was placed into certain roles in the short run when the pandemic began, clear thinking is required about the role of the National Centre for Disease Control (NCDC), and a systematic effort needs to commence on building state capacity in the chosen organization.

3.7.5. SCIENTIFIC RESEARCH
There is need to rethink the framework using which public resources are put to work through government research institutions, private research institutions, and private firms in order to achieve the requisite research capacity in the country that can be galvanized to address questions of importance to private and public decision-makers in India.

In the prevailing vision of science in India, there is a fusing of public expenditure and public production. It is more effective to use public funding through a grant mechanism to get the production of research out into non-government organizations. This creates greater competition and places management decisions about research organizations into the hands of non-government and private organizations that are better able to perform these functions. For an analogy, the National Aeronautics and Space Administration in the US is a contracting organization; it does not have a vast scientific workforce, it does not do research, design spacecraft, or build spacecraft (Shah 2019).

3.7.6. HEALTH STATISTICS
There is enormous value in building datasets and models around the questions of health. As an example, Rivers and George (2020) draw an analogy between the public goods of government-run weather data and forecasting, and the required public goods of government-run health data and associated forecasting. A particularly simple dataset, which can be highly influential for public health research, is the daily release of accurate statistics about births, deaths, and hospitalizations.

When tests take place in a clinical care setting, these data need to be assembled into a single database and made available in anonymized form to the research community. The Union Government, state governments, and city governments must all have the ability to create time-series survey data, where some or all parts of the country are put into intensive surveillance using periodic waves of testing of random samples. Public health officials require the ability to commission testing of a random sample of, say, health workers in a given city as part of their process of isolating the problem.

The development of electronic health records, with an open ecosystem of multiple but interoperable software systems at health care organizations, will help create a more information-rich environment, though there are grave concerns about the privacy of individual information. The National Digital Health Mission could potentially play a useful role in protecting individuals and improving the data quality and interoperability of electronic health records.

3.7.7. The Problem of Purchasing

When an epidemic gathers momentum, a surge in testing is required. This necessitates the ability of the government to purchase testing services from private persons. This, in turn, requires establishing state capacity in contracting (procurement, dispute resolution, contract renegotiation, and payments) in public health authorities at all three levels of government.

3.7.8. A Systematic Process for Constructing State Capacity

Many of the steps mentioned above (e.g., contact tracing and the role of the NCDC) require the systematic creation of organizational capability. Poor public administration in India in public health meant that a diverse array of public servants was pulled out of essential health (and non-health) services in order to prioritize COVID-19, and that has had its own adverse consequences. There is need for the systematic construction of organizational capabilities on all fronts so that a diverse array of state functions can harmoniously take place even in a crisis.

The lack of checks and balances in the foundational laws is a key source of arbitrary power and, thereby, low state capacity; a key feature of the road ahead lies in establishing checks and balances in law.

The road ahead involves designing laws, organization diagrams, process manuals, accountability mechanisms, training procedures, and putting in the homeostatic functions of contracts, finance, human resource management, facilities management, and transparency. The public administration dimensions of this problem are similar to the mainstream state capacity problems seen in India, for example, as analyzed in Srikrishna (2013); Ministry of Corporate Affairs (2016); Roy et al. (2019); and Kelkar and Shah (2019).

4. Health Care

There are two strengths that worked in India's favor in the pandemic in its early months. First, with young demographics, the fraction of those infected who required significant medical care as of this writing has been small. Second, there was more time to prepare, given that the pandemic came relatively late to India and with the additional months that were obtained through varying degrees of lockdown. By and large, this time was utilized to significantly galvanize the public sector health care system into action.

From the first principles of public economics, health care is largely a private good, with the special case of infectious disease where there is market failure in the form of positive externalities. When we think of the market for private health care, there is an important market failure in the form of asymmetric information. Most customers are not able to understand the extent to which the producer, doctor, or nurse acted in their best interests, or to be able to shop around and thus exert market pressure on pricing. There is thus a significant problem in consumer protection.

In India, there is one large health care organization—the government—which accounts for about a 30 percent market share of health care and about a 10 percent share of intensive care staff. The remainder of health care is produced by a large number of private health care firms within a competitive market structure. While in some other countries there is market failure in the form of excessive market power with a small number of health care firms, this is not a problem in India.

The prime focus of health policy in India has, however, been on the management, resourcing, and operation of health care organizations that the government controls. There has been little attempt at addressing market failure in the private market for health care, and in recognizing the important role of private health care providers, and utilizing them to achieve policy objectives.

4.1. The COVID-19 Surge in Health Care Requirements

As has been seen elsewhere in the world, the peak of the epidemic curve is associated with a surge in health care requirements that can overwhelm the health care system. In the Indian cities with the largest number of cases, Mumbai and Delhi, the health care system came under considerable stress. However, at the same time, in large parts of the country the epidemic did not enlarge sharply in early 2020. The timing of the epidemic in each city was different, but the features of the health care crisis in each city are similar and are reminiscent of those seen elsewhere in the world. As an example, Johnson (2020) is a recent story of the surge in Bengaluru.

Newspaper reports of the ICMR's statistical sampling in 70 districts in late April 2020 suggest that in a large fraction of the districts the prevalence of the disease was rather small. In April and May 2020, the expansion of cases was limited by the lockdown, which also helped forestall the possibility of capacity constraints in health care.

In a strategic view of the COVID-19 pandemic in India, the challenge lay in utilizing the levers of public health to flatten the epidemic curve while simultaneously enlarging health care capacity so as to minimize the extent to which surges took place that exceeded the health care system capacity. The overarching issue in the normative analysis of the Indian health care system in 2020 is to think about the extent to which health care capacity was indeed enlarged.

Indeed, looking into the deep future, COVID-19 has brought new attributes into the challenge of health policy. In order to address the possibility of an epidemic in the future that cannot be contained by public health alone, it will be important to plan for a health care system that has the capacity to scale up its services on demand. This will of course come at a cost. For example, it will mean holding in reserve capital goods such as hospital beds and ICUs, and paying for operating expenses, for example, salaries of intensivists who are underutilized in normal times.

How can meaningful capacity surges in health care be managed? The first path lies in building additional health care capacity through the one large health organization—the government. The public sector health care system has worked very hard so far in 2020 and has played a disproportionate role in addressing health care requirements. Indeed, without these capabilities, the outcomes in India would have been significantly worse. However, given initial conditions, where only about 30 percent of ICUs or ventilators, and an even smaller share of specialist staff were available, it was difficult to obtain the supply response needed through the public sector health care system. This approach also faced the constraints of operational capabilities and quality.

The other path lies in establishing contracts with the private sector. While this would face the complexities of government contracting, it would be attractive in several respects: (a) the private sector started out with about 70 percent capacity, and it is thus easier to obtain large expansions when working through the private sector and (b) the private sector is likely to have greater operational capabilities and quality.

For a city in India, there are many uncertainties about the magnitude of health care capacity required at a future date. A risk management perspective is useful in thinking about this sizing. It would be efficient for the government to establish contracts with private persons that would cover the cost of establishing enlarged facilities regardless of actual use, so that society would have the option of being able to utilize these facilities in the event of a surge in the disease.

4.2. Difficulties Faced by Private Health Care Organizations

In the epidemic, demand for health care other than for COVID-19 patients appears to have declined, perhaps through a combination of patients being afraid of infection at health care facilities, difficulties of transportation owing to the lockdowns, and financial constraints faced by households. Alongside this, some health care facilities pulled back from non-COVID-19 activities in order to prioritize COVID-19 activities, there were difficulties with the health care workforce, and some managers of health care facilities may have chosen to retreat from full-fledged operations. Monthly notifications of TB have dropped by 80 per cent, which gives a sense of the extent of the disruption (Ethiraj 2020).

The new government health care program, the *Pradhan Mantri Jan Arogya Yojana* (PMJAY), has become an important source of information about developments in health care. Smith et al. (2020) analyze the data for claims in PMJAY during the COVID-19 epidemic from January to June 2020. The value of claims dropped by 76 percent in the early lockdown phase. There was a slight decline in claims by women, the young, and the old. The number of active hospitals in the PMJAY system dropped by half at first, with private hospitals gradually recovering. Elective surgeries such as cataract or joint replacement at first dropped to near zero levels.

Table 1 shows the 2020 returns on the stock market index of health care firms after the returns of the overall market index is subtracted. This shows

TABLE 1. Excess Returns: Monthly Share Price Index of Health Care Firms Net of Overall Market Index during January–June 2020

2020	Returns (%)
January	14.0
February	−1.0
March	−27.0
April	11.0
May	−2.0
June	4.5

Source: CMIE Overall Share Price Index.

that in March 2020, with the lockdown, there was a 27 percent decline in health care stock prices reflecting these concerns. The large underlying declines in revenue driving the share price index are likely to have induced significant financial stress in private health care organizations. In an ideal world, private health care organizations should have been devoting their management skills to enlarging capacity; instead, their energies were significantly utilized in addressing their financial stress.

4.3. Protecting Health Care Workers

In the locations where the epidemic has surged, the health care system has faced significant constraints on the health care workforce. This reflects a combination of factors.

Given the substantial viral load that health care workers can be exposed to, many health care workers got sick and thus dropped out of the workforce. This problem was exacerbated by poor protocols in most Indian health care organizations. Concerns about possible sickness hampered labor force participation by some health care workers, particularly the elderly. In the lockdown, transportation constraints hindered the commute to work for junior staff. These problems added up to a decline in health care system capacity on account of the reduced workforce. Improved protocols, access to PPEs, and health insurance could help improve outcomes.

4.4. Health Care Financing

COVID-19-related health care expenses are a highly insurable risk; large expenditures are only incurred for a small fraction of the infected. One pathway for public resources to feed into health care financing lies in a government-run health care system. The other pathway lies in public financing of private health care.

Employees State Insurance (ESI) is a mandatory program for workers of large private firms that offers expansive benefits alongside mandatory payments by workers. In principle, ESI could be the kernel around which a significant health care arrangement could come about. However, in practice, ESI has become one more, large public sector health care organization, with a prime focus on building and operating health care organizations. For most compulsory participants in ESI, the promise of service delivery in practice is not matched by supply-side capabilities. ESI could significantly enlarge its outreach by shifting gears from an emphasis on production to an emphasis on contracting, where it could become a sophisticated purchaser of private health care services.

The many elements of government-funded health insurance schemes could also play an important role in health care financing for COVID-19. There were initial delays in enlarging package designs to encompass testing and treatment for COVID-19. There is a need to build institutional capacity in the operations of these programs in order to respond to the coming surge in requirements.

4.5. What Institutional Apparatus Would have Helped?

The private market for health care suffers from market failure in the form of asymmetric information. The conventional response of the state has emphasized instruments such as bans, price limits, and the commandeering of private facilities. It is desirable to address the market failure through a combination of private clubs, domestic and overseas certification, and sophisticated buyers (either public systems like ESI or PMJAY, or private health insurance companies), all centered around a small core of law and regulation. There is considerable complexity in identifying the minimal core of law and regulation that fits inside the envelope of what is feasible given the constraints on state capacity.

A key barrier that inhibits the relationship between public health policy and the private sector is that of contracting. Many government departments have low capacity in procurement, contract disputes, contract monitoring, contract renegotiation, and timely payments. Private persons have negative expectations of the extent to which the government will litigate or arbitrarily delay payments. Constraints in contracting have shaped up as a critical constraint inhibiting health policy.

At a practical level, in many cities there is an impending storm of the peak of the epidemic curve. The present landscape of actions by the Union Government, state governments, and city governments does not fully address the problem. It is in the self-interest of the health care industry and the business community in each city, and therefore of the city residents, to prepare better and to form local coalitions for coordination and action (Shah 2020d).

5. Conclusion

The pandemic has posed a huge challenge for health policy in all countries. There were significant weaknesses in Indian institutional arrangements before the pandemic commenced. These difficulties were partly grounded in the arrangements for health policy, and partly weaknesses of the homeostatic processes of the Indian State, such as in government contracting.

Some parts of the Indian health system have responded strongly to the pandemic. These include testing and health care in the public sector. At the same time, their pre-existing weaknesses have inhibited the scale of the response.

The stark light of the pandemic has created fresh insights on the difficulties and the priorities for reform. The enormous adverse consequences of the pandemic serve to reinforce the prioritization for public health. The possibilities for public health are summarized in one fact: Taiwan, a country of 23 million with strong travel links to China, has had 9 deaths so far. While the adequacy of resources is an important element of public health, the primary problem is that of institutional reform. Doing the institutional reform and then devoting resources would reflect the long-standing Indian tradition of scaling up resources into pathways that have proven themselves in delivering sound outcomes.

There is now considerable knowledge in the field of state capacity, on the tangible elements of institutional design, of the establishment of checks and balances, through which greater capability can be obtained. This knowledge can now be usefully brought into the field of health policy, with the accent on public health.

Appendix: Institutional Arrangements for Regulating Social Distancing

The pre-COVID-19 world of social interactions is infeasible as it will give rise to an infection surge that will overwhelm existing health care facilities. The other extreme, a complete lockdown for the entire country, has a large impact upon livelihoods. When GDP declines, this will in and of itself generate adverse health outcomes. As an example, infant mortality and maternal mortality go up when GDP declines. Similarly, the resources in the hands of the government that can possibly be brought to bear upon the COVID-19 epidemic are linked to GDP; when GDP declines, tax collections and the resources available to fight COVID-19 also decline.

The puzzle lies in finding a balance between these two extremes. If an environment is created of the state trying to prevent personal freedoms and people trying to surreptitiously regain personal freedoms, then the people will always succeed, and the health policy objectives of social distancing will be lost. The emergence of an adversarial relationship with people will hamper the everyday public health work of tracing, testing, isolating, and reducing pathways of transmission. When scientific progress comes about in the form of a vaccine, a prophylactic, or a cure, trusted public health channels are of the essence in rolling out these advances on a nationwide scale. This will be impeded if an environment of coercion and conflict is established.

For these reasons, there is need for democratic legitimacy for the chosen path of social distancing. The strategy for social distancing should involve a great deal of discussion and very little coercion. While the state can introduce information into this decision-making, ultimately, each individual and each organization has to make these trade-offs.

This starts with public health officials persuading individuals and organizations that there is an important threat. The government has made good progress in sending information into the populace about the dangers of the pandemic. If sickness or death takes place in a neighborhood, this will impact fear and concern in that neighborhood. Individuals will typically be amenable to thinking about this problem and changing their behavior in response to it. The sheer creation of accurate data and its timely release will create the requisite risk aversion.

Conversely, public health officials do not know enough about the life of each individual and each organization. The imposition of a single rulebook on all people at all times will induce difficulties. If anything, the imposition of a rulebook that lacks nuance and is insensitive to the particular conditions of each individual, household, or organization runs the risk of public health being seen as an out-of-touch imposition, leading to people devoting themselves to evasion.

Alongside social distancing measures (e.g., closing a *mandi* or modifying the working of a *mandi* in ways that lead to reduced disease transmission), there are a host of public health measures that need to be considered. This raises questions relating to the use of masks, enclosed spaces with recirculated air, disinfection protocols for public places, and the use of hand sanitizers and hand washing, among others. All these problems need to be analyzed at a local level, reflecting local constraints and local trade-offs.

Democratic legitimacy comes from expertise, information, persuasion, and the minimal use of coercion. A policy framework for social distancing may hence be envisioned as the following steps:

- There should be Green, Blue, and Red manuals for social distancing. The Green manual should have the mildest requirements and the Red manual should have the highest requirements.

- A group of academics and intellectuals should be organized that creates reference drafts of these three manuals at an all-India level. These draft manuals should then be released on a website for public commentary. There should be no state coercion around these manuals; they should only be inputs for public discourse.
- Each of these manuals should involve the minimal use of force. The bulk of the manual should involve reasoning and recommendations, not threats of state violence. A tiny portion of the manual should involve using powers under the Epidemic Diseases Act, 1897.
- Associated with these manuals should be the full reasoning about the logic behind the design of these manuals. Communication materials should be developed, which explain these manuals to officials and private citizens.

This work can be organized by the Ministry of Health and Family Welfare, the NITI Aayog, and academic institutions. The manuals should be given as intellectual inputs to cities/districts. Armed with this knowledge, officials in the rural districts and cities should debate with their local interest groups and adapt the manuals for their own use. For some places, it may be feasible to close down a *mandi*, but for another city it may be essential to keep *mandis* open and the response there may lie in the extent of safety procedures built into the working of *mandis*. These decisions are best made locally.

Each city would utilize the raw material of the three draft manuals made at an all-India level and come up with their own practical manuals that are grounded in their reality. We might thus have a Nagpur Green, a Nagpur Blue, and a Nagpur Red manual that are discussed and released in Nagpur. Manuals for different cities and districts would appear on the Internet, and their merits would be debated.

The bulk of each city or district manual would involve voluntary actions by various communities, associations, and organizations. The use of state coercion should be minimal. Local officials would have to manage this process of engaging with the community, developing these manuals, developing consensus around the design of the manuals, and getting to the right design of the manuals while using minimal state coercion.

Once a city/district has chosen its design of the Green/Blue/Red manuals, how might it transition between these manuals? When social distancing measures are brought in with greater predictability, economic activity can be better designed around this stochastic environment, and a given level of social distancing can then have a smaller impact upon economic activity and, eventually, GDP.

In order to achieve democratic legitimacy, predictability, and high compliance, each city should establish a Social Distancing Committee to control which manual is presently in use.[5] Designing the working of this Committee involves thinking about its composition and operations. Here are some suggestions.

Composition and Appointment of a Social Distancing Committee:

1. It should be made up of two officials (the most senior officials of the city government), three scientists, and two businesspersons, thus adding up to seven persons.
2. The appointment of these seven persons should be done by the city government.
3. All seven persons must be residents of the city and each must have at least six family members living in the city.
4. We may note that in a committee of seven, winning requires four votes. If the two city officials have made up their mind on a given idea, they have two votes in hand. For this idea to go through, they would require the support of two more votes from among the remaining five persons. Thus, we see that there is a healthy tension between having an important say for the officials and requiring that they carry at least two of the five other private citizens and their thought processes with them.

Operations of the Social Distancing Committee:

1. This committee should meet every Friday to review the current data about conditions in the city and the neighboring environment, and vote on a possible change over from one manual to another.
2. City officials and their associated researchers would make a presentation to the committee at the start of the meeting, which would provide the committee with the requisite information, based on which a decision can be made. This presentation would be released into the public domain.
3. Each individual in the committee should be required to release a one- or two-page of a rationale statement about why they voted in the way that they did. The public release of the voting record, and the rationale, would generate accountability. In the future, if it is clear (with the

---

5. These ideas draw on knowledge in the field of monetary economics on the working of monetary policy committees, for example, Shah (2014).

benefit of hindsight) that a decision to go to the Red manual was a mistake, this will generate an adverse impact upon the reputation of the individual. Meetings and voting should take place on a Friday and take effect from the next Tuesday, thus giving everyone three days to gear up for the changed setting.

4. This committee would also have the authority to modify the text of the three manuals over time. These decisions would also take place through voting, rationale statements, and transparency.

Such a committee process ensures that there is deliberation and democratic legitimacy in the decisions about social distancing. In their ordinary life, each of the seven persons would meet and hear the viewpoints of hundreds of persons, and all this knowledge would feed into thinking about the trade-offs and discovering low-cost mechanisms to improve public health that can be used to modify the manuals.

A well-known empirical fact in the history of epidemics is that democracies fare better in epidemics. The tools of public discussion, consensus building, transparency, and lack of the concentration of power will yield the best decisions. The democratic legitimacy of the Social Distancing Committee will help ensure that people cooperate with its decisions instead of trying to get around the constraints. The bulk of the actions envisioned in the three manuals would be voluntary actions of individuals and private organizations without bringing state coercion into the picture.

References

Agarwal, Natasha, and Harleen Kaur. 2020. "Information about COVID-19 in India." *The Leap Blog*, June 13. Available at https://blog.theleapjournal.org/2020/06/information-about-covid-19-in-india_13.html (accessed May 25, 2021).

Bajpai, Vikas. 2020. "Half-Truths and Twisted Data Won't Help Control COVID-19." *The Wire*, June 28. Available at https://science.thewire.in/health/covid-19-icmr-response-seroprevalence-survey-critique/ (accessed May 25, 2021).

Baker, Michael G., Nick Wilson, and Andrew Anglemyer. 2020. "Successful Elimination of COVID-19 Transmission in New Zealand." *New England Journal of Medicine*, 383: e56, DOI: 10.1056/NEJMc2025203. Available at https://www.nejm.org/doi/full/10.1056/NEJMc2025203 (accessed May 25, 2021).

Bansal, Samarth. 2020. "Indian Govt. Trots Out Meaningless Data as COVID-19 Cases Rocket despite Lockdown." *HuffPost*, May 20. Available at https://www.huffingtonpost.in/entry/india-coronavirus-cases-response-data-crisis_in_5ec49658c5b6956f4169fb4f (accessed May 25, 2021).

Ajay Shah **63**

Barnagarwala, Tabassum. 2020. "451 Missing Deaths in Mumbai, BMC Updating Records after Mismatch." *The Indian Express*, June 16. Available at https://indianexpress.com/article/cities/mumbai/mumbai-missing-covid-deaths-bmc-records-mismatch-6460939/ (accessed May 25, 2021).

Bhandari, Vrinda, and Faiza Rahman. 2020. "Constitutionalism during a Crisis: The Case of Aarogya Setu." *The Leap Blog*, May 25. Available at https://blog.the-leapjournal.org/2020/05/constitutionalism-during-crisis-case-of.html (accessed 25 May 2021).

Chandra Sharma, Neetu. 2019. "Why India Lacks Quality in Its Demographic and Health Data?" *Mint*, July 25. Available at https://www.livemint.com/news/india/why-india-lacks-quality-in-its-demographic-and-health-data-1564048796002.html (accessed May 25, 2021).

Cochrane, John H. 2020. "An SIR Model with Behavior." *The Grumpy Economist*, May 4. Available at https://johnhcochrane.blogspot.com/2020/05/an-sir-model-with-behavior.html (accessed May 25, 2021).

Das, Jishnu, Neelanjan Sircar, and Partha Mukhopadhyay. 2020. "A Blueprint for a Testing Strategy." *Hindustan Times*, April 22. Available at https://www.hindustantimes.com/analysis/a-blueprint-for-a-testing-strategy-analysis/story-OEx409xxBbAXbzLDV1diGI.html (accessed May 25, 2021).

Das, Mehul, Isalyne Gennaro, Sneha Menon, Anahita Shah, Kadambari Shah, Tvesha Sippy, and Priya Vedavalli. 2020. "Kerala's Strategies for COVID-19 Response: Guidelines and Learnings for Replication by Other Indian States", May 11 Mumbai: IDFC Institute. Available at http://www.idfcinstitute.org/site/assets/files/15617/kerala_strategies_for_covid-19_response_updated_may_11_2020-1.pdf (accessed May 25, 2021).

Ethiraj, Govindraj. 2020. "'COVID Will Set Back India's TB Programme by a Decade': Madhukar Pai." *IndiaSpend*, May 13. Available at https://www.indiaspend.com/covid-will-set-back-indias-tb-programme-by-a-decade/ (accessed May 25, 2021).

Gandhi, Monica, Deborah S. Yokoe, and Diane V. Havlir. 2020. "Asymptomatic Transmission, the Achilles' Heel of Current Strategies to Control COVID-19." *New England Journal of Medicine*, 382 (22): 2158–160.

ICMR COVID Study Group, COVID Epidemiology and Data Management Team, COVID Laboratory Team, and VRDLN Team, Indian Council of Medical Research. 2020. "Laboratory Surveillance for SARS-Cov-2 in India: Performance of Testing and Descriptive Epidemiology of Detected COVID-19, January 22– April 30, 2020." *Indian Journal of Medical Research*, 15 (5): 424–37. Available at http://www.ijmr.org.in/article.asp?issn=0971-5916;year=2020;volume=151;issue=5;spage=424;epage=437;aulast=ICMR (accessed May 25, 2021).

Isaac, T. N. Thomas, and Rajeev Sadanandan. 2020. "COVID-19, Public Health System and Local Governance in Kerala." *Economic & Political Weekly*, 55 (21), May 23. Available at https://www.epw.in/journal/2020/21/perspectives/covid-19-public-health-system-and-local-governance.html (accessed May 25, 2021).

Islam, Nazrul, Stephen J. Sharp, Gerardo Chowell, Sharmin Shabnam, Ichiro Kawachi, Ben Lacey, Joseph M. Massaro, Ralph B. D'Agostino, and Martin White. 2020. "Physical Distancing Interventions and Incidence of Coronavirus Disease 2019: Natural Experiment in 149 Countries." *British Medical Journal*, 370 (2020): m2743. Available at https://doi.org/10.1136/bmj.m2743 (accessed May 25, 2021).

Johnson, T. A. 2020. "Bengaluru Battle: Amid Spike, Shortage of Staff and ICU Beds with Ventilators." *The Indian Express*, July 6. Available at https://indianexpress. com/article/india/bengaluru-battle-amid-spike-shortage-of-staff-icu-beds-with-ventilators-6491895/ (accessed May 25, 2021).

Kaur, Harleen. 2020. "Can the Indian Legal Framework Deal with the COVID-19 Pandemic? A Review of the Epidemic Diseases Act." *Bar and Bench*, March 27. Available at https://www.barandbench.com/columns/can-the-indian-legal-frame-work-deal-with-the-covid-19-pandemic-a-review-of-the-epidemics-diseases-act (accessed May 25, 2021).

Kaur, Harleen, Ameya Paleja, and Siddhartha Srivastava. 2020. "Legal and Regulatory Framework for Laboratory Testing in India: A Case Study for COVID-19." *The Leap Blog*. Available at https://blog.theleapjournal.org/2020/07/ legal-and-regulatory-framework-for.html (accessed May 25, 2021).

Kelkar, Vijay, and Ajay Shah. 2019. *In Service of the Republic: The Art and Science of Economic Policy*. Bristol: Penguin Allen Lane.

———. 2020. "The Epidemic of 2020: Setting Course for a V-Shaped Recovery." *Business Standard*, April 7. Available at http://www.mayin.org/ajayshah/ MEDIA/2020/covid19_india.html (accessed May 25, 2021).

Kumar, Alok Prasanna. 2020. "Lawless Law-making in a COVID-19 World." *Economic & Political Weekly*, 55 (25), June 20. Available at https://www.epw. in/journal/2020/25/law-and-society/lawless-lawmaking-covid-19-world.html (accessed May 25, 2021).

Luo, Eric, Nicholas Chong, Clese Erikson, Candice Chen, Sara Westergaard, Edward Salsberg, and Patricia Pittman. 2020. "Contact Tracing Workforce Estimator." Washington, DC: Fitzhugh Mullan Institute for Health Workforce Equity, The George Washington University. Available at https://www.gwhwi.org/estima-tor-613404.html (accessed May 25, 2021).

Malani, Anup, Manoj Mohanan, Chanchal Kumar, Jake Kramer, and Vaidehi Tandel. 2020. "Prevalence of SARS-Cov-2 among Workers Returning to Bihar Gives Snapshot of COVID across India." *medRxiv*, June 28. Available at https:// www.medrxiv.org/content/10.1101/2020.06.26.20138545v1.full.pdf (accessed May 25, 2021).

Malani, Anup, Manoj Mohanan, Sanchit Balsari, and Anu Acharya. 2020. "Rethinking COVID-19 Testing Strategy." *The Hindu Business Line*, May 29. Available at https://www.thehindubusinessline.com/opinion/rethinking-covid-19-testing-strategy/article31697253.ece (accessed May 25, 2021).

Melnick, Edward R., and John P. A. Ioannidis. 2020. "Should Governments Continue Lockdown to Slow the Spread of COVID-19?" *British Medical Journal*, 369

(2020): m1924. Available at https://doi.org/10.1136/bmj.m1924 (accessed May 25, 2021).

Ministry of Corporate Affairs. 2016. "Report of the Working Group on the Building of the Insolvency and Bankruptcy Board of India." New Delhi: Government of India. Available at https://www.ibbi.gov.in/Wg-01%20Report.pdf (accessed May 25, 2021).

Morris, Loveday, and Luisa Beck. 2020. "While U.S. Struggles to Roll Out Coronavirus Contact Tracing, Germany Has Been Doing It from the Start." *The Washington Post*, May 25. Available at https://www.washingtonpost.com/world/europe/contact-tracing-coronavirus-germany/2020/05/24/7e59a668-93c1-11ea-87a3-22d324235636_story.html (accessed May 25, 2021).

Mukhopadhyay, Partha. 2020a. "Locking Down Is Not Enough. Ramp Up Testing." *Hindustan Times,* March 27. Available at https://www.hindustantimes.com/analysis/locking-down-is-not-enough-ramp-up-testing-writes-partha-mukhopadhyay/story-uInlUzJnkbca7iPXeysuUI.html (accessed May 25, 2021).

———. 2020b. "The Stability of Test Positivity in India." New Delhi: Centre for Policy Research, May 19. Available at https://www.cprindia.org/news/stability-test-positivity-india (accessed May 25, 2021).

Parsheera, Smriti. 2020. "Street-level Officials in India's COVID-19 Response." *The Leap Blog,* April 6. Available at https://blog.theleapjournal.org/2020/04/street-level-officials-in-indias-covid.html (accessed May 25, 2021).

Patnaik, Ila, Shubho Roy, and Ajay Shah. 2018. "The Rise of Government-funded Health Insurance in India" (Working Paper No. 18/231). New Delhi: National Institute of Public Finance and Policy.

Philip, Minu, Debraj Ray, and S. Subramanian. 2020. "Decoding India's Low COVID-19 Case Fatality Rate" (Working Paper No. 27896). Cambridge: National Bureau of Economic Research. Available at https://www.nber.org/papers/w27696 (accessed May 25, 2021).

Pritchett, Lant, and Michael Woolcock. 2004. "Solutions When *the* Solution Is the Problem: Arraying the Disarray in Development." *World Development*, 32 (2): 191–212.

Rajagopalan, Shruti, and Alexander Tabarrok. 2020. "Pandemic Policy in Developing Countries: Recommendations for India", Policy Briefs. Arlington, VA: Mercatus Center, George Mason University, April 9. Available at https://www.mercatus.org/publications/covid-19-policy-brief-series/pandemic-policy-developing-countries-recommendations-india (accessed May 25, 2021).

Rajan, S. Irudaya, and K. S. James. 2008. "Third National Family Health Survey in India: Issues, Problems and Prospects." *Economic & Political Weekly* 43, (48): 33–38, November 29.

Ramu, Swapnika. 2015. "MenAfriVac: A Novel Strategy for Building a Vaccine." *The Leap Blog*, May 10. Available at https://blog.theleapjournal.org/2015/05/menafrivac-novel-strategy-for-building.html (accessed May 25, 2021).

Rivers, Caitlin, and Dylan George. 2020. "How to Forecast Outbreaks and Pandemics: America Needs the Contagion Equivalent of the National Weather

Service." *Foreign Affairs*, June 29. Available at https://www.foreignaffairs. com/articles/united-states/2020-06-29/how-forecast-outbreaks-and-pandemics (accessed May 25, 2021).

Roy, Shubho. 2020. "Skepticism about Measurement: Hospital Beds Edition." *The Leap Blog,* June 24. Available at https://blog.theleapjournal.org/2020/06/ skepticism-about-measurement-hospital.html (accessed May 25, 2021).

Roy, Shubho, Ajay Shah, B. N. Srikrishna, and Somasekhar Sundaresan. 2019. "Building State Capacity for Regulation in India." In *Regulation in India: Design, Capacity, Performance*, edited by Devesh Kapur and Madhav Khosla. Oxford: Hart Publishing.

Rukmini, S. 2020a. "ICMR Data Shows India's COVID Testing Is Not in Right Shape–5 Things That Need Fixing." *The Print*, June 1. Available at https:// theprint.in/opinion/icmr-data-shows-indias-covid-testing-is-not-in-right-shape-5-things-that-need-fixing/433077/ (accessed May 25, 2021).

————. 2020b. "Why Audits, Reconciled Death Data Are Still Missing COVID Deaths." *IndiaSpend*, July 1. Available at https://www.indiaspend.com/why-audits-reconciled-death-data-are-still-missing-covid-deaths/ (accessed May 25, 2021).

Sadanandan, Rajiv. 2020. "Kerala's Response to COVID-19." *Indian Journal of Public Health* 4 (6): 99–101. Available at http://www.ijph.in/downloadpdf. asp?issn=0019-557X;year=2020;volume=64;issue=6;spage=99;epage=101;aul ast=Sadanandan;type=2 (accessed May 25, 2021).

Sané, Renuka. 2020. "Isolation: A Weak Link in Indian Public Health." *The Leap Blog,* March 20. Available at https://blog.theleapjournal.org/2020/03/isolation-weak-link-in-indian-public.html (accessed 25 May 2021).

Sané, Renuka, and Ajay Shah. 2021. "Excess Deaths in the COVID-19 Pandemic in India." *Preprint*. doi:10.2139/ssrn.3750679

Sethi, Nitin, and Kumar Sambhav Shrivastava. 2020. "Frustration in National COVID-19 Task Force." *Article 14*, January 27. Available at https://www. article-14.com/post/no-action-taken-frustration-in-national-covid-19-task-force (accessed May 25, 2021).

Shah, Ajay. 2014. "Designing the Monetary Policy Committee." *The Leap Blog*, January 25. Available at https://blog.theleapjournal.org/2014/01/designing-monetary-policy-committee.html (accessed May 25, 2021).

————. 2019. "Buy, Not Build, Spacecraft." *Business Standard,* September 9. Available at http://www.mayin.org/ajayshah/MEDIA/2019/isro_spillovers.html (accessed May 25, 2021).

————. 2020a. "Responding to the New Coronavirus: An Indian Policy Perspective." NIPFP Working Paper No. 309, March 11. Available at https://www.nipfp.org. in/media/medialibrary/2020/07/WP_309_2020.pdf (accessed May 25, 2021).

————. 2020b. "More Testing: From Concept to Implementation." *The Leap Blog*, April 12. Available at https://blog.theleapjournal.org/2020/04/more-testing-from-concept-to.html (accessed May 25, 2021).

Shah, Ajay. 2020c. "The de-Lockdown Needs a Better Institutional Foundation." *Business Standard*, May 4. Available at http://www.mayin.org/ajayshah/ MEDIA/2020/delockdown.html (accessed 25 May 2021).

———. 2020d, June 15. "COVID-19 in India in the Coming Months: The Puzzles Faced by Leaders of Health Care Organisations." *The Leap Blog*. Available at https://blog.theleapjournal.org/2020/06/covid-19-in-india-in-coming-months. html (accessed May 25, 2021).

Shah, Ajay, Sanhita Sapatnekar, Harleen Kaur, and Shubho Roy. 2019. "Financing Common Goods for Health: A Public Administration Perspective from India." *Health Systems & Reform*, 5 (4): 391–96.

Sharma, Jeevan Prakash, and Siddharth Premkumar. 2020. "India's Coronavirus Data Is Infected with Flaws. Numerophobia?" *Outlook*, June 22. Available at https://www.outlookindia.com/magazine/story/india-news-covid-19-special-why-indias-data-on-coronavirus-is-infected-with-flaws/303323 (accessed May 25, 2021).

Sharma, Smriti. 2016. "Problems of the Health Management Information System (HMIS): The Experience of Haryana." *The Leap Blog*, June 13. Available at https://blog.theleapjournal.org/2016/06/problems-of-health-management.html (accessed May 25, 2021).

Sinha, Amitabh. 2020. "Coronavirus Numbers Explained: Behind India's Unusual Spike in COVID-19 Deaths." *The Indian Express*, June 19. Available at https:// indianexpress.com/article/explained/coronavirus-numbers-explained-india-death-toll-mismatch-6462899/ (accessed May 25, 2021).

Smith, Owen, Parul Naib, Pulkit K. Sehgal, and Sheena Chhabra. 2020. "PMJAY under Lockdown: Evidence on Utilisation Trends" (PM-JAY Policy Brief). New Delhi: National Health Authority. Available at https://pmjay.gov.in/sites/default/ files/2020-06/Policy-Brief-8_PM-JAY-under-Lockdown-Evidence_12-06-20_ NHA_WB.pdf (accessed May 25, 2021).

Soucat, Agnes. "Financing Common Goods for Health: Fundamental for Health, the Foundation for UHC." *Health Systems & Reform*, 5 (4): 263–67.

Srikrishna, B. N. 2013. *Report of the Financial Sector Legislative Reforms Commission*, Vol. 1. New Delhi: Union Ministry of Finance, Government of India. Available at https://dea.gov.in/sites/default/files/fslrc_report_vol1_1.pdf (accessed May 25, 2021).

Sudhir, Amita, and Nachiket Mor. 2020. "Indicative Protocol for a First Level Oxygen Therapy Centre for Patients with Suspected or Confirmed COVID-19." *Preprint*. Available at file:///C:/Users/amehta/Downloads/ IndicativeProtocolforaFirstLevelOxygenTherapyCentreSudhirandMor300620 (accessed May 25, 2021).

Thomas, Suja. 2020. "Covid-19 in the Tropics: How Will High Heat and Humidity Shape the Outcomes?" *The Leap Blog*, May 4. Available at https://blog.the-leapjournal.org/2020/05/covid-19-in-tropics-how-will-high-heat.html (accessed May 25, 2021).

Triggle, Nick. 2020. "Coronavirus: Track and Trace System in Place from June—PM." *BBC News*, May 20. Available at https://www.bbc.com/news/uk-52741331 (accessed May 25, 2021).

To view the entire video of this IPF session and the General Discussion that ended the session, please scan this QR code or use the following URL https://www.youtube.com/watch?v=U1mmv_uUoYE

Comments and Discussion[*]

Chair: **Rajesh Bhushan**
Secretary, Ministry of Health and Family Welfare, Government of India

K. P. Krishnan
NCAER & former Secretary, Ministry of Skill Development and Entrepreneurship

Given my experience in government, the lesson that I want to start with is that for a number of complex questions of public policy, very often what is required is a good understanding of something as basic as information asymmetry and the two initial characteristics of public goods, namely, non-rival and non-excludable. Whether it is finance, urban development, land, skills, or cooperatives, these public good concepts can explain far more than what people realize. And not understanding or not applying them can also explain many egregious mistakes in public policy. The Kelkar–Shah book (2019), from which a lot of Ajay's presentation today comes, applies these principles very sensibly.

This paper draws mostly the right conclusions. I want to go a little beyond the paper and relate my remarks to what I am observing of COVID-19 and the government's response.

The first point I want to make is that public goods have a jurisdictional dimension, particularly important in a federal country. India's Constitution provides for three levels of government and distributes responsibilities across them. As economists, we should study whether the principles of public goods and their jurisdictional dimension are embedded in that distribution of constitutional responsibilities. The Constitution's 7th Schedule deals with the distribution of responsibilities between the Union and the states for both legislative and executive powers. The 11th and 12th Schedules, added in 1992, deal with the powers of rural panchayats and urban municipalities. The 7th Schedule has three lists: the Union, the State, and the Concurrent. The third is somewhat peculiar to India, as not many

---

[*] To preserve the sense of the discussions at the India Policy Forum, these discussants' comments the views expressed at the IPF and do not necessarily take into account revisions to the conference version of the paper in response to these and other comments in preparing the final, revised version published in this volume. The original conference version of the paper is available on NCAER's website at the links provided at the end of this section.

other countries have a concurrent list over which both the Union and the states have jurisdiction.

Where does public health figure on these lists? Item 6 on the State List includes public health, sanitation, hospitals, and dispensaries, so *prima facie* public health is a state responsibility. However, dig deeper and item 28 on the Union List mentions port quarantine, including related hospitals, in the context of shipping. In the present context, item 81 on the Union List is about inter-state migration and inter-state quarantine—it would appear that some founding father of the Constitution actually visualized a pandemic. Even more to the point, item 29 in the Concurrent List says, "Prevention of the extension from one State to another of infectious or contagious diseases...." Looking to the third tier of local government, the Constitution's 11th Schedule contains item 23, referring to "health and sanitation, including hospitals, primary health centers, and dispensaries," which leaves little doubt when read with Article 243G relating to panchayats. In parallel, item 6 of the 12th Schedule, when read with Article 243W of the Constitution dealing with urban municipalities, assigns public health and sanitation to urban municipalities.

I wanted to make the point that public health is allocated to state governments as well as local governments, but there are many elements of public health relating to contagious diseases and pandemics that are also in the Union and Concurrent Lists. So one could say either of the following: (a) there is confusion and a lack of clarity on this issue or (b) public health is indeed complex, and there are elements that are national, state-level, and local, requiring close coordination between them. These issues speak directly to the topic of the paper on state capacity and institutional design.

Second, let me turn to the Disaster Management Act of 2005, the lynchpin of the Government of India's initial response to the pandemic using the Act's provisions extensively. The Act defines a disaster as a catastrophe, a mishap, a calamity, or a grave occurrence arising from natural or man-made causes or by accident or negligence. But disaster management also includes prevention, mitigation, and reduction of the risk of any disaster or the severity of its consequences. The National Disaster Management Authority (NDMA) constituted under this Act under the Home Ministry has a large number of powers that include steps for disaster mitigation, prevention, and preparedness.

Section 11 of the Act mandates the NDMA to draw up a national plan for disaster management and has a requirement, again mandatory, that it needs to be reviewed and updated annually. I think that, at some point, this is something that should be looked at by all agencies concerned with public accountability.

In light of these constitutional and legislative issues concerning public health disasters, what are the questions we should pose for future research arising from Ajay Shah's paper? First, is fighting a pandemic a national public good, a regional public good, or a local public good—how do we unpack this? Clearly, there are elements of all three involved. Migration rights need to be dealt with nationally. However, ICU beds and oxygen supplies perhaps need to be dealt with at the state level. The examples that Ajay quoted of Tamil Nadu, Kerala, and subsequently Mumbai, which have been successful in contact tracing and enforcing quarantine, clearly show that this is best done at the municipal and panchayat levels. I think we have to break this broad entity called "public health" into its many constituent elements and do a more detailed analysis of their nature and characteristics in building state capacity.

Second, the NDMA clearly had its work cut out in preparing a national plan to combat COVID-19 in January 2020 when we formally reported cases that the Ministry of Health and Family Welfare was aware of, not in large numbers, but certainly the beginnings of what looked like a pandemic. By the end of the first lockdown, we clearly should have had a revised national plan ready. Monday morning quarterbacking is easy and in retrospect we all have excellent vision, but I think in terms of lessons to be learnt, not getting this right led to a lot of problems.

I want to highlight a final data problem before I conclude: the wrong unit or locus for decision-making clearly led to a lot of perverse behavior. One perversity that I am aware of is in a cross-roads district through which a lot of thoroughfare traffic passes. A large public charity was ready to set up an excellent mobile COVID-19 testing facility offering free testing. The district magistrate banned it under the Disaster Management Act since he was concerned that his district count of COVID-19 would go up. We have seen other districts and states doing this. The absence of more coherent planning and a deeper understanding of the public good nature of the fight against a pandemic led to many such perverse consequences.

Based on Ajay's paper and other data that are coming in, there is a good opportunity for us to research these serious public economics and public health questions.

Reference

Kelkar, Vijay, and Ajay Shah. 2019. *In Service of the Republic: The Art and Science of Economic Policy*. Gurgaon: Penguin Random House.

Randeep Guleria
Director, All India Institute of Medical Sciences

I would like to start by complimenting Ajay Shah for an excellent paper. It is really good at flagging the challenges that we are facing on COVID-19. Let me start with the situation pre-COVID-19 and then see what the health sector did when COVID-19 came into India in a big way and what it should continue to do.

Prior to COVID-19, health care was dominated by the private sector roughly in a 70:30 ratio, with a lot of out-of-pocket expenditures. The government had a lot of schemes, including PMJAY and *Ayushman Bharat* that were making a difference, but a large section of the middle class had the problem of having to pay out of pocket—you could go into an ICU and really lose all your savings. We saw that a lot because we had to shift patients to the All India Institute of Medical Sciences not because the patients were not being managed properly, but because the families had just run out of money. Then there was public sector underinvestment and issues of the quality of care, especially in smaller cities and district hospitals. We were already facing an increasing burden of non-communicable diseases (NCDs). The disease burden in India shifted somewhere around 2003 from communicable diseases to NCDs, and now almost 60 percent of the Indian disease burden is NCDs, including diabetes, cancers, and chronic respiratory diseases.

There were also huge human resource challenges, such as a shortage of doctors and health personnel in both urban and rural India. Much effort was being made to increase medical colleges, to get the private sector hospitals to become teaching centers, to start Diplomate of National Board courses, and to get nurses to become nurse practitioners. We were also looking at the concept of family physicians, a concept that was missing in India with the move towards specialists, which was not working in smaller cities and district hospitals. So, this was the background when the SARS-CoV-2 pandemic hit us.

India faced immediate challenges. It is not that India was totally unprepared or that, in recent history, it had never anticipated a pandemic. In 2005, and even as early as 2000, there was talk in the government of planning for a pandemic. The Government of India had set up a joint monitoring group to look at outbreak management at the time of the Zika virus. We had discussions about this in 2003 after SARS, and in responding to H5N1 bird or avian flu, which caused a significant amount of poultry deaths in Maharashtra, West Bengal, and the Northeast. Luckily, the virus did not exhibit sustained human transmission, though it had a case fatality rate of more than 60 percent. At that point of time, there was a huge pandemic concern in India and globally. We had the H1N1 pandemic in 2009. So there were lessons that we had learnt. But still, you are never really prepared for a pandemic until it really hits you.

The government was proactive early. We had early screening at airports and the very aggressive initial lockdown gave us time to prepare. We had COVID-19 care centers, COVID-19 hospitals, and COVID-19 ICUs. Oxygen facilities were actually made available and ventilators, to some extent, were also made available. There were issues on testing and training that we handled.

But there were a lot of downsides we faced, and those are the lessons that we need to really look at. First was the decline in private sector involvement. I mentioned that the private sector has been big in health care, but when it came to the pandemic, the involvement was much less, and this put a lot of stress on the already strained government health sector. A strategy needs to be developed to get more private sector involvement when it comes to outbreak management because the bulk of ICU and ventilator care still lies in the private sector. In a large number of district and smaller hospitals, we do not have oxygen supply, which can be easily made available. Second, on equipment and personnel, we did not have a large number of ventilators and critical care specialists, and this became one of the major issues.

Third, aggressive contact tracing, which the paper discusses very well, was another major challenge. The biggest problem was the stigma that got associated with COVID-19. We need an effective public outreach program to help people get over their stigma. I know many individuals who had classical COVID-19 symptoms—fever, cough, or shortness of breath—but refused to get themselves tested, and many then went into respiratory failure and had to be rushed to the hospital. Faced with this stigma, contact tracing cannot work well. I know that in certain areas of New Delhi, where stigma was prominent, this led to an increased disease burden and cluster formation in that area. So, under-reporting led to surges.

Fourth, testing was also a huge challenge, and the paper brings this out. When we started—and we had realized this way back in 2009 when looking at H1N1—there were very few, good quality virology labs in the country, and that became a big challenge. Our virology lab framework was designed initially with support from the US Centers for Disease Control and Prevention and the National Institute of Virology in Pune, but this was geared to influenza surveillance. Virology labs need a lot of investment in infection control to come up to BSL2 (Biosafety Level-2) standards, and this was something which was not available at the beginning. This was upscaled during the lockdown. We got medical colleges to build labs and start testing, and from when we had just about 100–150 labs, we have now gone to over 1,000 labs and the number of tests from 10,000–20,000 to 200,000 per day. Here again, the challenge remains persuading the private medical colleges to invest in setting up testing labs and to ramp up testing. We need a public–private partnership arrangement here.

Finally, the paper mentions the need for good data on the pandemic: data on antibodies, those who have tested positive, the mortality rate, or even just hospital data. We have to look at what comorbidities are: we really have no idea. Does malnutrition serve as a risk factor for severe COVID-19? Does past history of tuberculosis serve as a risk factor? If you have underlying bad lungs, do you get more severe COVID-19? We have a younger population, but we have a higher number of diabetics; so are the younger people who are diabetic more prone to develop COVID-19? We need data to answer many of these research questions. We need to develop an electronic national health database that can be used even after the pandemic because it will help on disease surveillance.

The challenge will be to identify who will collect the data and ensure that they are collected correctly. Doctors, who are already overburdened, cannot do it. The paper notes that often states try to hide the data because they want to show that they are doing better than others. If fatalities are undercounted, infection rates are low because you are asked to test less people, then data credibility is the casualty, and we need to look at this. We also need to make sure the data are readily available to researchers in a timely way. If we have a national database that is available to all research-ers, they can then do a deep dive into the data and help come up with solutions that could help save lives and help in better policy design and operational management. This is something that we really need to develop in the long term, not only for COVID-19 but also for post-COVID-19 management as we look to the shift toward NCDs that needs a lot of data if we are to respond effectively.

I will conclude by recapping the lessons we have learnt so far—we need to increase investment in health, we need to focus on primary health, we need aggressive surveillance, and we need to have a good public–private partnerships so that the private sector can come on board quickly. There has also been a lot of talk that we need an incremental, insurance-based approach so that health care becomes a right in India.

General Discussion

Participants in the General Discussion included **Karthik Muralidharan, Rohini Somanathan, Pankaj Shrivastava, C. N. Raghupati Cavale**, and **Subhomoy Bhattacharjee.**

To get a sense of the richness of this discussion, we invite you to view the video of the General Discussion segment of this IPF session. Please use the appropriate hyperlink on the IPF 2020 Program available at the links below.

The session video and all slide presentations for this IPF session are hyperlinked on the IPF Program available by scanning this QR code or going to

https://www.ncaer.org/IPF2020/Agenda/Agenda_IPF_2020.pdf

BARRY EICHENGREEN*
University of California, Berkeley

POONAM GUPTA†
World Bank

RISHABH CHOUDHARY‡
Indira Gandhi Institute of Development Research
World Bank

Inflation Targeting in India: An Interim Assessment§

ABSTRACT   This paper provides an assessment of India's inflation targeting regime. It shows that the Reserve Bank of India (RBI) is best characterized as a flexible inflation targeter: contrary to criticism, it does not neglect changes in the output gap when setting policy rates. The paper does not find that the RBI became more hawkish following the transition to inflation targeting; on the contrary, adjusting for inflation and the output gap, policy rates became lower, not higher. Some evidence suggests that inflation has become better anchored: increases in actual inflation excite inflation expectations less, which is indicative of improved anti-inflation credibility. The question is whether the shift to inflation targeting has enhanced the credibility of monetary policy such that the RBI is in a position to take extraordinary action in response to the COVID-19 crisis. The paper argues that the rules and understandings governing inflation targeting regimes come with escape clauses, allowing central banks to suspend their inflation targets temporarily under specific circumstances such as those provided by the COVID-19 pandemic. The paper provides evidence that inflation targeting central banks were able to respond more forcefully to the COVID-19 crisis, consistent with the idea that inflation expectations were better anchored, providing more policy room for maneuver.

Keywords: Inflation Targeting, Monetary Policy, India

JEL Classification: E5, E52

   * *eichengr@berkeley.edu*
   † *pgupta@ncaer.org*
   ‡ *rchoudhary@worldbank.org*
   § We thank Kenneth Kletzer, Rakesh Mohan, Raghuram Rajan, Rajeswari Sengupta, Venkat Bhargav Sreedhara, and participants at the India Policy Forum, July 13–16, 2020, for helpful comments.

1. Introduction

Monetary policy in India has a checkered history. The Reserve Bank of India (RBI) has followed a variety of policy strategies over the years. Following a long period of fiscal dominance during which the central bank was expected to monetize budget deficits, the fiscal framework was reformed and strengthened in the early years of the current century, allowing the RBI to exert more independence and bring inflation down to levels characteristic of other low- and middle-income (LMI) countries. This transition culminated in the inflation-targeting (IT) agreement of February 2015 and an amended RBI Act in May 2016, which gave the central bank a statutory inflation target. At this point, the RBI adopted a full IT framework, emulating international best practice.

These changes being recent, their consequences have been the subject of little systematic analysis. Moreover, their efficacy is now being subjected to the mother of all stress tests in the form of the COVID-19 pandemic. We think that four years of experience is just enough for a preliminary analysis and that the challenge of the pandemic makes it important to extract lessons from that experience.

Some of the lessons we draw may be surprising. Contrary to conventional wisdom that the RBI should focus on core inflation and "look through" volatile and transient food price inflation, we find that food price inflation can de-anchor expectations and spill over into core inflation; by implication, monetary policy should respond. We show that the RBI is best characterized as a flexible inflation targeter: contrary to criticism, it does not neglect changes in the output gap when setting policy. We do not find that the RBI became more hawkish following the transition to IT; on the contrary, adjusting for inflation and the output gap, policy rates became lower, not higher. We find some evidence that inflation has become better anchored: increases in actual inflation do less to excite inflation expectations, indicative of improved anti-inflation credibility. Consistent with this conclusion, a number of inflation-related outcomes (the level and volatility of inflation, the stability of inflation expectations, and the behavior of ancillary variables such as the exchange rate and equity markets) are more stable than before.

Finally, we ask whether the RBI, having gained credibility with the shift to IT, is in a position to take extraordinary steps in response to COVID-19. We argue that this is the case, and that rules like those governing modern IT regimes come with implicit escape clauses allowing central banks credibly committed to those regimes to deviate, under exceptional circumstances, without untoward consequences. Specifically, we argue that the better anchoring of inflation expectations has enhanced the scope for the RBI to respond to an exceptional shock like the COVID-19 pandemic—a shock that is (a) independently verifiable and (b) not of the authorities' own making—despite the fact that inflation was already running at the top of the target range and that COVID-19, as a negative supply shock, might be expected to raise inflation. We provide evidence that inflation-targeting central banks were able to respond more forcefully to the COVID-19 crisis, consistent with the idea that inflation expectations were better anchored, giving them more policy room for maneuver.

Section 2 starts with an overview of the evolution of India's monetary policy framework, placing the shift to IT within a broader historical context. Section 3 describes different measures of inflation for India with an eye toward determining which have the greatest utility for policy. Section 4 estimates reaction functions for the RBI that can be used to place its policy actions in an international comparative perspective. It asks whether and how the reaction functions changed with the shift to IT. Sections 5 and 6 look at how the behavior of macroeconomic and financial variables, including inflation expectations and pass-through, changed, if at all, with the shift to IT. Section 7 looks at the RBI's response to the COVID-19 pandemic, after which Section 8 concludes the paper.

2. India's Monetary Policy Framework[1]

India's monetary policy framework has evolved over recent decades (for a comprehensive summary, see Appendix Table A.1). In the first two decades following Independence, there was no formal framework for monetary policy. Policy regulated credit availability with an eye toward the needs of the current Five-Year Plan.[2] With enactment of the Banking Regulation Act in 1949, banks were required to maintain a Statutory Liquidity Ratio (SLR) in the form of gold, cash, and approved securities. Other policy instruments included the discount rate (bank rate), reserve requirements, and open market operations (OMOs).

---

1. This section draws on Mohan and Ray (2018), Das (2020), and Hutchison et al. (2013). See also Mohan and Kapur (2009) and Patra and Kapur (2012) for discussions of the evolution of monetary policy in India. Dua (2020) provides a discussion of the IT framework, and Patnaik and Pandey (2020) compare features of India's IT framework with that of other countries.

2. Monetization of the budget deficit by the RBI increased after the Second Five-Year Plan, leading to an increase in statutory liquidity ratio to 25 percent from 20 percent.

The monetary policy framework in place since the end of the 1960s (when the major banks were nationalized) through the mid-1980s is often described as one of "credit planning," during which policy operated via the SLR and the Cash Reserve Ratio (CRR), a specified minimum fraction of total customer deposits that commercial banks must hold in cash or as deposits with the central bank. The SLR was used to finance the budget deficit, the CRR to neutralize the effect of deficit financing on inflation.[3] Deposits at public sector banks and credit supplied by them expanded rapidly, resulting in a rapid increase in the broad money supply: the money stock increased by 17.5 percent a year during the 1970s and the first half of the 1980s, compared to less than 10 percent during the previous decade. Since the period featured modest economic growth (about 4 percent a year), this resulted in relatively high inflation (averaging 8.8 percent). Das (2020) contends that traditional monetary policy instruments, such as the bank rate and OMOs, proved inadequate for regulating credit growth, money supply, and inflation, owing to fiscal dominance.[4]

From the mid-1980s through the late 1990s, the RBI employed a "monetary targeting with feedback" framework in which the broad money supply was set in line with projected GDP growth and inflation. The move to this framework coincided with financial sector reforms and increasingly market-determined interest and exchange rates. Price stability was the central objective of monetary policy, with 5–7 percent as the target range for inflation. (This is different from saying that the central bank adopted a monetary policy strategy of inflation targeting, where such a framework involves additional elements, as described below.) Although the RBI introduced various money market instruments in the late 1980s, including commercial

---

3. The SLR was raised from 25 percent of the bank's Net Demand and Time Liabilities (NDTL) in 1969 to 37 percent by July 1985, while the CRR was raised from 3 percent of the bank's NDTL in 1969 to 9 percent by 1985.

4. Recall that the RBI was not independent and was expected to finance the budget deficit with no questions asked. As Ghate and Kletzer (2016) put it:

> Fiscal dominance and financial repression have been hallmarks of Indian monetary policy for decades. The Reserve Bank of India was designated as the banker for the government and authorized to grant advances to the Government of India in the Reserve Bank of India Act of 1934. These advances became *ad hoc* three-month Treasury Bills continuously held by the RBI in a process of automatic monetization of government debt. The RBI simply funded the public sector budget deficit through periods of rising public debt and inflation until the 1990s. In 1997, the authorization to issue such *ad hoc* Treasury Bills ended and was replaced by a system of Ways and Means advances. The RBI continues in its debt management role for the Government of India. In 2006, RBI's participation in the primary market for government debt ceased, and India completed the transition to market-determined yields on government bonds.

paper and certificates of deposit, the money market was thin and illiquid due to low volumes. Fiscal dominance in the form of significant automatic monetization of budget deficits by the central bank remained a monetary policy fact of life.

As the economy was further liberalized, the practice of automatic debt monetization through the central bank's purchases of treasury bills was eliminated.[5] This allowed the RBI to adopt a multiple indicator approach as of April 1998. In addition to taking into account trends in growth and inflation, the central bank now took into consideration additional macroeconomic variables such as credit growth, the exchange rate, the trade balance, unemployment, and the stance of fiscal policy. The decade that followed was also marked by greater fiscal discipline, enforced starting in 2003 through a newly enacted Fiscal Responsibility and Budget Management (FRBM) Act, which prohibited the RBI from purchasing government securities on the primary market, and by continued financial sector liberalization and interest rate deregulation.

As a result of these changes, interest rates gradually became the main instrument of monetary policy. From the late 1990s through the early 2000s, the bank rate was used to signal the policy stance. In April 1999, the RBI introduced an Interim Liquidity Adjustment Facility (ILAF) under which liquidity was injected at the bank rate and withdrawn at the reverse repo rate (the rate at which the RBI borrows from the banks). By November 2004, this had developed into a full-fledged Liquidity Adjustment Facility (LAF) in which the repo rate (the rate at which the banks borrow from the RBI) provided the upper bound of the policy interest rate corridor, while the reverse repo rate provided the lower bound. If liquidity was ample, the operative rate was the reverse repo rate; when it was scarce, it was the repo rate. From 2011, a revised corridor was redefined as a fixed width of 200 basis points. The repo rate was placed in the middle, with the reverse repo rate 100 basis

---

5. There were two kinds of treasury bills: "ordinary treasury bills" were placed with banks and retails investors at market rates as per a weekly schedule of borrowing, and "ad hoc bills" could be placed only with the RBI, at below market rates when required. "Ad hoc" connotes that there was no schedule for issuance. In 1994, the RBI and the government signed an agreement specifying limits on the automatic monetization of budget deficits. In March 1997, another agreement was then signed under which ad hoc treasury bills were replaced by Ways and Means Advances, through which the government could borrow from the RBI subject to limits. It was agreed that these advances would not be a regular source of deficit financing but only cover day-to-day mismatches in receipts and payments of the government. Note that as part of the COVID-19 policy response, the borrowing limits under Ways and Means Advances were increased for both Central and state governments, and the number of consecutive days for which government advances could be overdrawn was also increased.

points below it, and a Marginal Standing Facility (MSF) rate 100 basis points above it (at which commercial banks could borrow overnight up to 1 percent of their net demand and time liabilities to meet liquidity shocks).

Further changes were introduced in September 2014 to coincide with the move to formal inflation targeting (see Patra et al. 2016). An expert committee (Reserve Bank of India 2014) had recommended that the RBI should manage liquidity by offering term repos of different tenors. This led to the ending of unlimited accommodation of liquidity needs at the fixed LAF repo rate; providing most central bank liquidity through term repo auctions; fine-tuning operations through repo/reverse repo auctions of maturities ranging from intra-day to 28 days; allowing market participants to hold central bank liquidity for a longer period; and progressively reducing the SLR.

The government and the RBI then signed an inflation-targeting agreement in February 2015 and amended the RBI Act in May 2016.[6] The inflation target was set by the government in consultation with the RBI.[7] Accordingly, the government announced via the Official Gazette that 4 percent Consumer Price Index (CPI) inflation would be the target from August 5, 2016, with an upper tolerance limit of 6 percent and a lower limit of 2 percent. It further announced that the government would constitute a six-member Monetary Policy Committee (MPC), including three ex-officio members from the RBI: the Governor of the Bank (who would also be its Chairperson); the Deputy Governor in charge of monetary policy; and one officer to be nominated by its Central Board. The other three members would be appointed by the government. The members would hold office for four years and could not be reappointed.

The RBI was required to organize at least four meetings of the MPC annually, following a schedule published in advance.[8] It was asked to publish a Monetary Policy Report every six months explaining the sources of inflation. It was to provide forecasts of inflation for a period ranging from 6 to 18 months; the resolution adopted by the Committee; further details on the 14th day after every meeting of the MPC, including the minutes of the proceedings of the meeting; the vote and the statement of each member of the MPC; and a document explaining steps to be taken to implement the decisions of the MPC. Finally, if the inflation target was not met, the RBI was required to submit a report detailing the reasons for failure to achieve it; remedial actions; and the estimated time period within which the inflation

---

6. For details, see amendment to the RBI Act, 1934, inserted by the Finance Act, 2016, Chapter III F, Monetary Policy.

7. With the possibility of revisiting it after five years.

8. The first meeting of the MPC was held on October 3 and 4, 2016.

target could be achieved. The agreement specified that the RBI would be deemed to have missed its target if inflation exceeded 6 percent, or declined below 2 percent, for three straight quarters.

3. Measures of Inflation

Inflation in India has averaged 8 percent or more since the 1980s, except in the early 2000s, when it averaged 4 percent and, more recently, when inflation fell with the move to inflation targeting (see Table 1). Inflation rates have exceeded average global inflation for the most part (Figure 1), while fluctuations have broadly tracked those in other LMI countries aside from 2009–2015. Basu et al. (2015) attribute India's relatively high inflation during this period to budget deficits and monetary policy accommodation in the years that coincided with national elections.

TABLE 1. Average Inflation Rates in India, the World, and in Low- and Middle-Income Countries (%)

	1981–85	1986–90	1991–95	1996–2000	2001–05	2006–10	2011–15	2016–19
India	9.3	8.5	10.5	7.7	4.0	8.8	7.9	4.0
LMI	10.8	9.3	13.7	6.6	5.3	6.3	4.5	3.2
World	9.3	6.8	8.7	4.8	3.5	4.9	3.0	2.0

Source: World Bank's World Development Indicators (WDI) for LMI countries and the world, Ministry of Statistics and Programme Implementation, CEIC for India, authors' calculations.

FIGURE 1. Long-term Inflation Rate (Consumer Prices) in India and Its Co-movement with Global and LMI Inflation

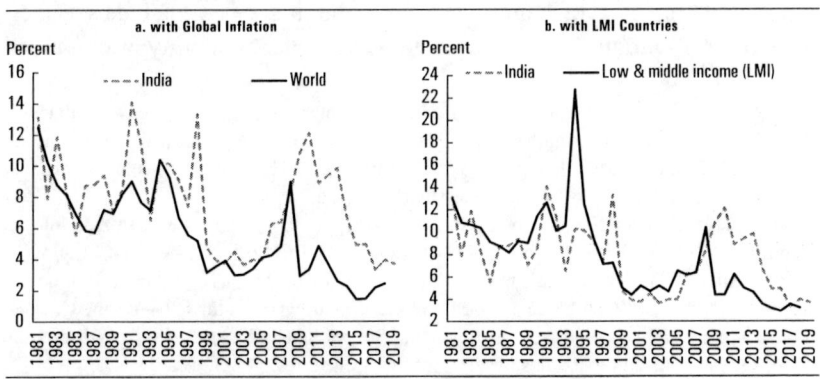

Source: WDI, Authors' calculations.

On the basis of correlations like these, some authors (e.g., Chhibber 2020) have argued that Indian inflation is heavily influenced by global developments, reducing the effectiveness of monetary policy. We analyzed the correlation of global inflation and Indian headline, food, and fuel inflation series at monthly, quarterly, and annual frequencies. It turns out that Indian inflation is *not* highly correlated with global inflation. For the most part, there is no systematic time pattern in these correlations.[9]

3.1. Alternative Measures

A challenge for monetary policy generally is the measurement of inflation. This is true for India, where there was no composite Cost of Living Index before 2011. Instead, there existed separate CPI series for industrial workers, agricultural workers, and nonagricultural rural workers. The CPI for industrial workers (CPI-IW) was commonly used as a proxy for the composite CPI.[10]

A unified CPI series has been available since January 2011. It can be used to calculate monthly year-over-year inflation starting in January 2012. While the RBI used the Wholesale Price Index (WPI) in monetary policy analysis until about March 2014, it now utilizes the headline CPI.[11] The WPI consists of the prices of bulk transactions of goods in the domestic market. It includes manufacturing and commodities but not services (see Table 2).

CPI inflation has been higher than WPI inflation on average. While the average difference between CPI and WPI inflation was 0.4 percent between 1997 and 2009, it widened to 3.2 percent in 2009–2019. Divergences between the two series can be attributed to both food inflation (which has a higher weight in the CPI) and manufacturing inflation (which has a larger weight in the WPI).

The question is: Which series should the RBI target? The WPI may not be the best for two reasons. First, it places a large weight on oil and commodity prices, which are volatile; second, it does not include services. Headline CPI inflation is also affected by volatile commodity prices, albeit

---

9. Results available on request. These findings are not surprising: food prices in India have been much more stable than global prices because they are administered, while energy prices were similarly more stable than global prices until about 2015, and co-move more strongly with global prices after they became more market-based.

10. There have been five different CPI series: CPI-Combined, CPI–IW, CPI Agricultural Labor (CPI–AL), CPI Rural Labor (CPI–RL), and the CPI Urban Non-Manual Employees (CPIUNME). The last one of these has been discontinued. The weights of different components in the baskets for CPI-Combined and CPI–IW are similar, whereas the CPI–AL and CPI–RL have a larger weight on food, nearly 70 percent. See Mohan and Ray (2018) for a discussion of the composition and dynamics of different inflation series.

11. When estimating reaction functions, we follow this practice, using the CPI inflation starting 2012 and WPI inflation before that.

TABLE 2. Composition of the Wholesale Price Index and the Headline Consumer Price Index

WPI		CPI	
Primary products/food	22.6	Food, beverages, and tobacco	48.2
Fuel	13.2	Fuel and light	6.8
Manufactured	64.2	Housing	10.1
		Miscellaneous	28.3
		Clothing and footwear	6.5

Source: CEIC, Ministry of Statistics and Programme Implementation.

to a lesser extent than the WPI. More importantly, food prices account for nearly half of the CPI, and food prices are often heavily affected by sector-specific, non-monetary factors such as weather and harvests. Insofar as shocks to food prices are transient, there is an argument that the RBI should look through them.[12] Such arguments favor a core (non-food, non-fuel) CPI. The counterarguments favoring headline inflation are that (a) it is easier to explain to the public and thus more effective in anchoring expectations and (b) food inflation feeds back into core inflation and hence needs to be tamed lest it becomes structural and strongly entrenched.[13]

The choice of WPI or CPI is inconsequential if the two series co-move closely. But this is not generally the case, as shown in Figure 2. In the period 2014 Q3 to 2016 Q4, for example, WPI inflation (headline) averaged −1.2 a quarter, while CPI inflation (headline) averaged more than 5 percent a quarter.

12. It has been argued (by Banerjee 2020 and others) that IT has led to a worsening of the agricultural terms of trade and declining rural/agricultural incomes. Variants of this argument are that the government has grown more reluctant to raise support prices for agricultural products because it wishes to help the RBI to lower inflation, or that it has grown more reluctant because it fears the wider repercussions on the economy of the RBI raising interest rates in response. We find the first variant implausible (helping the RBI hit its inflation target is not a government priority). The second variant amounts to the statement that government support for the rural sector costs the economy as a whole through either higher inflation or higher interest rates. The 2015 IT agreement reflected a consensus that paying these costs in the form of inflation was more costly than paying them in the form of interest rates. We do not see what has changed.

13. Cecchetti (2007) and Mohanty (2014) recommend targeting headline inflation. JPMorgan (2018) uses a modified version of core inflation, which besides food and fuel further excludes elements that may be impacted by fuel prices. They term this measure "core-core CPI" and suggest that India should target core or core-core inflation. The argument runs that instead of core inflation converging to food/headline inflation, it is food/headline inflation that converges to core inflation in India. Hence, an elevated core inflation can be undesirable and ought to be monitored and targeted directly. As we show below, we do not find evidence to support the argument.

FIGURE 2.   Consumer and Wholesale Price Inflation

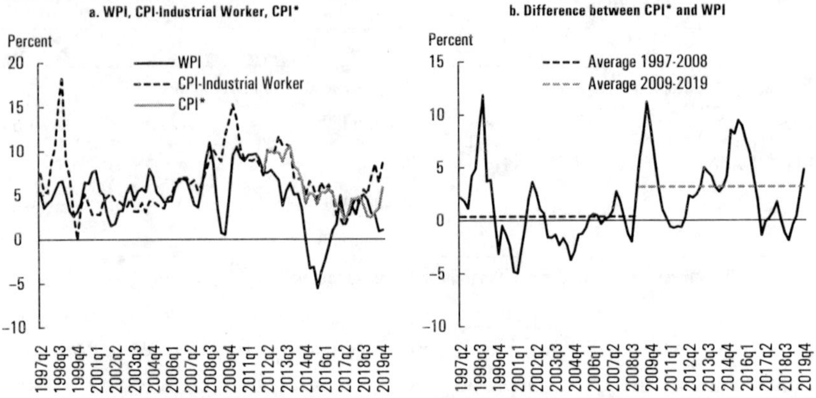

a. WPI, CPI-Industrial Worker, CPI*

b. Difference between CPI* and WPI

Source: Ministry of Statistics and Programme Implementation, CEIC.
Note: *CPI inflation series consists of CPI-Industrial Workers until 2011, and CPI-Combined from 2012 onward.

The correlation between WPI headline and CPI headline inflation has not been very high, though it rose in the last decade and is significantly greater than zero at the 95 percent confidence level (see Table 3). Given the relative composition of their baskets, it is unsurprising that WPI headline inflation is correlated more strongly with WPI core inflation, and that CPI headline inflation is correlated more strongly with food inflation. Their respective food and core inflation series are correlated more strongly than their respective headline inflation series.[14]

3.2. Persistence

Contrary to popular presumption, food price inflation has not been higher than core and headline inflation (Table 4).[15] Neither is it more persistent. We estimate first-order autocorrelation coefficients for rolling windows of 20, 30, and 40 quarters. The coefficients for core and headline inflation are higher than that for food price inflation.[16] Nor has inflation persistence declined over time (in contrast to evidence for the US, e.g., Fuhrer 2010).

14. These patterns have not changed in the last decade.
15. See Appendix B for details.
16. Unit root tests conducted on all inflation measures provide mixed results. While we cannot reject the null of unit root for core inflation at the 5 percent level using both ADF and PP tests (implying high persistence), but for food, fuel, and headline inflation, we reject the null of unit root when the lag length considered for ADF and PP tests is less than 4.

TABLE 3.   Correlation Matrix of Inflation Measures

A: 1997 Q2–2008 Q4						
Inflation Measure	WPI Headline	WPI Food	WPI Core	CPI Headline	CPI Food	CPI Core
WPI Headline	1					
WPI Food	0.34*	1				
WPI Core	0.82*	0.20	1			
CPI Headline	0.32*	0.90*	0.09	1		
CPI Food	0.41*	0.93*	0.26	0.94*	1	
CPI Core	−0.04	0.63*	−0.32*	0.81*	0.58*	1
B: 2009 Q1–2019 Q4						
Inflation Measure	WPI Headline	WPI Food	WPI Core	CPI Headline	CPI Food	CPI Core
WPI Headline	1					
WPI Food	0.55*	1				
WPI Core	0.93*	0.27	1			
CPI Headline	0.58*	0.91*	0.39*	1		
CPI Food	0.34*	0.89*	0.10	0.92*	1	
CPI Core	0.77*	0.74*	0.67*	0.86*	0.61*	1

Source: Authors' calculations.
Note: *denotes significance at the 5% level.

TABLE 4.   Level and Volatility of CPI Inflation and Its Components (Quarterly Data from 1997 Q2–2019 Q4)

	Mean	Standard Deviation	Coefficient of Variation
CPI	6.41	3.31	0.52
CPI Food	6.29	5.01	0.80
CPI Fuel	6.96	4.96	0.71
CPI Core	6.47	2.76	0.43

Source: Authors' calculations.

We also calculate the largest autoregressive root or dominant root in the univariate autoregressive process for each inflation series. In the long run, the effect of a shock will be dominated by this largest root. The dominant roots confirm that core and headline inflation are more persistent than food price inflation. The sum of autoregressive coefficients gives a similar result: high persistence across inflation series and higher persistence of core inflation.

Yet another measure of persistence is the impulse half-life, that is, the number of periods it takes for the impulse response to fall below 0.5 following a unit shock. This measure also confirms the higher persistence of core inflation (see Appendix B). The half-life for headline inflation is estimated at around four quarters, and for core inflation at around five quarters. These findings are consistent with the earlier results of Ball et al. (2016), who similarly document the shorter duration of food price shocks.

We estimate a vector autoregression (VAR) model to identify the timing relationship between food price inflation and core inflation.[17] We treat food and core inflation as endogenous and fuel inflation as exogenous (as given largely by global economic conditions).[18] We estimate specifications with 2, 4, and 8 lags. Food price inflation has a larger and more consistent impact on core inflation than vice versa. The impact is significant for two quarters. Fuel inflation does not impact food or core inflation at a quarterly frequency. Granger causality tests in Table 5 further suggest that food inflation Granger-causes core inflation. This result is robust to different lag lengths. In contrast, there is no evidence that core inflation Granger-causes

T A B L E   5 .   Granger Causality Wald Tests (VAR Model)

Dependent Variable (y)	Explanatory Variable (x)	F	df	df_r	Prob > F	Does x Granger-cause y?
Lag length 2						
Food inflation	Core inflation	2.4129	2	81	0.0960	No
Core inflation	Food inflation	3.4081	2	81	0.0379	Yes
Lag length 4						
Food inflation	Core inflation	3.3246	4	73	0.0147	Yes
Core inflation	Food inflation	3.3435	4	73	0.0143	Yes
Lag length 8						
Food inflation	Core inflation	0.6982	8	61	0.6917	No
Core inflation	Food inflation	2.9597	8	61	0.0073	Yes

Source: Authors' calculations.
Notes: Granger causality is based on a 5% significance level; "No" indicates that we fail to reject the null hypothesis: x does not Granger-cause y.

17. Data is from 1997 Q1 to 2019 Q4. We use the standard splicing method to expand our CPI 2011–12 inflation series, which starts from 2012 onwards. Prior to 2012, CPI–IW inflation has been used for each component—food, fuel, and core.

18. India being a net importer of fuel, its base price is determined globally, and retail prices by the base price and taxes. During the earlier period in the analysis, the retail price was administered.

food inflation. Put differently, past values of food inflation help predict core inflation, but past values of core inflation do not help predict food inflation.

Contrary to popular perception, we do not find food price inflation to be higher, more volatile, or persistent than core inflation. There is evidence, however, that the changes in food inflation lead to subsequent changes in core inflation, but not the other way around. This reinforces a finding of Mishra and Roy (2012).[19] We confirm that this relationship has not changed post IT.

Other authors (e.g., Chhibber 2020) have suggested that the RBI should "look through" (i.e., disregard) movements in food price inflation on the grounds that food prices are volatile, and that focusing on them distorts the conduct of policy. In responding to food price inflation, the central bank will be focusing on the transitory inflation threat and neglecting other more important objectives of policy. We find, on the contrary, that food price inflation feeds through to core inflation as producers mark up the prices of other products. Central banks in advanced economies have been able to look through fluctuations in food and fuel price inflation without consequences for core inflation and therefore, without jeopardizing their inflation targets. In India, where food is a much more important component of consumption baskets, this may not be the case. This is not an argument that the central bank should react to each and every movement in headline and food inflation. But it does suggest that neglecting food price inflation that diverges from the target for an extended period of time can have negative consequences.

4. Reaction Functions

We now ask whether monetary policy decisions are influenced more by the output gap or inflation, whether the reaction function has changed with the adoption of inflation targeting, whether the output gap and inflation carry different weights in the reaction function at high and low values, and whether the reaction function is different for headline and core inflation.[20]

---

19. This is consistent with Ball et al. (2016), who show that changes in headline inflation feed into expected inflation and future core inflation. Raj et al. (2020) evaluate several possible measures of core inflation and similarly find that headline inflation does not converge to core inflation.

20. Rangarajan (2020) suggests that IT in India is flexible in the sense that "what inflation targeting demands is that when inflation goes beyond the comfort zone, the exclusive concern of monetary policy must be to bring it back to the target level. When inflation is within the comfort zone, authorities can look to other objectives."

All estimated reaction functions include the output gap and inflation but, in an augmented version, we also include the lagged policy rate, the percentage change in the exchange rate, and the budget deficit or government borrowing.

A number of earlier papers have estimated reaction functions for the RBI (see Appendix Table A.4). These studies find that the output gap is important (Hutchison et al. 2013; Mohanty and Klau 2004) and that the exchange rate also matters, especially from the late 1990s when it became more flexible. Inflation, in general, has a much smaller coefficient, both absolutely and relative to the Taylor rule benchmark of 1.5.

These analyses typically use quarterly data, since quarterly GDP growth is available from 1997; we follow this standard practice.[21] For inflation, we use the WPI inflation until 2013 and the CPI inflation thereafter, since these are the inflation rates monitored by the RBI.

For the policy rate, we adopt two approaches. First, we construct a composite policy rate series in the manner of Patra and Kapur (2012).[22] This is based on the series that was used by the RBI at the time for monetary policy purposes, as detailed in Table 6 and Figure 3a. In the second approach, we use the bank rate for the period 1997–2001 and the repo rate from 2002 onwards[23] (See Figure 3b). The exchange rate is calculated as quarter-over-quarter percentage change in the nominal exchange rate with respect to the US dollar. The budget deficit and market borrowing variables are highly seasonal at a quarterly frequency, so we adjust them

TABLE 6. Effective Policy Rates

	Duration	
Instrument	Month	Quarter
Bank rate	January 1996–February 2002	1996 Q1–2002 Q1
Reverse repo rate	March 2002–June 2006	2002 Q2–2006 Q2
Repo rate	July 2006–November 2008	2006 Q3–2008 Q4
Reverse repo rate	December 2008–May 2010	2009 Q1–2010 Q2
Repo rate	June 2010–present	2010 Q3–present

Source: Based on information in Patra and Kapur (2012).

21. Papers estimating reaction functions at a monthly frequency use the Index of Industrial Production as a proxy for output, which we regard as unreliable.

22. The bank rate, the repo rate, and the reverse repo rate are available as monthly averages and end-of-the-month values. The results are insensitive to the two series. In the results reported here, we have used monthly averages.

23. The two series are highly correlated, as is evident in Figure 4.

FIGURE 3.   **Policy Rates**

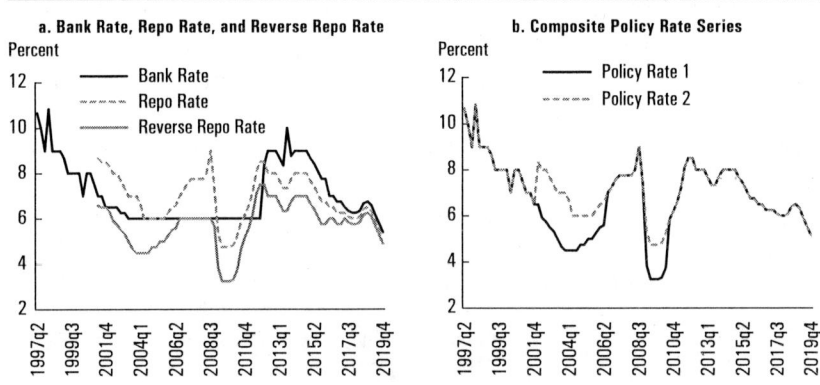

a. Bank Rate, Repo Rate, and Reverse Repo Rate

b. Composite Policy Rate Series

Source: RBI, CEIC.   Source: Authors' calculations.
Note: The first composite policy rate series is based on the policy rates at different points in time, as per
Table 6. In the second composite policy rate series, the bank rate is used for the period 1996–2001 and the
repo rate from 2002 onwards. The correlation between the two policy rate series is 0.93.

for seasonality and express them as a percentage of the seasonally-adjusted nominal GDP.[24]

The output gap is measured as the difference between the seasonally adjusted real GDP and its trend obtained via the Hodrick-Prescott filter (as in Patra and Kapur 2012) and expressed as a percentage of seasonally adjusted real GDP.[25] Summary statistics and correlations for these variables are presented in the Appendix Table A.4.[26] The policy rate is positively and significantly correlated with the output gap and exchange rate depreciation. It is also positively correlated with inflation, though the correlation is weaker and significant only at the 10 percent level.

We estimate the following baseline specification of the reaction function using OLS:

$$epr_t = \alpha_0 + \alpha_1 gap_t + \alpha_2 \text{inflation}_t + \epsilon_t \tag{1}$$

where, epr_t is the effective policy rate; gap_t denotes the output gap expressed as a percentage of GDP; and inflation_t denotes the inflation measure as targeted by the RBI. We assess if the policy rate is different after

24. We use both X-11 and X-13 ARIMA SEATS to seasonally adjust these series. The choice of filter does not seem to matter in the results.

25. The quarterly real GDP series is seasonally adjusted using the X-11 algorithm (of the US Department of Commerce).

26. The policy rate is most persistent (or inertial), followed by inflation. The output gap and exchange rate are least persistent, as per their AR(1) coefficients.

TABLE 7.   Monetary Policy Reaction Functions (Dependent Variable is the Effective Policy Rate)

	I	II	III	IV
Inflation	0.11	0.06	0.08***	0.08***
	(1.25)	(0.62)	(3.23)	(2.86)
Output gap (% of GDP)	0.36***	0.40***	0.20***	0.21***
	(4.43)	(4.96)	(2.65)	(2.64)
Inflation targeting		−0.82***		−0.07
		(2.98)		(0.75)
Lagged effective policy rate			0.85***	0.85***
			(18.00)	(17.85)
Constant	6.17***	6.56***	0.48*	0.53*
	(13.27)	(11.29)	(1.73)	(1.80)
Observations	91	91	90	90
Adjusted R^2	0.11	0.13	0.89	0.89

Source: Authors' calculations.
Notes: Robust t statistics in parentheses. *, **, and *** indicate significance at 10, 5, and 1 percent, respectively.

controlling for the output gap and inflation once the country moved to IT by including a dummy for the period since IT in the regression.

In all variants in Table 7, the output gap has a positive and significant coefficient, as anticipated. Inflation also has a positive coefficient.[27] When we add the lagged policy rate as an explanatory variable (Woodford's version of the Taylor Rule, Woodford 2011), its coefficient indicates significant inertia. The output gap and inflation remain positive as before.

We also include a dummy variable for the IT period to address the concern that interest rates have been higher post IT. On the contrary, we find that rates have been lower once one accounts for inflation and the output gap, though not always significantly so.[28]

27. It is significantly less than the standard Taylor rule benchmark of 1.5. The coefficients on the output gap and inflation are similar to those in other papers estimating the reaction function for India, including Hutchison et al. (2013); Patra and Kapur (2012); Singh (2010); and Mohanty and Klau (2004). Bhoi et al. (2019) estimate a reaction function for 2000–18, using the weighted average call money rate as the policy rate and similarly find the coefficient on the output gap to be larger post IT.

28. We also included two additional terms interacting inflation and the output gap with this same IT dummy. The coefficient on the output gap was consistently positive, and that on inflation consistently negative, though a dozen or so quarterly observations for the IT period do not give us sufficient variation and degrees of freedom to estimate these coefficients reliably and precisely.

Policy rates were lowered dramatically during the Global Financial Crisis. Was this reaction unusual, given that growth slowed sharply between 2007 and 2008? When we add a dummy for the Global Financial Crisis, its coefficient is negative and significant, confirming that the RBI moved more quickly than predicted by its standard reaction function. Another question is whether policy rates react to the inflation series that the RBI tracks formally or to one or more of the CPI inflation series. When we include different inflation series in the reaction function, the results suggest that monetary policy responds to headline and core inflation but not to food inflation.

We also ask if the weights on the output gap and inflation are different in periods when these variables take on unusually high or low values. Contrary to previous suggestions, we do not find evidence of such threshold effects.[29]

While there is evidence of autocorrelation in our OLS estimates, when we correct the standard errors using Newey–West correction, the significance levels are unaffected. Previous studies have used GMM for estimating the reaction function on the grounds that OLS coefficients may suffer from endogeneity and simultaneity bias. When we do so, the coefficients of inflation and output gap are similar to the OLS estimates obtained when we include the lagged policy rate. When we do not include the lagged policy rates, the GMM estimates of the coefficients for both inflation and the output gap are larger and more significant than the OLS estimates (see Appendix D).

Some scholars believe that even though India formally moved to inflation targeting in September 2016, it had de facto started paying more attention to the level of inflation and had announced a glide path for inflation starting in 2014.[30] In lieu of the formal inflation targeting, we define another dummy

29. Specifically, we define dummies for very high values of inflation as when it exceeds 9 percent; for a very large output gap as when it exceeds 1.5; for very low levels of inflation as when inflation is below 3 percent; and for a low output gap as when it is below –1.5. The cutoffs have been selected at about top 10 percent or bottom 10 percent of the observations for inflation and the output gap. We include one of these dummy variables at a time in the regressions. The only coefficient that is significant at a 10 percent level is for a high output gap. This coefficient is negative, indicating that at a very high GDP growth rate (and output gap), the policy rate does not increase proportionately.

30. Mohan and Ray (2018) note that while IT was formally adopted in 2016, the monetary policy framework of the RBI had started tilting towards IT from 2014, and after Raghuram Rajan joined the RBI as governor. The RBI started publishing a biannual Monetary Policy Report to provide an assessment of the overall macroeconomic conditions as well as forecasts of inflation and growth. It also put forth the objective to lower CPI inflation to below 8 percent by January 2015, and below 6 percent by January 2016.

that takes a value 1 from 2014 Q1 onwards. This variable does not show up as significant or impact our other results. When we add the budget deficit or the government's market borrowings (both as a percentage of GDP), their coefficients are insignificant.

5. Outcomes Pre- and Post-Inflation Targeting

Studies of the impact of inflation targeting have reached different conclusions depending, inter alia, on the countries, the period, and the measures considered. We tabulate these studies in Appendix F (Table F.1). For emerging market economies, there is evidence of lower inflation under IT, but the results for inflation volatility are less consistent.[31] There is no clear consensus on the effects of IT on output growth—Brito and Bystedt (2010) find a significant negative effect on growth while other studies (Gemayel et al. 2011; Naqvi and Rizvi 2009) find insignificant effects of IT on growth. Gonçalves and Salles (2008) find that IT reduces output volatility, whereas Batini and Laxton (2007) find no such evidence.

We now compare the behavior of a range of economic and financial variables before and after the adoption of IT in India. We compare percentage changes and, where appropriate, volatility. Unless noted otherwise, the data are again quarterly and extend from 1997 through 2019. Our baseline specification is of the form:

$$y_t = \alpha_0 + \alpha_1 IT_t + \alpha_2 GFC_t + \alpha_3 \text{Post-GFC}_t + \epsilon_t^y \qquad (2)$$

where, y_t denotes the outcome variable; IT_t, GFC_t, and Post-GFC$_t$ denote the inflation targeting dummy (Q3 2016–Q4 2019), the Global Financial Crisis (GFC) dummy (Q3 2008–Q1 2009), and a post-GFC dummy (Q2 2009–Q4 2019), respectively.[32] CPI headline, core and food inflation are all lower in the IT period, as shown in Table 8.[33] While CPI inflation increased after the GFC, all measures of CPI inflation declined after the shift to IT. CPI headline inflation declined by 4.9 percentage points relative to the post-GFC average, and food inflation declined even more sharply by 6.9 percentage

31. Vega and Winkelried (2005), Batini and Laxton (2007), Lin and Ye (2007), and Gemayel et al. (2011) conclude that inflation volatility is significantly lower after IT, whereas Gonçalves and Salles (2008) and Brito and Bysted (2010) find any difference to be insignificant.

32. We acknowledge that this framework cannot strictly establish any causal effects of IT, since we have not controlled for confounding factors and developments.

33. In an alternative specification, we control for the output gap and see an even sharper decline in headline inflation.

TABLE 8. Inflation is Lower after Inflation Targeting

	WPI Inflation	CPI Headline Inflation	CPI Core Inflation	CPI Food Inflation
Inflation Targeting	−1.53	−4.91***	−3.29***	−6.91***
	(1.56)	(8.23)	(5.76)	(6.12)
Global Financial Crisis dummy	2.65	3.98***	0.26	7.79***
	(1.46)	(7.14)	(0.61)	(7.81)
Post Global Financial Crisis dummy	−0.66	3.14***	2.31***	4.20***
	(0.70)	(4.43)	(3.46)	(4.05)
Constant	5.13***	5.55***	5.87***	5.11***
	(20.50)	(11.63)	(14.60)	(7.12)
Observations	91	91	91	91
Adjusted R^2	0.06	0.29	0.17	0.27

Source: Authors' calculations.
Notes: Robust t statistics in parentheses; *, **, and *** indicate significance at 10, 5, and 1 percent, respectively.

points. WPI inflation also declined by 1.5 percent, though the change is not statistically significant.

The same analysis for inflation volatility, calculated as the quarterly average of the 15-month rolling standard deviation of monthly inflation series, shows lower inflation volatility after the adoption of IT, except in the case of food price inflation, over which the central bank arguably has less control. Plotting this volatility measure (Figure 4) indicates that, except for food price inflation, volatility is lower after the shift to IT relative to the preceding decade. This is borne out in Table 9 where, except for food price inflation, the volatility of all measures of inflation has declined.

Figure 5 and Table 10 indicate no change in exchange rate depreciation or appreciation (computed as an average of daily changes), foreign exchange reserves, or portfolio debt flows. However, portfolio equity flows are somewhat smaller (as a percentage of GDP) under the IT regime. Yields on government debt are smaller, on average, by about 90 basis points, after the adoption of IT.

We measure the exchange rate and equity market volatility by the standard deviation of percentage changes in the daily value of the rupee to the dollar exchange rate and equity markets, respectively. Table 11 suggests that the exchange rate and equity markets have become less volatile under IT. Measuring the volatility of portfolio flows as the standard deviation of daily flows (measured in USD billions) within a quarter, we note that their average volatility has increased since the GFC, but it has not changed with the shift to IT, relative to the post-GFC period average.

FIGURE 4. Inflation and Its Volatility

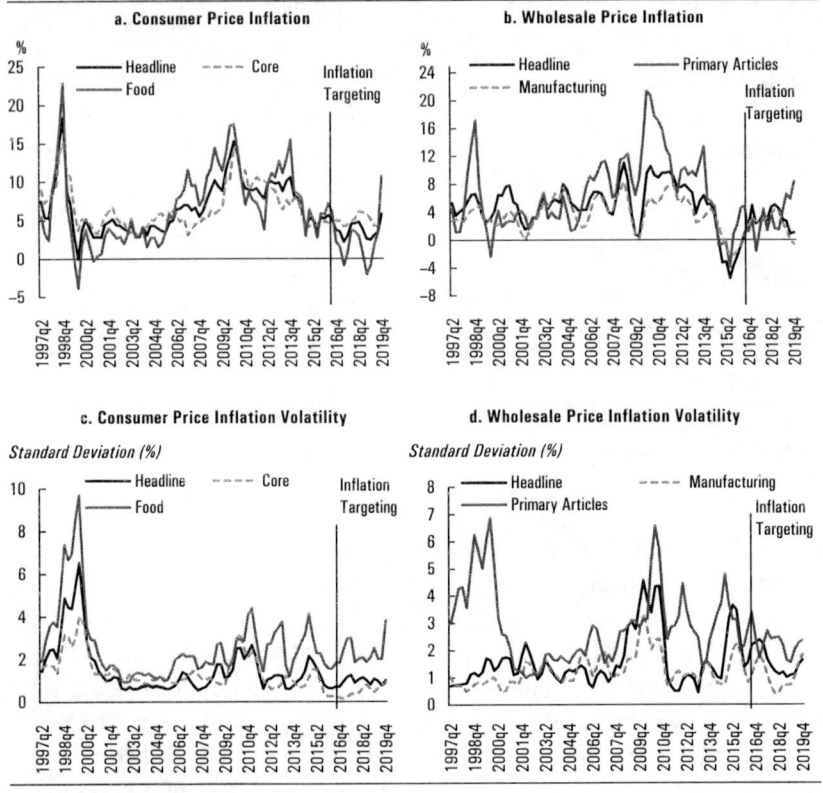

Source: CEIC, Author's calculations.
Note: Inflation volatility is computed as a 15-month rolling standard deviation of the monthly inflation series, which is then averaged at a quarterly frequency.

The weighted average call rate (WACR), the interest rate at which banks lend overnight money to one another, is the RBI's operating target under its IT framework. Table 11 suggests that its volatility has declined under IT relative to the post-GFC period.

In sum, the exchange rate, the stock market, and the call money rate all became less volatile following the adoption of inflation targeting. In contrast, the volatility of portfolio capital flows has not changed (Figure 6).

In Table 12, we ask whether IT impacted output growth and its volatility. We use year-on-year percentage changes in the Index of Industrial Production (IIP) as a proxy for output growth.[34] Volatility is defined as the

---

34. We use the IIP instead of GDP growth as the IIP is available at a monthly frequency.

T A B L E 9 .   Inflation Volatility under IT

	Volatility of CPI Inflation			Volatility of WPI Inflation		
	Headline	Core	Food	Headline	Primary Articles	Manufacturing
Inflation	−0.42***	−0.80***	−0.28	−0.48*	−0.99***	−0.41**
Targeting	(3.32)	(5.01)	(1.26)	(1.69)	(3.92)	(2.17)
Global Financial	−0.12	−0.65***	−0.31	1.65***	0.33	0.62***
Crisis dummy	(0.43)	(5.15)	(0.73)	(18.80)	(1.34)	(9.95)
Post Global	−0.31	−0.27	−0.13	0.80***	0.59*	0.42***
Financial Crisis	(1.23)	(1.44)	(0.36)	(3.12)	(1.84)	(2.86)
dummy						
Constant	1.71***	1.57***	2.73***	1.26***	2.69***	1.09***
	(7.53)	(13.03)	(8.37)	(22.43)	(11.49)	(18.38)
Observations	91	91	91	91	91	91
Adjusted R^2	0.02	0.19	−0.03	0.19	0.04	0.11

Source: Authors' calculations.
Notes: Robust t statistics in parentheses; *, **, and *** indicate significance at 10, 5, and 1 percent, respectively.

15-month rolling standard deviation of the year-on-year percentage changes (which is then averaged at a quarterly frequency). There is no evidence of a change in the rate of growth, but volatility is lower under IT relative to the post-GFC average.

We do not find changes in the rate of growth of the government total, revenue (operating and recurrent), or capital spending under the IT regime. The rate of growth of interest payments is somewhat smaller, which is probably a reflection of lower bond yields.

Finally, we looked for evidence that the transmission of policy impulses to banking and financial markets improved with the adoption of IT. Historically, evaluations of transmission in India have been mixed. Mishra et al. (2016) examined the strength of transmission using a structural VAR methodology. They found that a tightening of policy is associated with a significant increase in bank lending rates. Although pass-through to the lending rates is only partial, they conclude that their result for India compares favorably with the results for other developing countries. Consistent with these findings, Acharya (2017) and Dua (2020) argue that transmission to the money market and long-term interest rates is rapid and relatively complete, but that bank deposit and lending rates adjust more slowly and less completely.

We collated monthly data on government bonds yields of 1-, 2-, 5-, and 10-year maturities, treasury bill rates, and average lending rates on

FIGURE 5.   **Exchange Rates and Reserves**

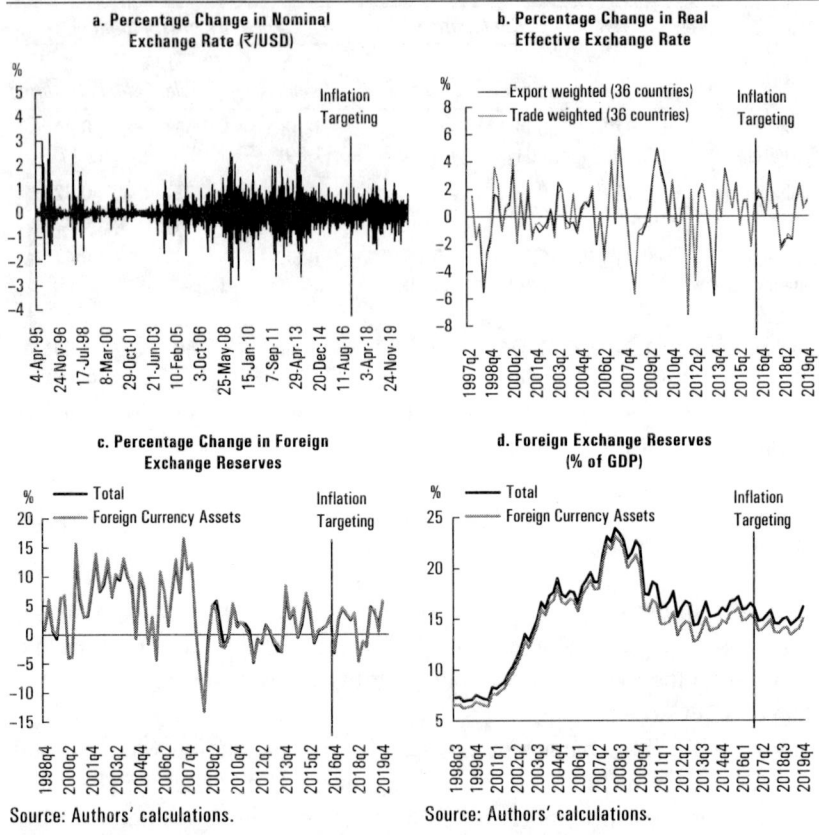

Source: Authors' calculations.

Note: Foreign exchange reserves are expressed as a percentage of annual (calendar year) GDP in panel d.

new and outstanding loans. We used the repo rate as the relevant policy rate. Table 13 confirms that transmission is greater for treasury bill and short-tenure bonds. Transmission to government bonds yields and bill rates improved somewhat following the adoption of IT. Transmission to bank lending rates is relatively weak, as other authors have shown, and has not improved with the adoption of IT.

6. Are Expectations Better Anchored?

Kose et al. (2019) find that long-term inflation expectations have declined in the past two decades in both advanced economies, and emerging markets

TABLE 10. Exchange Rates, Reserves and Portfolio Flows

	Nominal Exchange Rate (% Change)	Trade Weighted REER (% Change)	% Change in Reserves (q-o-q)	Portfolio Equity Flows (% of GDP)	Portfolio Debt (% of GDP)	G-Sec Secondary Market 10-Year Maximum Yield
Inflation	−0.63	−0.08	0.47	−0.74***	−0.23	−0.91***
Targeting	(0.66)	(0.13)	(0.47)	(3.06)	(1.03)	(5.69)
Global Financial	5.83***	−0.87**	−13.12***	−1.56***	0.06	−0.56
Crisis dummy	(2.75)	(2.25)	(4.34)	(6.95)	(0.24)	(0.90)
Post Global	0.70	0.39	−5.08***	0.18	0.34***	−0.15
Financial Crisis dummy	(0.83)	(0.64)	(4.89)	(0.80)	(2.70)	(0.41)
Constant	0.38	0.09	6.37***	0.75***	0.05	8.49***
	(1.02)	(0.26)	(7.28)	(5.29)	(1.60)	(24.87)
Observations	91	91	85	84	84	86
Adjusted R^2	0.08	−0.02	0.32	0.14	0.05	0.03

Source: Authors' calculations.
Notes: Robust t statistics in parentheses; *, **, and *** indicate significance at 10, 5, and 1 percent, respectively.

and developing economies (EMDEs). Although inflation expectations are less well anchored in EMDEs, their sensitivity to domestic and global shocks has declined. They suggest that an IT regime and greater central bank transparency are associated with better anchoring.[35]

Studies of India similarly suggest that expectations have become better anchored in recent years. For example, Asnani et al. (2019) analyze the inflation expectations of households and find that inflation expectations have become better anchored during the IT period; in particular, there is only limited spillover from food inflation to food and non-food inflation expectations in the IT period.[36]

---

35. Lower public debt and greater trade openness are also associated with better anchoring of expectations. Using monthly survey data from Consensus Economics for a sample of 22 EMDEs and 14 advanced economies in a structural VAR model, Davis and Presno (2014) similarly find that the introduction of IT is associated with a statistically significant reduction in the response of inflation expectations (12 months ahead) to shocks in oil prices and observed inflation.

36. Benes et al. (2017) and Patra and Ray (2010) similarly found that lagged inflation, as well as current and lagged changes in fuel and food prices, significantly affected inflation expectations prior to IT.

FIGURE 6. Volatility of Macrofinancial Indicators

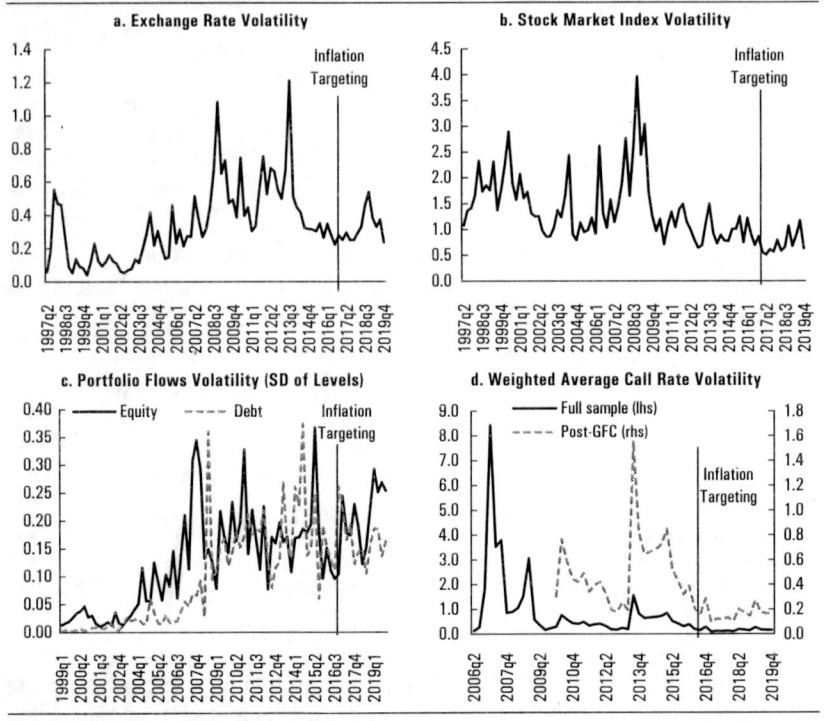

Source: Authors' calculations, CEIC, RBI.
Note: "lhs" is left-hand-side axis, and "rhs" is right-hand-side axis.

TABLE 11. Volatility of Financial Variables

	Exchange Rate Volatility	SENSEX Volatility	WACR Volatility	Portfolio Equity Volatility	Portfolio Debt Volatility
Inflation Targeting	−0.17***	−0.38***	−0.31***	0.02	−0.01
	(3.84)	(3.82)	(5.51)	(0.99)	(0.50)
Global Financial Crisis dummy	0.58***	1.47***	−0.59	0.04*	0.17**
	(4.89)	(3.62)	(0.55)	(1.77)	(2.30)
Post Global Financial Crisis dummy	0.28***	−0.42***	−1.84**	0.10***	0.15***
	(6.36)	(3.58)	(2.12)	(5.58)	(12.33)
Constant	0.22***	1.54***	2.32***	0.08***	0.02***
	(10.18)	(19.02)	(2.68)	(5.64)	(6.28)
Observations	91	91	55	84	84
Adjusted R^2	0.45	0.43	0.30	0.33	0.69

Source: Authors' calculations.
Notes: Robust t statistics in parentheses; *, **, and *** indicate significance at 10, 5, and 1 percent, respectively. WACR = weighted average call rate.

TABLE 12. Industrial Production and Government Expenditure

	IIP (% Change)	Volatility of IIP	Total Government Expenditure (% Change)	Revenue Expenditure (% Change)	Capital Expenditure (% Change)	Interest Payments (% Change)
Inflation Targeting	-0.88 (1.02)	-0.99*** (3.36)	-1.58 (0.42)	-1.43 (0.44)	9.31 (0.41)	-5.45 (1.39)
Global Financial Crisis dummy	-6.98** (2.15)	3.28*** (5.60)	23.95** (2.42)	26.23** (2.27)	-6.80 (0.42)	2.52 (0.30)
Post Global Financial Crisis dummy	-3.68*** (4.24)	1.22*** (4.17)	-0.90 (0.30)	-2.63 (1.11)	-0.55 (0.03)	2.08 (0.63)
Constant	7.85*** (13.11)	2.19*** (17.49)	12.54*** (5.39)	13.61*** (8.66)	22.35 (1.52)	11.60*** (4.95)
Observations	91	91	87	87	87	87
Adjusted R^2	0.24	0.33	0.08	0.19	-0.03	-0.02

Source: Authors' calculations.
Notes: Robust t statistics in parentheses; *, **, and *** indicate significance at 10, 5, and 1 percent, respectively.

TABLE 13. Transmission of the Policy Rate

	One-year Government Bond Yield	91-Day Treasury Bill Rate	Bank Lending Rate on Outstanding Loans	Bank Lending Rate on New Loans
Repo rate	0.94*** (20.25)	1.15*** (20.23)	0.61*** (12.56)	0.64*** (17.77)
IT	-1.35*** (2.99)	-0.41 (0.89)	0.87** (1.99)	-0.12 (0.34)
Repo rate × IT	0.33*** (4.59)	0.18** (2.59)	-0.23*** (3.38)	-0.06 (1.03)
Constant	0.12 (0.38)	-1.52*** (3.93)	7.30*** (19.49)	6.31*** (23.00)
Observations	232	233	102	71
Adjusted R^2	0.59	0.59	0.91	0.91

Source: Authors' calculations.
Notes: Robust t statistics in parentheses; *, **, and *** indicate significance at 10, 5, and 1 percent, respectively.

The RBI has been conducting its Inflation Expectations Survey of Households since 2005, recording survey respondents' perceptions of current inflation and expectations of inflation three months, and one year ahead. The survey records both qualitative and quantitative responses. It was conducted quarterly (in March, June, September, and December) until March 2014. At that point, two additional rounds in May and November were added to align it with the bimonthly monetary policy review cycle.

The RBI has also been conducting a survey of professional forecasters since the second quarter of 2007–08, drawing responses from forecasters with both financial and non-financial institutions. Initially, the survey was conducted at a quarterly frequency, but this was changed to bi-monthly in 2014–15. The survey collects annual quantitative forecasts for two financial years (the current year and next year) and quarterly forecasts for five quarters (the current quarter and next four quarters). We analyze how the inflation expectation series for India has changed since the implementation of IT. For the analysis below, we use both the household and professional forecaster series averaged at quarterly frequencies.[37] We use the CPI inflation expectations of professional forecasters and compare household and professional forecasts with CPI inflation.[38]

Both professional forecasts and households' expectations of inflation declined with the shift to IT (Table 14). Even so, household expectations of inflation consistently exceed actual inflation, and the deviation has not declined. Figure 7 shows that the average of professional forecasts has been

TABLE 14.   Inflation Expectations Declined after Inflation Targeting

	Households' Expectations			Professional Forecasters' Expectations			
	Current	1 Quarter Ahead	1 Year Ahead	1 Quarter Ahead	2 Quarters Ahead	3 Quarters Ahead	4 Quarters Ahead
Inflation Targeting	−1.22*** (2.70)	−0.94** (2.06)	−1.27** (2.59)	−4.08*** (9.50)	−3.39*** (9.13)	−2.89*** (9.46)	−2.74*** (8.16)
Constant	9.47*** (22.48)	9.82*** (22.98)	10.52*** (23.95)	8.29*** (20.90)	7.83*** (22.10)	7.44*** (26.04)	7.26*** (26.42)
Observations	54	54	54	45	45	45	30
Adjusted R^2	0.03	0.01	0.03	0.51	0.47	0.50	0.44

Source: Authors' calculations.
Notes: Robust t statistics in parentheses; *, **, and *** indicate significance at 10, 5, and 1 percent, respectively.

37. We restrict our analysis to a quarterly frequency in order to have comparable results across sectors.

38. We use the CPI combined inflation series from 2012 onwards and prior to that, the CPI–IW. Professional forecasters' expectations are for the CPI–IW prior to 2014, and for the combined series from 2014 onwards.

FIGURE 7. CPI Inflation and Household and Professional, One-quarter and Four-quarter Ahead Inflation Expectations

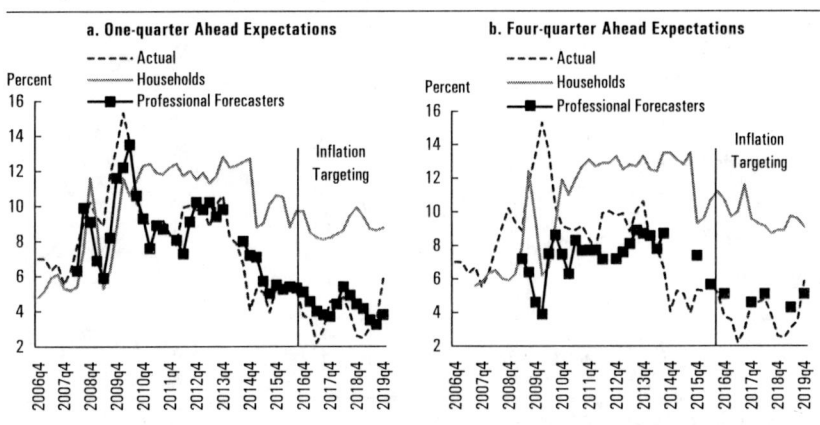

Source: CEIC, RBI.
Note: Data for One-quarter and Four-quarter ahead expectations for professional forecasters is not available for some quarters. We report mean expectations for both the household and professional forecasters' series.

close to actual inflation, while household expectations have often exceeded actual inflation. In the last few years, and particularly since the shift to IT, expected inflation has declined, in line with the decline in actual inflation. However, households' expectations have declined less than actual inflation and continue to be higher (by about 3 percentage points).

In addition, while household inflation expectations continue to display considerable variation around their mean and median, professional forecaster expectations show a smaller range since the shift to IT, consistent with firmer anchoring (see Figure 8).

6.1. Do Shocks to Current Inflation Influence Expectations about Future Inflation?

To assess whether shocks to current inflation influence expectations about future inflation, we regress expected inflation q quarters ahead on current inflation. Our baseline specification is:

$$E_t \pi_{t+q} = \beta_0 + \beta_1 \pi_t + \epsilon_t \qquad (3)$$

$E_t \pi_{t+q}$ denotes expectations at time t of inflation in period $t+q$ and π_t denotes CPI inflation in period t. The coefficient β_1 captures the extent to which current inflation exerts an influence on current expectations about inflation in period $t+q$. If inflation expectations are well-anchored, then one

FIGURE 8. Inflation Expectations (One Quarter Ahead) before and after IT

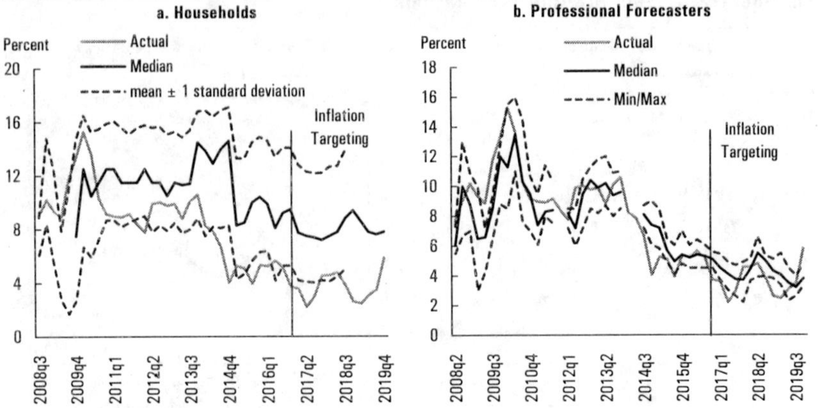

Source: CEIC, RBI, Authors' calculations.
Note: Prior to 2014, professional forecasters' expectations are for CPI–IW, and from 2014 onwards for the combined series.

would expect β_1 to be small and insignificant.[39] Since our goal is to assess whether inflation expectations have become better anchored under IT, we also estimate:

$$E_t \pi_{t+q} = \beta_0 + \beta_1 \pi_t + \beta_2 IT_t + \beta_3 \pi_t \times IT_t + \epsilon_t \tag{4}$$

For household expectations, we find that, for a 1 percentage point increase in current inflation, expectations about one-quarter and one-year ahead inflation increase by about 40 basis points (Table 15). The magnitude of this pass-through has remained the same since the shift to IT (β_3 is insignificant). For the professional forecasters, the pass-through from inflation to expectations has declined significantly since the shift to IT.

6.2. Do Inflation Expectations Feed into Actual Inflation?

To assess whether inflation expectations feed into actual inflation, we estimate the following specification:

$$\pi_t = \beta_0 + \underbrace{\beta_1 \pi_{t-1}}_{\text{persistence}} + \underbrace{\beta_2 E_{t-1} \pi_t}_{\text{expectations}} + \underbrace{\beta_3 \text{output gap}_t}_{\text{supply-side shock}} + \epsilon_t \tag{5}$$

39. For households, we use three-month and one-year ahead mean inflation expectations and for professional forecasters, we use one- to four-quarter ahead mean (CPI) inflation expectations.

T A B L E 1 5 .   Do Shocks to Current Inflation Affect Inflation Expectations?

	Households' Expectations		Professional Forecasters' Expectations			
	1 Quarter Ahead	1 Year Ahead	1 Quarter Ahead	2 Quarters Ahead	3 Quarters Ahead	4 Quarters Ahead
CPI Inflation	0.40***	0.41***	0.70***	0.50***	0.30***	0.13
	(3.17)	(3.09)	(10.26)	(5.74)	(3.56)	(1.23)
IT	1.18	0.42	0.50	0.34	−0.06	−0.43
	(0.91)	(0.29)	(0.62)	(0.39)	(0.08)	(0.42)
CPI Inflation × IT	−0.08	0.05	−0.32*	−0.35**	−0.36***	−0.42***
	(0.48)	(0.20)	(1.95)	(2.31)	(2.83)	(3.57)
Constant	6.50***	7.10***	2.31***	3.52***	4.83***	6.06***
	(5.34)	(5.71)	(3.80)	(4.86)	(7.15)	(6.12)
Observations	54	54	45	45	45	30
Adjusted R^2	0.12	0.15	0.87	0.72	0.62	0.45

Source: Authors' calculations.
Notes: Robust t statistics in parentheses; *, **, and *** indicate significance at 10, 5, and 1 percent, respectively.

The expectation term is the expectation of current inflation in the previous quarter. Lagged inflation captures the persistent nature of inflation, and the output gap controls for supply-side shocks. As before, the output gap is defined as the difference between seasonally adjusted GDP and potential GDP, expressed as a percentage of seasonally adjusted GDP. β_1 captures the magnitude of pass-through from inflation expectations to actual inflation. To compare the strength of any feedback from expectations to actual inflation pre- and post-IT, we interact the expectations term with an IT dummy.

The estimated results are presented in Table 16. Pre-IT, there is no pass-through from households' expectations to actual inflation. However, a 1 percentage point increase in professional forecaster's expectations about the next quarter's inflation implies, on an average, an increase in inflation in the next quarter by about 40 basis points. This impact of inflation expectations on inflation has become muted under IT, again consistent with better anchoring.

7. COVID-19 and Credibility

The question of the day is how an inflation-targeting central bank should respond to an exceptional shock like the COVID-19 pandemic. In practice, we have seen central banks around the world, including those in EMDEs, cut

TABLE 16. Do Inflation Expectations Feed into Actual Inflation?

	Dependent Variable: CPI Inflation (%)			
	Households' Expectations		Professional Forecasters' Expectations	
Lagged inflation	0.90***	0.90***	0.62***	0.61***
	(8.36)	(8.46)	(4.46)	(4.38)
Inflation Expectations	−0.10	−0.11	0.39**	0.41**
	(1.14)	(1.34)	(2.66)	(2.66)
IT	6.14*	5.85	2.77	2.75
	(1.79)	(1.64)	(1.51)	(1.48)
Inflation Expectations × IT	−0.75**	−0.71*	−0.73**	−0.70*
	(2.09)	(1.90)	(2.09)	(1.97)
Output gap (% of GDP)		−0.12		−0.09
		(0.93)		(0.81)
Constant	1.72**	1.91**	0.13	0.03
	(2.04)	(2.25)	(0.14)	(0.04)
Observations	53	53	44	44
Adjusted R^2	0.84	0.84	0.86	0.86

Source: Authors' calculations.
Notes: Robust t statistics in parentheses; *, **, and *** indicate significance at 10, 5 and 1 percent, respectively.

interest rates sharply and engage in a wide range of credit-market operations. This response contrasts with the response to past external crises affecting EMDEs when central banks were reluctant to cut interest rates significantly for fear of fanning inflation expectations. That inflation expectations in a number of EMDEs are now better anchored than before, we would argue, is part of the explanation for why they have been able to do more.[40]

This is the case for India. On March 27, 2020, the RBI cut the repo rate by 75 basis points, the reverse repo rate by 90 basis points, and the CRR by 1 percent.[41] It followed this by another 25 basis points reduction in the reverse repo rate and lowered the liquidity coverage ratio required of banks to 80 percent of the previous requirement. The RBI then further reduced the repo rate by 40 basis points on May 22, for a total reduction of 115 basis points

40. We would not deny that there is also a role for Federal Reserve (and advanced country central bank policy in general) in the contrast. That the Fed responded so aggressively to the crisis opened up space for central banks, including in EMDEs, to do more.

41. In addition, the requirement of minimum daily CRR balance maintenance was also reduced from 90 percent to 80 percent for three months, while the borrowing limit for the marginal standing facility was increased from 2 percent to 3 percent of the SLR.

FIGURE 9.   Inflation and Monetary Policy during the Pandemic

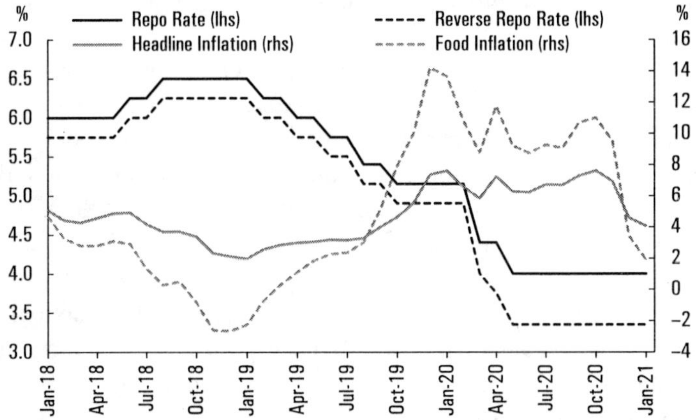

Source: RBI, CEIC.
Note: "lhs" is left-hand-side axis, and "rhs" is right-hand-side axis.

between March and May 2020. The reverse repo rate was also decreased by 40 basis points on May 22, 2020.

The RBI took these steps despite the fact that consumer price inflation in March (according to figures published in mid-April) was running at 5.91 percent, at the top of the RBI's 2–6 percent target range and down only slightly from 6.58 percent in February (Figure 9). It did so despite the possibility that CPI inflation might accelerate further, given the impact of the lockdown and other supply-side disruptions on food prices and of exchange rate depreciation on the cost of imports. Thus, the fact that inflation expectations had become better anchored allowed the RBI to temporarily disregard the fact that inflation was already at the top of the Bank's target range and to respond to this exceptional shock.

Three further literatures speak of the consequences of such actions. One is concerned with how an inflation-targeting central bank should respond to supply shocks, COVID-19 related lockdowns, and disruptions to supply chains and production, that is, a negative supply shock. Monetary policy is an awkward instrument for dealing with the consequences of supply shocks, since it operates mainly on aggregate demand rather than aggregate supply.[42] The dilemma for MPC members is that raising the policy rate

---

42. Other non-monetary policies of central banks designed to buttress the liquidity and stability of specific financial assets and even institutions can be thought of as supply-side interventions insofar as they prevent credit-market disruptions from interfering with supply.

in response to the inflationary consequences of a negative supply shock will only worsen the output shortfall, but reducing rates will only worsen the inflation overshoot.[43]

Thus, the standard advice for an inflation-targeting central bank is to cut rates—or at least to refrain from raising them—if the negative supply shock is temporary. If the shock is temporary, there will be higher prices and inflation now but lower prices and less inflation, or even deflation, in the future. The central bank should therefore be able to "look through" today's inflation when setting rates. For an economy frequently subject to supply shocks, this is an argument for the central bank to adopt a relatively long horizon when formulating its inflation forecast. When supply shocks, both positive and negative, tend to fall disproportionately on food and fuel prices, this is an argument for focusing not on headline CPI, which includes them, but core CPI, which does not.

There are three caveats to these points. First, the COVID-19 pandemic has elements of both a negative supply shock and a negative demand shock, as firms halt investment projects and households increase their precautionary saving and see their incomes fall. The negative demand shock may only materialize with a lag, and it may be smaller in India than elsewhere insofar as households living close to the margin of subsistence have little scope for reducing spending. But demand-side considerations point in the direction of interest rate cuts, insofar as they imply weaker inflation going forward.

Second, this logic assumes that the negative supply shock from COVID-19 is temporary. Unfortunately, there is also a scenario in which the shock, if not permanent, is at least very persistent—that it will require continuous or repeated lockdowns and distancing, with associated disruptions to trade and production, until a vaccine is successfully identified, manufactured and distributed, or until herd immunity develops. A permanent shock of this sort, which is inflationary, ceteris paribus, suggests raising rates.

Third, even if the shock is transient, there is the danger that allowing inflation to stray above the top of the target range may un-anchor inflation expectations. Agents may see current inflation above target as evidence that the central bank has lost control of the inflation process, igniting a wage–price spiral. Thus, if monetary policy lacks credibility, the costs of monetary accommodation of the shock will be greater. This is something that, in principle, can be inferred from observed measures of inflation expectations.

---

43. Especially since a classic negative supply shock will not increase the output gap—it will only reduce actual output, since potential output has fallen, while increasing unemployment.

This last observation is taken up in the second relevant literature, that on escape clauses for inflation-targeting central banks. The question here is whether an inflation-targeting central bank can invoke an exceptional event—unavoidable circumstances that provide a temporary reprieve from performing its obligations under a contract, which is the definition of *force majeure*—and depart from its inflation target without damaging its credibility. *Force majeure* clauses are included in a variety of private contracts in both civil law and common law countries. Few central banks include them in descriptions of their IT regimes. The Czech National Bank is a rare case of a central bank that, when establishing its inflation target in 1998 and revising it in 2001, specified escape clauses. These included major changes in the world prices of raw materials and energy, major changes in the exchange rate not due to domestic economic fundamentals, major changes in regulated prices, step changes in indirect taxes, and natural disasters. Heenan et al. (2006) report that, at the time of their writing, only five inflation-targeting central banks specified exceptions in their target definitions; most of these pertained to administered prices and indirect taxes.[44] Some central banks have added escape clauses to their monetary policy statements in exceptional circumstances. Thus, the MPC of the Bank of England added an explicit financial stability escape clause to their bank rate forward guidance in 2013.

Heenan et al. (2006) argue that the advantages of explicit escape clauses are likely to be limited. As they note, the central bank would have to identify the shock, explain the impact, detail its policy response, and forecast the inflation path whether or not there was a formal escape clause. They worry that formal escape clauses are overly legalistic and may divert the public communications of the central bank from the underlying macroeconomic issues toward the technical details of the escape clause itself.

In addition, there is a closely related literature on exchange rate escape clauses concerned with the circumstance under which an exchange-rate targeting central bank can alter the target. Obstfeld (1997) warns that exchange rate escape clauses can be destabilizing. If the escape clause permits or requires the policymaker to alter or suspend the target when certain economic and financial conditions obtain, investors anticipating the possibility that the escape clause will be invoked may take actions that produce those very conditions.

Grossman and van Huyck (1988) specify the conditions under which invoking an escape clause will not result in reputational damage (under

44. They do not specify these, but the three we are aware of are New Zealand, the Philippines, and the Czech Republic.

which it will not diminish the credibility of the policy regime or be destabilizing). First, the shock must be independently verifiable. Second, the shock must not be of the central bank's own making. COVID-19 clearly satisfies these conditions. These conclusions suggest that central banks, including the RBI, may be able to temporarily exceed their inflation targets without damaging their credibility—assuming, that is, that the other preconditions discussed above are met.

Third, and finally, there is a literature on the optimal degree of discretion in monetary policy (e.g., Athey et al. 2005). It may be that the full extent of the shock is not independently verifiable, so the Grossman–van Huyck conditions are not satisfied. But the central bank may know better—it may have private information about the severity of the shock. This is plausibly the case of the Coronavirus pandemic, when estimating its effects requires epidemiological modeling and estimates of the behavioral response. Knowing that a major negative shock is coming, the central bank may then have good reason to cut rates even though inflation is currently running above target.

The question is whether it can do so without damaging its credibility. The main threat to credibility, Athey et al. (2005) argue, is that the central bank may abuse those same discretionary powers in the future, for example, by overly stimulating the economy in the manner of the classic time inconsistency problem. The solution, they show, is a cap on the target rate of inflation that penalizes the central bank when that target is exceeded. This kind of reputational or political penalty is precisely what IT is designed to apply. This, in turn, suggests that an inflation-targeting central bank should have more room than other central banks to cut rates in this situation because it is granted more discretion and invites less damage to its credibility.

So did IT give central banks, in general, and the RBI in particular, more room for maneuver? In Table 17, we show policy rate changes between December 2019 and May 2020, together with the 2019 rate of inflation, for 70 emerging and developing countries, distinguishing between IT and non-IT central banks and India. The cut in policy rates is larger for IT than non-IT central banks, despite the fact that IT central banks had less "space" (their policy rates started out closer to zero). The contrast is suggestive of greater anti-inflation credibility that makes for more policy room for maneuver.

In Table 18, we regress the change in the policy rate over the same period on a dummy variable for IT central banks, the lagged policy rate, and the lagged rate of inflation. The resulting estimates confirm that IT central banks lowered their policy rates by more, even after controlling

TABLE 17.   Policy Response to COVID-19 by IT and Non-IT Central Banks

	IT	Non-IT	India
Number of countries	27	43	
Average policy rate at end-2019	4.70	5.27	5.15
Average policy rate change between December 2019 and May 2020 (percentage points)	−1.31	−0.90	−1.15
Average inflation rate during 2019	3.13	3.19	3.7

Source: Data from Haver Analytics and Authors' calculations. Inflation is the monthly average during 2019.

TABLE 18.   Change in Policy Rate during the COVID Crisis

	Change in Policy Rate		
Dependent Variable	I	II	III
Inflation targeting dummy	−0.41	−0.48**	−0.47*
	(1.57)	(2.04)	(1.96)
Policy rate at end-2019		−0.12***	−0.09*
		(2.82)	(1.97)
Inflation at end-2019			−0.06
			(0.94)
Constant	−0.90***	−0.25	−0.23
	(5.74)	(1.18)	(1.02)
Observations	70	70	70
Adjusted R^2	0.02	0.23	0.22

Source: Authors' calculations.
Notes: Robust t statistics in parentheses; *, **, and *** indicate significance at 10, 5, and 1 percent, respectively.

for inflation and the level of the policy rate.[45] This suggests that inflation targeting, or more accurately the complex of institutional arrangements associated with it, had a payoff in terms of greater policy credibility and room for maneuver in the COVID-19 crisis.[46]

45. We find the same thing when we construct the dependent variable as the change in policy rate as a percentage of lagged rate.

46. IT frameworks are not assigned randomly, of course. The literature suggests several approaches to instrumenting IT status. Virtually, all of them produced negative coefficients on the IT specification in Table 18, although significance levels varied. The coefficient in question was significantly less than zero when the instrumental variable was real GDP in 2010 US dollars (on the grounds that larger economies adopt IT while smaller ones prefer to peg the exchange rate), the World Bank measure of voice and accountability (on the grounds that IT tends to be adopted in countries with a culture of transparency), and regulatory quality (on the grounds that IT requires administrative capacity that is common to monetary policy and other forms of regulation).

8. Conclusion

Inflation targeting in India is barely four years old, which has hindered earlier efforts at performance evaluation. Here, we take advantage of the limited accumulation of data to analyze what, if anything, changed with the advent of IT. We show that the RBI is best characterized as a flexible inflation targeter: contrary to some assertions and criticisms, it does not neglect changes in the output gap when setting policy rates. We do not find that the RBI became more hawkish following the transition to IT; on the contrary, adjusting for inflation and the output gap, policy rates became lower, not higher. We find some evidence that inflation has become better anchored: increases in actual inflation do less to excite inflation expectations, indicative of improved anti-inflation credibility. This is consistent with the fact that a number of other inflation-related outcomes are more stable post-IT than before.

Finally, we ask whether the shift to IT has enhanced the credibility of monetary policy such that the RBI is in a position to take extraordinary action in response to the COVID-19 crisis. We argue that the rules and understandings governing IT regimes come with escape clauses allowing central banks to temporarily disregard their inflation targets under specific circumstances that may be satisfied by the COVID-19 pandemic. Cross-country comparisons confirm that IT, in conjunction with related institutional arrangements, have provided benefits in terms of additional policy room for maneuver in this crisis.

Appendix A

TABLE A.1. India's Monetary Policy Framework

	Initial Phase 1935–49	Developmental Years 1949–69	Credit Planning 1969–85	Monetary Targeting 1985–98	Multiple Indicator Approach 1998–2015	Flexible Inflation Targeting 2016 onward
Objective	Sterling–rupee parity	Development and stability	Financing economic growth and ensuring price stability	Inflation and growth	Inflation and growth	Price stability while simultaneously focusing on growth when inflation is under control
Target	Exchange rate	Administering supply and demand of credit	Priority sector credit targeting	Reserve money (M0) was used as the operating target, and Broad money (M3) as an intermediate target	Multiple indicators: rates, credit, external, fiscal variables, and expectations survey used for growth and inflation projections	Headline CPI inflation
Operating procedure (instruments)	Bank rate, OMOs, CRR	Bank rate, reserve requirements, and OMOs	Bank rate, reserve requirements, selective credit controls, and OMOs	Bank rate and reserve requirements (CRR, SLR)	Direct: CRR, SLR; Indirect instruments: repo operations under LAF and OMOs	Repo rate as intermediate target and WACR as the operating target
Additional comments		1. The focus of monetary policy was on regulating liquidity in the system through OMOs—by buying and selling of government securities—so as to maintain exchange rate parity; 2. CRR was to be used in exigencies rather than as an active instrument of credit control. The RBI used selective credit control and moral suasion to restrain banks from extending credit for speculative purposes.	1. SLR requirement prescribed for banks emerged as a secured source for government borrowings; 2. In the 1960s, inflation was considered to be structural and inflation volatility primarily caused by agricultural failures, so there was greater reliance on selective credit controls.	1. Monetary targeting was flexible to accommodate changes in real GDP growth. In practice, it was an indicative monetary targeting framework with a feedback from real economic activity; 2. CRR was used as the primary instrument for monetary control; 3. By the second half of the 1990s, the RBI was able to move away from direct instruments to indirect market-based instruments in its liquidity management operations.	Some of these instruments, including changes in reserve requirements, standing facilities and OMOs were meant to affect the quantum of marginal liquidity, while changes in policy rates, such as the Bank rate and reverse repo/repo rates were the instruments for changing the price of liquidity.	

Source: Mohanty (2017); Das (2020).

TABLE A.2. Description of Variables Used in the Analysis

Variable	Description
CPI inflation	This measure is the "2011–12 CPI headline inflation" series from 2012 Q1 onwards. Prior to 2012 Q1, it is the CPI–IW headline inflation.
CPI food inflation	This measure is the "2011–12 CPI food inflation" series from 2012 Q1 onwards. Prior to 2012 Q1, it is CPI–IW food inflation.
CPI core inflation	This measure is the "2011–12 CPI core inflation" series (i.e., headline excluding food and beverages, and fuel and light) from 2012 Q1 onwards. Prior to 2012 Q1, it is CPI–IW core inflation.
WPI (manufacturing/food) inflation	The three measures of WPI inflation—WPI, WPI manufacturing, WPI food—are spliced using standard splicing methodology. For instance, if the new inflation rate series starts from 2012 Q1, we consider the new series from thereon, and prior to that, the inflation rate as implied by the old series is considered.
Inflation	This inflation measure is defined as: $$Inflation_t = \begin{cases} CPI\ Inflation_t, \text{ if } t \ge Q1\ 2014 \\ WPI\ Inflation_t, \text{ if } t \le Q4\ 2013 \end{cases}$$ This definition of headline inflation has been used while estimating the central bank's reaction function.
Core inflation	This inflation measure is defined as: $$Core\ Inflation_t = \begin{cases} CPI\ Core\ Inflation_t, \text{ if } t \ge Q1\ 2014 \\ WPI\ Manufacturing\ Inflation_t, \text{ if } t \le Q4\ 2013 \end{cases}$$ This definition of core inflation has been used while estimating the central bank's reaction function.
Food inflation	This inflation measure is defined as: $$Food\ Inflation_t = \begin{cases} CPI\ Food\ Inflation_t, \text{ if } t \ge Q1\ 2014 \\ WPI\ Food\ Inflation_t, \text{ if } t \le Q4\ 2013 \end{cases}$$ This definition of food inflation has been used while estimating the central bank's reaction function.
Exchange rate	We use the quarter-on-quarter percentage point change in the INR/USD exchange rate. Thus, $$Exchange\ rate_t = 100 \times \left(\frac{INR/USD_t}{INR/USD_{t-1}} - 1 \right)$$ where t denotes the quarter.
Output gap	We apply the Hodrick-Prescott filter to the seasonally-adjusted quarterly real GDP series and then express the output gap as a percentage of GDP. Seasonal adjustment is carried out using the X-11 filter. The output gap obtained by applying X-13 ARIMA SEATS for seasonal adjustment, is very similar to the one obtained using the X-11 method.

(Table A.2 Contd.)

Variable	Description
IT dummy	The inflation targeting period starts from 2016 Q3 because in May 2016 an amendment was made to the RBI Act, 1934, to provide a statutory basis for the implementation of the flexible IT framework. We consider the start date from the third quarter as the Act was amended in the middle of the second quarter. Thus, $$T_t = \begin{cases} 1, \text{if } t \ge Q3\,2016 \\ 0, \text{otherwise} \end{cases}$$
Global Financial Crisis dummy	This denotes the Global Financial Crisis period, that is, Q3 2008–Q1 2009. Thus, $$GFC_t = \begin{cases} 1, \text{if } Q3\,2008 \le t \le Q1\,2009 \\ 0, \text{otherwise} \end{cases}$$
Post-Global Financial Crisis dummy	This denotes the post-Global Financial Crisis period, that is, Q2 2009–Q4 2019. Thus, $$Post\,GFC_t = \begin{cases} 1, \text{if } Q2\,2009 \le t \le Q4\,2019 \\ 0, \text{otherwise} \end{cases}$$ Our last sample point is Q4 2019.
Effective policy rate	We define the effective policy rate as in Patra and Kapur (2012) $$\text{Effective Policy Rate}_t = \begin{cases} \text{Bank rate}_t, & \text{if } Q2\,1997 \le t \le Q1\,2002 \\ \text{Reverse repo rate}_t, & \text{if } Q2\,2002 \le t \le Q2\,2006 \\ \text{Repo rate}_t, & \text{if } Q3\,2006 \le t \le Q4\,2008 \\ \text{Reverse repo rate}_t, & \text{if } Q1\,2009 \le t \le Q2\,2010 \\ \text{Repo rate}_t, & \text{if } Q3\,2010 \le t \le Q4\,2019 \end{cases}$$ The bank rate, repo rate, and reverse repo rate represent the average value in a quarter.
Fiscal deficit, fiscal deficit (% of GDP)	We aggregate the Central government's monthly fiscal deficit at a quarterly frequency. To compute the fiscal deficit to GDP ratio, we seasonally adjust both series using X-11 and X-13 ARIMA SEATS and construct two measures of deficit based on different filters applied.
Market borrowings, market borrowings (% of GDP)	We aggregate the Central government's monthly market borrowings data at a quarterly frequency. To compute the market borrowings to GDP ratio, we seasonally adjust both series using X-11 and X-13 ARIMA SEATS. Both seasonal filters give very similar results.
Portfolio flows: Equity and debt	We use daily portfolio flows (equity and debt) data as published by the National Securities Depository Limited.
IIP	The IIP series has been spliced using the standard splicing method. The year-on-year growth rates starting 1996 are based on the 1993–94 series; from April 2006 onwards, they are based on the 2004–05 series; and from April 2013 onwards, they are based on the 2011–12 series.

(Table A.2 Contd.)

(Table A.2 Contd.)

Additional Data Used for Analysis in Section 7: COVID and Credibility

Variable	Description
Population	We use population data for the year 2018. For regression analysis, we transform the population sum into the log level (Source: WDI).
Real GDP (constant 2010 USD)	Data are in constant 2010 USD. Dollar figures for GDP are converted from domestic currencies using the 2010 official exchange rates. We use the 2018 values and convert them into log terms for analysis. (Source: WDI, World Bank national accounts data, and OECD National Accounts data files).
Real GDP per capita (constant 2010 USD)	GDP per capita is gross domestic product divided by mid-year population. Data are in constant 2010 USD. We use the 2018 values and convert them into log terms for analysis. (Source: WDI, World Bank national accounts data, and OECD National Accounts data files).
Trade (% of GDP)	Trade is the sum of the exports and imports of goods and services measured as a share of gross domestic product. We use the values for 2018. (Source: WDI, World Bank national accounts data, and OECD National Accounts data files).
Central bank independence weighted index	(Source: Garriga, Ana Carolina. 2016. "Central Bank Independence in the World: A New Data Set," *International Interactions*, 42 (5): 849-868. DOI: 10.1080/03050629.2016.1188813) The Central Bank Independence measure is based on rules pertaining to legislative reforms, policy formulation, etc., which are coded and combined into a single weighted index. We use values for 2012 (the latest reported year).
Governance indicators	The Worldwide Governance Indicators report on six broad dimensions of governance over the period 1996–2018—voice and accountability, political stability and absence of violence, government effectiveness, regulatory quality, rule of law, and control of corruption. We use the percentile ranks for the year 2018 to conduct our analysis and construct an average governance indicator (rank) by simply averaging the percentile ranks over six categories of reported indicators (Source: World Bank).
Financial development index and related indices	We use nine indices that summarize how developed financial institutions and financial markets are in terms of their depth, access, and efficiency. These indices are then aggregated into an overall index of financial development (financial development index). All indices are for year 2017 (latest available). (Source: IMF Strategy, Policy and Review Department)

Source: Authors' compilation.

TABLE A.3. Inflation Basket in Various CPI Series

	CPI-Combined	CPI–IW	CPI Agricultural Labor (CPI–AL)	CPI Rural Labor (CPI–RL)
Base year	*2012*	*2001*	*1986–87*	*1986–87*
Weights of major groups				
Food, beverages, tobacco	48.24	48.47	72.94	70.47
Fuel and light	6.84	6.42	8.35	7.9
Housing	10.07	15.29	–	–
Clothing and footwear	6.53	6.58	6.98	9.76
Miscellaneous	28.32	23.32	11.73	11.87
Total	100	100	100	100
Compiling agency	CSO, GoI		Labour Bureau, GoI	

Source: Central Statistics Office (CSO), Ministry of Statistics and Programme Implementation, Government of India (GoI); Labour Bureau, GoI.

TABLE A.4. Correlation Coefficients between the Different Variables and their Summary Statistics

	Policy Rate	Output Gap	Inflation	Exchange Rate Depreciation	Fiscal Deficit/ GDP	Government Market Borrowing
Policy rate	1					
Output gap	0.35*	1				
Inflation	0.19	0.15	1			
Exchange rate depreciation	0.30*	−0.07	0.18	1		
Fiscal deficit/GDP	0.09	−0.32*	0	0.17	1	
Government market borrowing	−0.13	−0.27*	0.02	−0.06	0.49*	1

Source: Authors' calculations.
Notes: *indicates that the correlation coefficient is significant at the 1 percent level. Correlation between policy rate and inflation is significant at the 10 percent level.

Appendix B: Further Analysis of the Food-Price-Core-Inflation Pass-through

We use a VAR model to identify the pass-through effect of food inflation on core inflation and vice versa. Our sample goes from 1997 Q1 to 2019 Q4. We splice the respective CPI series using standard splicing methods to arrive at CPI food, core, and fuel inflation. In particular, we have used the CPI–IW variant prior to 2012 Q1 and new CPI food/fuel/core 2011–12 series post that.

Our VAR model includes food and core inflation as endogenous variables and fuel inflation as exogenous. We select a lag length of 8 using the information criteria.[47] For fuel inflation, we consider 4 lags as exogenous to the model. As an additional check, we implement the same model by replacing each variable by its first difference (the optimal lag length changes to 4 with first difference specification).

a. *Persistence of shocks:* We find that inflationary shocks are quite persistent, that is, the shock to food or core inflation does not dissipate in the next period but stays intact for almost three quarters and eventually converges to lower levels. For instance, in Figure B.1d., we see that a one Cholesky standard deviation shock to food inflation stays intact until the fourth quarter and tends to vanish fully only after a year. The same is true for the core inflation shock as is evident from Figure B.1a.

b. *Pass-through from food to core inflation:* Figure B.1c shows the orthogonal impulse response of one Cholesky standard deviation shock to food inflation with core inflation as the response. The effect of the food inflation shock shows up after one quarter lag and tends to spiral up, albeit at a slower pace, until it starts moderating after the eighth quarter.

c. *Pass-through from core to food inflation:* In the orthogonal impulse response of one Cholesky standard deviation shock to core inflation

FIGURE B.1. **Orthogonal Impulse Response**

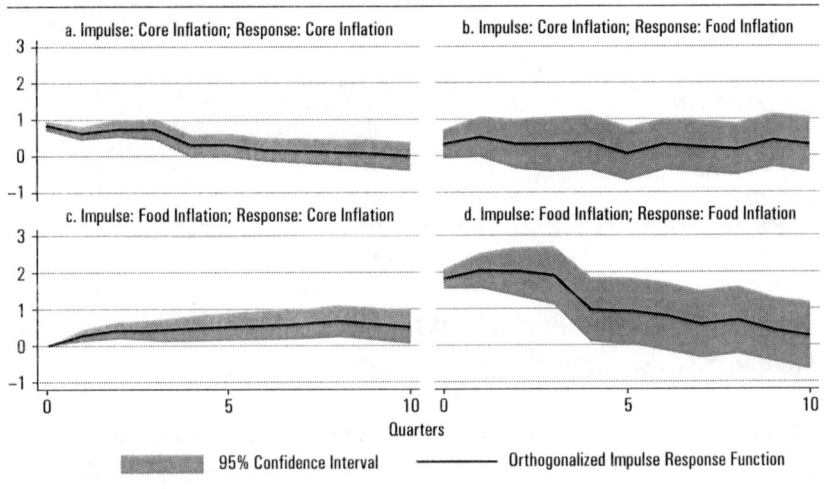

Source: Authors' calculations.

47. Optimal lag length is selected using both Schwarz Bayes and Akaike information criteria.

with food inflation as the response, the results suggest no pass-through from core to food inflation despite an immediate jump in the point estimate of the orthogonal impulse response. The extreme wide confidence intervals signal the insensitivity of food inflation to core inflation shocks. This is not surprising given that food inflation in India is largely driven by supply-side shocks such as rain, and weather and climatic conditions.

d. *Results using first difference specification:* The persistence results as described in point (a) remain consistent with this first difference specification. However, the argument for the pass-through effects from food to core inflation weakens as the confidence interval around the impulse response widens. The results also suggest an immediate pass-through from core inflation to food inflation, which points to the role of channels other than supply shocks. The immediate pass-through from core to food inflation is very short-lived and dies out in the third quarter.

Appendix C: Inflation Persistence

C.1. First-Order Autocorrelations
We construct the rolling window estimates of first-order autocorrelation for headline, core, food, and fuel inflation (similar to Pivetta and Reis [2007], Fuhrer [2010]). We consider three windows for rolling sample autocorrelation with length 20, 30, and 40 quarters. Headline and core inflation display similar time variation in their autocorrelation and a very high degree of persistence with their autocorrelation coefficients lying in the range of 0.8–0.9, based on a 10-year rolling window (see Figures C.1a and C.1b). Food inflation persistence, as measured by the first-order autocorrelation, appears to have declined from being highly persistent in 2010 (having a correlation coefficient slightly above 0.9); the autocorrelation coefficient has hovered around 0.8 in the recent quarters.

C.2. Dominant Root of the Univariate Time Series Process
We now consider Largest autoregressive root (LAR) or "dominant root" implied by the univariate autoregressive process for inflation as a measure of persistence. Consider an AR(p) model:

$$y_t = \theta_0 + \sum_{i=1}^{p}\theta_i y_{t-i} + \epsilon_t$$

(C1)

FIGURE C.1. First-order Autocorrelation for Alternative Inflation Measures

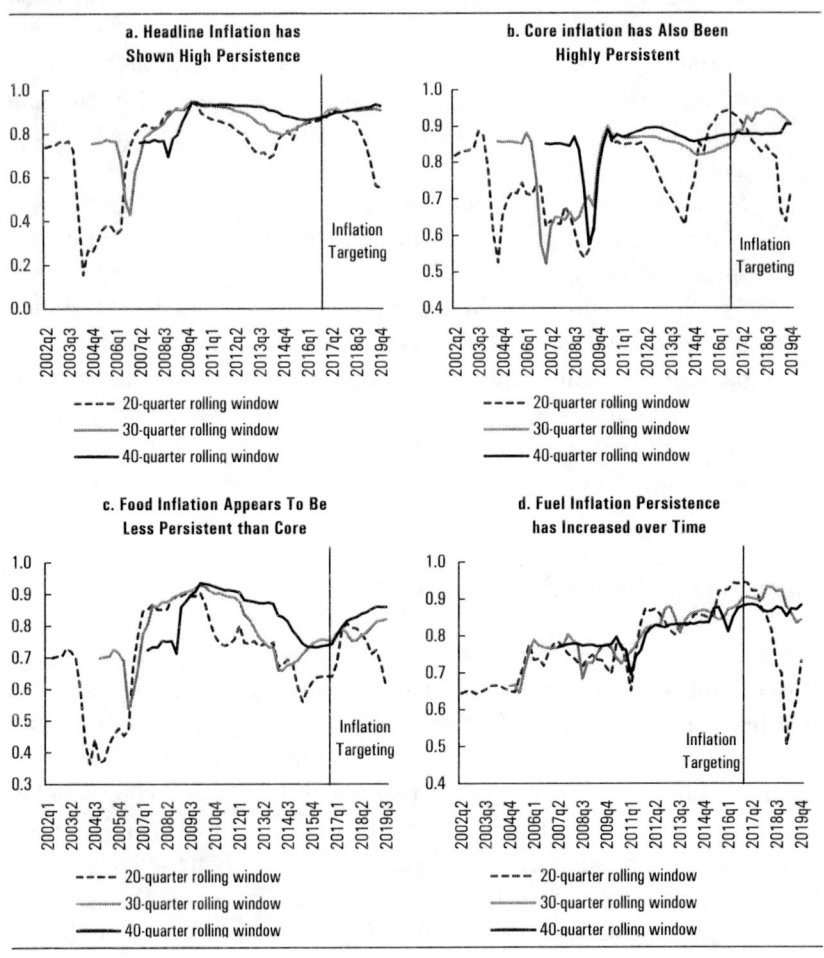

Source: Authors' calculations.

The lag polynomial obtained from the AR(p) model can written as:

$$L(p) = \left(1 - \theta_1 L - \theta_2 L^2 - \dots \theta_p L^p\right) \tag{C2}$$

which can be factored and expressed as:

$$L(p) = \left((1 - \beta_1 L)(1 - \beta_2 L)(1 - \beta_3 L)\dots(1 - \beta_p L)\right) \tag{C3}$$

where the β_i coefficients are ordered according to their size, with β_1 the largest. In the long run, the effect of a shock on inflation will be dominated

TABLE C.1.   Dominant AR Root for Inflation Measures 1997 Q2–2019 Q4

CPI Inflation Series	Dominant AR Root			
	$p = 1$	$p = 2$	$p = 3$	$p = 4$
Headline	0.85	0.71	0.72	0.66*
Core	0.87	0.84	0.76	0.77*
Food	0.80	0.69	0.58	0.74*
Fuel and light	0.81	0.54*	0.76*	0.74*

Source: Authors' calculations.
Notes: 1. * denotes complex roots.
2. Results are based on maximum likelihood estimation (MLE) of AR(p) model.

by this largest root: in the case where β_1 is one, the series has a unit root, and all shocks are permanent. The advantage to the LAR measure is that it effectively measures how close a given inflation series is to having a unit root, that is, how close to permanent a given shock will be. A disadvantage, however, is that the other roots beyond the unit root are ignored, while they matter too in practice, for example, a series with a β_2 of coefficient of 0.8 will display more persistence than one with 0.2.

Table C.1 summarizes the results. All the measures of inflation are highly persistent, as suggested by their dominant AR roots. Comparing across the measures, we find core inflation to be relatively more persistent than food inflation. It is worth noting that the AR roots are estimated using OLS estimation and are likely to be biased downward.

C.3. Sum of Autoregressive Coefficients

Another widely used persistence measure is the sum of autoregressive coefficients (SARC). For this measure, the AR(p) measure chosen above for each of the inflation indices is estimated, and the θ coefficients in the equation are summed. SARC is a widely used method for assessing persistence, first proposed with some modifications in Andrews and Chen (1994), who present it as a better single number estimate of long-term dynamics than unit root tests. However, it also has shortcomings, particularly those that relate to oscillating dynamics. If some of the θ coefficients are positive and others are negative, the sum will be close to zero despite what could be near-infinite dynamics. Table C.2 presents the SARC estimates for different AR models with varying lag lengths. This measure also suggests a high degree of persistence across all four measures of inflation with persistence being relatively higher in core inflation than food or fuel inflation. For the AR(1) model, the SARC estimates are very close to the

TABLE C.2.   **Sum of AR Coefficients for Inflation Measures 1997 Q2–2019 Q4**

CPI Inflation Series	Sum of AR Coefficients			
	$p = 1$	$p = 2$	$p = 3$	$p = 4$
Headline	0.85	0.82	0.82	0.81
Core	0.88	0.87	0.85	0.82
Food	0.81	0.78	0.77	0.74
Fuel and light	0.81	0.75	0.69	0.70

Source: Authors' calculations.
Note: Results are based on the OLS estimation of the AR(p) model.

dominant AR roots for all four inflation measures. Some of the observed difference in the SARC estimates and dominant AR root estimates could be attributed to the estimation methodology, as the former is estimated using OLS while the latter is estimated using MLE. Among the first four measures of persistence considered so far, none of them has quantified the time until which an inflation shock persists in the economy. The best way to visualize this is by analyzing the impulse response function estimated from a univariate or a multivariate time series model. However, to quantify the cut-off time period until which the shock lasts, we analyze another measure known as half-life.

C.4. Half-Life

Another measure for estimating persistence is calculating the impulse half-life. For this method, an impulse response function for each of the AR(p) models is derived. The number of periods required to reduce the impulse response function below 0.5 from an initial unit shock is the half-life. Unlike the previously described methods, this produces integral measures of persistence. For an AR(1) model, a simplified formula is used to calculate half-life, as described below:

$$\text{Half-life (in periods)} = \frac{\log(0.5)}{\log(\theta_1)} \tag{C4}$$

where θ_1 is the coefficient on AR(1) term in the AR(1) model. Table C.3 presents the half-life estimates based on OLS estimation of AR(1) model for different inflation components. The results suggest a higher persistence of core inflation as the shock's half-life is around five quarters while that of food and fuel is about three quarters. The half-life for headline inflation is estimated to be around four quarters.

T A B L E C . 3 .   Half-life for Inflation Measures 1997 Q2–2019 Q4

CPI Inflation Series	Half-life
Headline	4.12
Core	5.16
Food	3.12
Fuel and light	3.38

Source: Authors' calculations.
Note: Results are based on the OLS estimation of the AR(1) model. Half-life, here, is measured in terms of number of quarters.

Appendix D: GMM Estimates of the Monetary Policy Reaction Function

Below in Table D.1 we present results from the GMM estimation of the reaction function. In columns (1), (2), (5), and (6), inflation is instrumented

T A B L E D . 1 .   Estimation of the Monetary Policy Reaction Function

	(1)	(2)	(3)	(4)
Inflation	0.33***	0.30***	0.19**	0.26***
	(4.15)	(3.70)	(2.56)	(3.01)
Output gap (% of GDP)		0.37***	0.56***	0.53***
		(5.24)	(4.20)	(4.14)
Lagged effective policy rate				
Constant	4.81***	4.99***	5.74***	5.36***
	(10.48)	(11.36)	(14.91)	(11.80)
Observations	87	87	87	87
Adjusted R^2	0.00	0.12	0.12	0.09
	(5)	(6)	(7)	(8)
Inflation	0.11***	0.10***	0.09***	0.09***
	(3.79)	(3.22)	(3.45)	(3.27)
Output gap (% of GDP)		0.19***	0.22***	0.21***
		(3.07)	(3.79)	(3.65)
Lagged effective policy rate	0.86***	0.82***	0.85***	0.85***
	(19.30)	(17.59)	(19.27)	(20.31)
Constant	0.27	0.59**	0.49*	0.45*
	(0.93)	(1.98)	(1.87)	(1.77)
Observations	87	87	87	87
Adjusted R^2	0.86	0.89	0.89	0.89

Source: Authors' calculations.
Notes: Robust t statistics in parentheses. $^*p < 0.10$, $^{**}p < 0.05$, $^{***}p < 0.01$.

by its four lags while the output gap is treated as exogenous; in columns (3) and (7), the output gap is instrumented by its four lags, while inflation is treated as exogenous; and in columns (4) and (8), the output gap and inflation are both assumed to be endogenous and are instrumented by four lags of inflation and the output gap.

Appendix E: Previous Estimates of Monetary Policy Reaction Functions for India: A Review

The theoretical model built by Taylor (1993) is used widely as a workhorse for the empirical estimation of monetary policy reaction functions. The model assumes the policy rate as a function of inflation and output gaps. Many studies have estimated the monetary reaction function for India. We list some of them below.

1. **Virmani (2004)** estimated India's monetary policy reaction function by using the Taylor (1993) rule as well as the McCallum (1988) rule augmented with a change in the real effective exchange rate. The sample period was from the third quarter of 1992 to the fourth quarter of 2001. From the OLS and GMM estimations, it was found that the backward-looking Taylor rule captures the evolution of the short-term interest rate reasonably well, as does the backward-looking McCallum rule.

2. **Mohanty and Klau (2004)** extended the Taylor rule to include changes in the real effective exchange rate and examined how the central bank changes the policy rate in response to inflation, the output gap, and the exchange rate. They used quarterly data from 1995 to 2002 in 13 emerging economies, including India. Empirical results of OLS and GMM for India showed that all the explanatory variables are significant with the expected signs, and that the interest rate responds to exchange rate volatility more than inflation and the output gap.

3. **Ranjan et al. (2007)** find a significant response of the Monetary Policy Index (MPI)[48] to the output and inflation gaps over the period 1951–2005 (coefficient on output gap: 0.88 and on inflation gap: 0.52).

---

48. The MPI their analysis uses is a composite index of policy actions, defined as the geometric mean of the index of the Bank rate, CRR, and SLR.

Both these coefficients go up (output gap: 1.89, inflation gap: 1.65) when the sample is restricted to begin in 1992. When the output gap is replaced by its first lag, the coefficient values decline in almost all the models in both periods. The authors estimate three different measures of the output gap and the results are robust to the choice of such a measure, though the coefficient on the output gap changes slightly.

4. **Inoue and Hamori (2009)** empirically estimate India's monetary policy reaction function by applying the Taylor (1993) rule and its open-economy version that employs dynamic OLS. The analysis uses monthly data of IIP (as a proxy for output), WPI, REER, and the call rate (as interest rate) from April 1998 to December 2007. When the simple Taylor rule was estimated for India, the output gap coefficient was statistically significant, and its sign was found to be consistent with the theoretical rationale; however, the same was not true of the inflation coefficient. After including the exchange rate, the coefficients of the output gap and the exchange rate had statistical significance with the expected signs, whereas the results of inflation remained the same as before.

5. **Hutchison et al. (2010)** estimate an exchange-rate-augmented Taylor rule for India over the period 1980 Q1 to 2008 Q4. They investigate monetary policy changes between pre- and post-liberalization periods in order to capture the potential impact of macroeconomic structural changes on the RBI's monetary policy conduct. Overall, the authors find that the output gap seems to matter more to the RBI than inflation, there is greater sensitivity to consumer price inflation, exchange rate changes do not constitute an important policy factor, and the post-1998 conduct of monetary policy seems to have changed in the direction of less inertia.

6. **Singh (2010)** estimates the monetary policy reaction function for the Indian economy for the period 1951–2009. The function has exchange rate and interest rate smoothing terms in addition to the inflation gap and the output gap. In addition to estimating for the whole period, the author also estimates these functions separately for the period up to 1988 and thereafter. The coefficients have expected signs in most of the models. While the coefficients are significant in very few models in the pre-1989 period, in the remaining period, these coefficients are significant in most of the models. This is in line with the findings of Ranjan et al. (2007). The interest rate smoothing

term is highly significant in most of the models, more in the pre-1989 period than after that.

7. **Hutchison et al. (2013)** estimate a time-varying Taylor-type rule for India during 1987 Q1 to 2008 Q4 using IIP (as a proxy for output), WPI, call money market rate, and the nominal exchange rate. They find that the conduct of monetary policy over the last two decades can be characterized by two regimes—hawk and dove. In the first of these two regimes, the central bank reveals a greater relative (though not absolute) weight on controlling inflation vis-à-vis narrowing the output gap. The central bank, however, was found to be in the "dove" regime through about half of the sample period, focusing more on the output gap and exchange rate targets to stimulate exports rather than moderating inflation.

8. **Kumawat and Bhanumurthy (2016)** model the monetary policy response function for India, for the period April 1996 to July 2015. Using the 91-day Treasury bill rate as the policy rate, they find that monetary policy has been responsive to the inflation rate, output gap, and exchange rate changes during this period but with substantial time-varying behavior in the reaction function. The regime shift tests show that the transition is driven by the inflation gap as well as by exchange rate changes. Another important finding is that there is a high degree of inertia in the policy rates.

Appendix F

TABLE F.1. Literature Comparing the Macroeconomic Performance Pre- and Post-inflation Targeting

Author	Sample		Estimation Methodology	Conclusions
	Countries	Time		
Ball and Sheridan (2005)	20 OECD members (all developed and moderate inflation economies): 7 IT and 13 NIT	1960–2001	Cross-section OLS (difference-in-difference approach)	No evidence that IT improves macroeconomic performance as measured by the behavior of inflation, output, or interest rates.
Vega and Winkelried (2005)	World; 23 IT and 86 NIT		Propensity score matching	IT has helped in reducing the level and volatility of inflation in the countries that adopted it.
Gonçalves and Salles (2008)	36 EMEs: 13 IT	1980–2005	Cross-section OLS	Compared to non-targeters, developing countries adopting the IT regime experienced greater drops not only in inflation but also in growth volatility.
Mishkin and Schmidt-Hebbel (2007)	21 IT (8 AEs and 13 EMEs); 13 NIT AEs; 21 post-IT; 21 pre-IT; Stationary IT; 13 NIT AEs	1990–2005	Cross-section OLS, IV Panel	IT helps countries achieve lower inflation in the long run, have a smaller inflation response to oil-price and exchange rate shocks, strengthen monetary policy independence, improve monetary policy efficiency, and obtain inflation outcomes closer to target levels. The performance attained by industrial–country inflation targeters generally dominates the performance of emerging economy inflation targeters and is similar to that of industrial non-IT countries.
Batini and Laxton (2007)	21 IT; 29 NIT	1985–2004	Cross-section OLS	Targeting is associated with lower inflation, lower inflation expectations, and lower inflation volatility in the initial years of operation. There are no visible adverse effects of targeting on output, and performance along other dimensions—such as the volatility of interest rates, exchange rates, and international reserves—has been favorable.

(Table F.1 Contd.)

(Table F.1 Contd.)

Author	Sample Countries	Time	Estimation Methodology	Conclusions
Lin and Ye (2007)	AEs: 7 IT	1985–1999	Propensity score matching	IT has no significant effects on either inflation or inflation variability in these seven countries. Evidence from long-term nominal interest rates and income velocity of money also supports the window-dressing view of IT.
Brito and Bystedt (2010)	EMEs: 13 IT and 46 NIT	1980–2006 (annual)	Various panel models	No evidence that the IT regime results in lower inflation in developing countries. There is evidence of lower output growth during IT adoption.
Calderón and Schmidt-Hebbel (2010)	World: 24 IT; 73 NIT	1975–2005 (annual)	Multivariate structural inflation model; panel models: fixed effects, random effects, and system GMM	Controlling for high inflation and hyperinflation episodes, IT regimes and fixed exchange rate regimes are associated with lower inflation.
Gemayel et al. (2011)	EMEs: 10 IT; 29 NIT	1990–2008 (annual)	Cross-section OLS, panel estimation (via GMM)	IT is associated with lower inflation and inflation volatility. There is no robust evidence of an adverse impact on output.
Pontines (2011)	22 Industrial, 52 developing; 23 IT (10 industrial, 13 developing)	1985–2005 (annual)	Treatment effect regression that jointly estimates the probability of being an inflation targeter and the outcome equation (considers the problem of self-selection in the countries' decision to be an inflation targeter).	Nominal and real exchange rate volatility are lower in IT countries than in countries that do not target inflation.
Rose (2007)	23 IT; 42 countries in the control group (selected based on real GDP and population)	Jan 1990–Dec 2005 (monthly)	Difference-in-difference (comparing pre- and post-IT while controlling other factors)	Inflation targeters have lower exchange rate volatility and less frequent sudden stops of capital flows than similar countries that do not target inflation. IT countries do not have current accounts or international reserves that look different from other countries.

Source: Authors' compilation.
Note: IT stands for inflation targeting countries, NIT for non-inflation targeting countries, EMEs for emerging market economies, and AEs for advanced economies.

References

Acharya, Viral. 2017. "Monetary Transmission in India: Why Is It Important and Why Hasn't It Worked Well?" (Inaugural Aveek Guha Memorial Lecture). Mumbai: Tata Institute of Fundamental Research, November 16.

Andrews, Donald W. K., and Hong-Yuan Chen. 1994. "Approximately Median-Unbiased Estimation of Autoregressive Models." *Journal of Business and Economic Statistics*, 12 (2): 187–204.

Asnani, Swati, Pankaj Kumar, and Shekhar Tomar. 2019, December 18. "Does Inflation Targeting Anchor Inflation Expectations? Evidence from India" (Paper presented at the 15th ISI-CSH Annual Conference on Growth and Development, held at Indian Statistical Institute, New Delhi).

Athey, Susan, Andrew Atkeson, and Patrick Kehoe. 2005. "The Optimal Degree of Discretion in Monetary Policy." *Econometrica*, 73 (5): 1431–475.

Ball, Lawrence M., Anusha Chari, and Prachi Mishra. 2016. "Understanding Inflation in India." *India Policy Forum*, 12: 1–45. New Delhi: National Council of Applied Economic Research.

Ball, Lawrence M., and Niamh Sheridan. 2005. "Does Inflation Targeting Matter?" In *The Inflation Targeting Debate*, edited by B. Bernanke and M. Woodford. Chicago; London: University of Chicago Press.

Basu, Kaushik, Barry Eichengreen, and Poonam Gupta. 2015. "From Tapering to Tightening: The Impact of the Fed's Exit on India." *India Policy Forum*, 11: 1–66. New Delhi: National Council of Applied Economic Research.

Batini, Nicoletta, and Douglas Laxton. 2007. "Under What Conditions Can Inflation Targeting be Adopted? The Experience of Emerging Markets." In *Monetary Policy under Inflation Targeting*, edited by F. Mishkin, K. Schmidt-Hebbel, and N. Loayza, 467–506. Santiago: Central Bank of Chile.

Benes, Jaromir, Kevin Clinton, Asish George, Joice John, Ondra Kamenik, Douglas Laxton, Pratik Mitra, G. V. Nadhanael, Hou Wang, and Fan Zhang. 2017. "Inflation-Forecast Targeting for India: An Outline of the Analytical Framework" (IMF Working Paper WP/17/32). Washington, DC: International Monetary Fund.

Bhoi, Barendra Kumar, Abhishek Kumar, and Prashant Mehul Parab. 2019. "Aggregate Demand Management, Policy Errors and Optimal Monetary Policy in India" (IGIDR Working Paper No. 2019-029). Mumbai: Indira Gandhi Institute of Developmental Research.

Brito, Ricardo D., and Brianne Bystedt. 2010. "Inflation Targeting in Emerging Economies: Panel Evidence." *Journal of Development Economics*, 91 (2010): 198–210.

Calderón, Cesar and Klaus Schmidt-Hebbel. 2010. "What Drives Inflation in the World?" In *Inflation in an Era of Relative Price Shocks*, edited by R. Fry, C. Jones, and C. Kent, 138–77. Sydney: Reserve Bank of Australia and Centre for Applied Macroeconomic Analysis of the Australia National University.

Cecchetti, Stephen. 2007. "Core Inflation Is an Unreliable Guide." *The Financial Times*, March 1.

Chhibber, Ajay. 2020. "With Food and Fuel Consumer Price Index Surges, It's Time to Rethink the Inflation Target Regime." *Economic Times*, January 24.

Das, Shaktikanta. 2020. "Seven Ages of India's Monetary Policy" (Reserve Bank of India Governor's Speech, St Stephen's College, University of Delhi), January 24.

Davis, J. Scott and Ignacio Presno. 2014. "Inflation Targeting and the Anchoring of Inflation Expectations: Cross-country Evidence from Consensus Forecasts," Globalization Institute Working Papers 174, Dallas: Federal Reserve Bank of Dallas.

Dua, Pami. 2020. "Monetary Policy Framework in India." *India Economic Review*, 55 (1): 117–154.

Fuhrer, Jeffrey C. 2010. "Inflation Persistence." In *Handbook of Monetary Economics*, Vol. 3, edited by Benjamin M. Friedman and Michael Woodford, 423–86. New York: North Holland.

Garriga, Ana Carolina. 2016. "Central Bank Independence in the World: A New Data Set." *International Interactions*, 42 (5): 849–868.

Gemayel, Edward R., Sarwat Jahan, and Alexandra Peter. 2011. "What Can Low-Income Countries Expect from Adopting Inflation Targeting?" (IMF Working Paper No. WP/11/276). Washington, DC: International Monetary Fund, November.

Ghate, Chetan, and Kenneth Kletzer, eds. 2016. *Monetary Policy in India: A Modern Macroeconomic Perspective*. New Delhi: Springer India.

Gonçalves, Carlos Eduardo S., and João M. Salles. 2008. "Inflation Targeting in Emerging Economies: What Do the Data Say?" *Journal of Development Economics*, 85 (1–2): 312–318.

Grossman, Herschel, and John Van Huyck. 1988. "Sovereign Debt as a Contingent Claim: Excusable Default, Repudiation, and Reputation." *American Economic Review*, 78 (5): 1088–1097.

Heenan, Geoffrey, Marcel Peter, and Scott Roger. 2006. "Implementing Inflation Targeting: Institutional Arrangements, Target Design and Communications" (IMF Working Paper WP/06/278). Washington, DC: International Monetary Fund.

Hutchison, Michael, Rajeswari Sengupta, and Nirvikar Singh. 2010, September 18. "Estimating a Monetary Policy Rule for India." *Economic & Political Weekly*, 45 (38): 67–68.

———. 2013. "Dove or Hawk? Characterizing Monetary Policy Regime Switches in India." *Emerging Markets Review*, 16 (2013): 183–202.

Inoue, Takeshi, and Shigeyuki Hamori. 2009. "An Empirical Analysis of the Monetary Policy Reaction Function in India" (IDE Discussion Paper No. 200). Chiba: Institute of Developing Economies, Japan External Trade Organization (JETRO).

JPMorgan. 2018. "Is Inflation Dead? A Discussion" (Economic Research). Mumbai: JP Morgan Chase Bank, April.

Kose, M. Ayhan, Hideaki Matsuoka, Ugo Panizza, and Dana Vorisek. 2019. "Inflation Expectations: Review and Evidence" (World Bank Policy Research Paper No. 8785). Washington, DC: World Bank.

Kumawat, Lokendra, and N. R. Bhanumurthy. 2016. "Regime Shifts in India's Monetary Policy Response Function" (Working Paper No. 16/177). New Delhi: National Institute of Public Finance and Policy.

Lewis, W. Arthur. 1954. "Economic Development with Unlimited Supplies of Labour." *The Manchester School,* 22 (2): 139-191.

Lin, Shu, and Haichun Ye. 2007. "Does Inflation Targeting Really Make a Difference? Evaluating the Treatment Effect of Inflation Targeting in Seven Industrial Countries." *Journal of Monetary Economics,* 54 (8): 2521-2533.

Mccallum, Bennet T. 1988. "Robustness properties of a rule for monetary policy" *Carnegie-Rochester Conference Series on Public Policy,* 29: 173-203.

Mishkin, Frederic S., and Klaus Schmidt-Hebbel. 2007. "Does Inflation Targeting Make a Difference?" In *Monetary Policy under Inflation Targeting,* edited by F. Mishkin, N. Loayza and K. Schmidt-Hebbel, 291-372. Santiago: Central Bank of Chile.

Mishra, Prachi, and Devesh Roy. 2012. "Explaining Inflation in India: The Role of Food Prices." *India Policy Forum,* 8: 139-223. New Delhi: National Council of Applied Economic Research.

Mishra, Prachi, Peter Montiel, and Rajeswari Sengupta. 2016. "Monetary Transmission in Developing Countries: Evidence from India" (IMF Working Paper No. 16/167). Washington, DC: International Monetary Fund, December.

Mohan, Rakesh, and Muneesh Kapur. 2009. "Managing the Impossible Trinity: Volatile Capital Flows and Indian Monetary Policy" (SCID Working Paper No. 401). Stanford: Stanford University.

Mohan, Rakesh, and Partha Ray. 2018. "Indian Monetary Policy in the Time of Inflation Targeting and Demonetization" (Working Paper No. 4). New Delhi: Brookings India.

Mohanty, Deepak. 2014. "Why Is Recent Food Inflation in India So Persistent?" (Speech delivered at the Annual Lalit Doshi Memorial Lecture, St Xavier's College, Mumbai), January 13.

Mohanty, Madhusudan, and Marc Klau. 2004. "Monetary Policy Rules in Emerging Market Economies: Issues and Evidence" (BIS Working Paper No. 149). Basel: Bank for International Settlements.

Naqvi, Bushra, and Syed Kumail Abbas Rizvi. 2009. "Inflation Targeting Framework: Is the Story Different for Asian Economies?" (MPRA Paper No. 19546). Germany: University Library of Munich.

Obstfeld, Maurice. 1997. "Destabilizing Effects of Exchange-Rate Escape Clauses." *Journal of International Economics,* 43 (1-2): 61-77.

Patnaik, Ila, and Radhika Pandey. 2020. "Moving to Inflation Targeting" (NIPFP Working Paper No. 316). New Delhi: National Institute of Public Finance and Policy.

Patra, Michael D., and Muneesh Kapur. 2012. "Alternative Monetary Policy Rules for India" (IMF Working Paper No. 12/118). Washington, DC: International Monetary Fund.

Patra, Michael D., and Partha Ray. 2010. "Inflation Expectations and Monetary Policy in India" (IMF Working Paper No. 10/84). Washington, DC: International Monetary Fund.

Patra, Michael D., S. Pattanaik, J. John, and H.K. Behera. 2016. "Global Spillovers and Monetary Policy Transmission in India" (RBI Working Paper Series No. 03/2016). New Delhi: Reserve Bank of India.

Pivetta, Frederica, and Ricardo Reis. 2007. "The Persistence of Inflation in the United States." *Journal of Economic Dynamics and Control*, 31 (4): 1326–1358.

Pontines, Victor. 2011. "The Nexus between Inflation Targeting and Exchange Rate Volatility" (Staff Papers No. sp84). Kuala Lumpur: South East Asian Central Banks (SEACEN) Research and Training Centre.

Raj, Janak, Sangita Misra, Asish Thomas George, and Joice John. 2020. "Core Inflation Measures in India: An Empirical Evaluation using CPI Data" (RBI Working Paper Series No. 05). New Delhi: Reserve Bank of India, May 12.

Rangarajan, Chakravarty. 2020. "The New Monetary Policy Framework—What It Means" (NIPFP Working Paper Series No. 20/297). New Delhi: National Institute of Public Finance and Policy.

Ranjan, R., R. Jain, and S. C. Dhal. 2007. "India's Potential Economic Growth: Measurement Issues and Policy Implications." *Economic & Political Weekly*, 42 (17): 1563–1572.

Reserve Bank of India. 2014. "Report of the Expert Committee to Revise and Strengthen the Monetary Policy Framework" (Chairman: Dr Urjit Patel). Mumbai: Reserve Bank of India. Available at https://www.rbi.org.in/SCRIPTs/PublicationReportDetails.aspx?UrlPage=&ID=743 (accessed April 20, 2021).

Rose, Andrew K. 2007. "A Stable International Monetary System Emerges: Inflation Targeting Is Bretton Woods Reversed." *Journal of International Money and Finance*, 26 (5): 663–681, September.

Singh, Bhupal. 2010. "Monetary Policy Behaviour in India: Evidence from Taylor-Type Policy Frameworks" (Staff Study SS [DEAP]: 2/2010). Mumbai: Reserve Bank of India.

Taylor, John B. 1993. "Discretion versus policy rules in practice." *Carnegie-Rochester Conference Series on Public Policy,* 39: 195–214, North-Holland.

Vega, Marco, and Diego Winkelried. 2005. "Inflation Targeting and Inflation Behavior: A Successful Story?" *International Journal of Central Banking*, 1 (3): 153–175.

Virmani, Arvind. 2004. "Operationalizing Taylor-Type Rules for the Indian Economy" (Technical Report). Ahmedabad: Indian Institute of Management.

Woodford, Michael. 2001. "The Taylor Rule and Optimal Monetary Policy." *American Economic Review*, 91 (2): 232–237.

Comments and Discussion[*]

Chair: **Rakesh Mohan**
Yale Jackson Institute & Centre for Social and Economic Progress

Kenneth Kletzer
University of California, Santa Cruz

The authors have written an exceptionally clear, informative, and thorough paper, integrating empirical analysis with insightful and well-supported interpretations. I am particularly interested in having an interim assessment of inflation targeting for India available. It does seem early to perform an interim appraisal of a monetary policy regime that has not quite completed its fourth year, but inflation targeting will face review in 2021. Although less critical than public health and other interventions to alleviate individual hardship, monetary policy everywhere is tackling a major macroeconomic challenge due to COVID-19. The authors wisely combine a discussion of the role for monetary policy in the present crisis with the retrospective analysis of the current policy regime. The result is a valuable analytical paper accessible and informative to policymakers.

The appraisal of inflation targeting in India follows a well-used, appropriate empirical practice in the area. It also follows a substantial literature on Indian inflation, the importance of food price inflation in India, and the effects of adopting inflation targeting in emerging market and middle-income economies. I discuss the paper in the context of the following four topics.

The first concerns the appropriate measure of inflation to adopt as the operative inflation target. The paper begins with an overview of the comparison of the unified CPI, component-wise CPIs, and the WPI, and provides a very clear explanation as to why the CPI is the more meaningful and useful measure of inflation. This is expected, but it is convincingly done. The authors then address the attention given to food price inflation by policymakers and commentators. The authors' comparisons of the volatility,

* To preserve the sense of the discussions at the India Policy Forum, these discussants' comments reflect the views expressed at the IPF and do not necessarily take into account revisions to the conference version of the paper in response to these and other comments in preparing the final, revised version published in this volume. The original conference version of the paper is available on NCAER's website at the links provided at the end of this section.

persistence, and interactions of food inflation, core inflation, and headline inflation replicate and update the findings from others, including two previous papers presented at the NCAER India Policy Forum itself in 2011 and 2015. Food inflation remains less persistent than headline or core inflation, and the volatilities have quite similar magnitudes. Combining the CPI and the CPI for industrial workers for a longer time series, the authors show that food inflation predicts core inflation, but core inflation does not predict food inflation. They conclude that the standard core inflation measure, all items less food and fuel, provides an inferior inflation target than headline inflation, which incorporates the long-run effects of food inflation.

Although the Granger-causality tests in the text are supplemented by vector autoregressions in the Appendix, earlier papers have also demonstrated these results using cointegration and vector error correction models. Among these is the 2011–12 IPF paper by Prachi Mishra and Devesh Roy, who also argue that because the conventional exclusionary measure of core inflation does not converge to headline inflation in the long run, headline inflation is the more appropriate measure for an inflation target. Laurence Ball, Anusha Chari, and Prachi Mishra in the 2015–16 IPF use disaggregated sectoral price data and propose the use of trimmed mean or median inflation as a better guide for targeting inflation. One observation they make is that food and fuel contribute about two-thirds of the upper 10 percent tail of quarterly price changes. This is consistent with the similar volatility and shorter duration of food price shocks shown by the authors of this paper. Ball et al. (2015–16), however, use the Phillips curve to assess the choice of a core inflation measure. I strongly recommend to the current authors adding references to both previous IPF papers, perhaps including some comparisons to the present paper. There are also two recent RBI papers, one published this year, that I recommend the authors take a look at (Raj et al. 2020; Rath et al. 2000). Although it is common, I recommend a little temperance using the phrase "the pass-through of inflation" to describe Granger-causality. There is a natural explanation, involving price and wage-setting behavior, why food-specific shocks such as weather cause overall inflation to rise, but the test actually just shows prediction. Further, monetary policy reaction functions should affect this statistical relationship.

The second point in the paper concerns the importance of output growth, or the output gap, in the Reserve Bank's policy goals under inflation targeting. The RBI implements a flexible inflation target. The paper does a convincing job demonstrating so by showing that the output gap plays no less of a role in determining changes in the effective policy rate after the inception of inflation targeting than it did before. The monetary policy rule regressions further confirm that policy rate changes respond to headline inflation and not additionally to food inflation. Hopefully, writers in the business press will take note.

Sections 5 and 6 address what I think is the third major point. This is the assessment of the performance of the inflation targeting regime. Does it appear to be a success so far? As we go through Section 5, inflation in the CPI, as well as headline, core, and food inflation, is significantly, and economically, lower after inflation targeting than before, whether the change in the policy regime is dated at the formal start in 2016 or when the RBI began adopting the procedures of inflation targeting in 2014. The volatility of all measures of inflation, with the exception of food inflation, are also lower. The overall absence of effects on exchange rates, foreign reserves, and portfolio flows, as well as the reductions in the volatility of exchange rates, the stock market, and the call rate, are all checks on the plus side. Indeed, India fares better than most emerging market and middle-income countries in the various cross-country studies compiled in the Appendix. It seems to me that inflation targeting in India is doing very well so far.

Another important question in this assessment is whether progress has been made towards anchoring inflation expectations since the adoption of inflation targeting. The evidence is ambiguous. The survey of inflation expectations for households continues to illustrate tremendous persistence in their inflation expectations. The slow decline in expected inflation in response to the decrease in inflation over several years and the large 3 percent difference between the inflation expected by households and actual inflation are disconcerting. Since the introduction of the RBI's survey of inflation expectations for professional forecasters, actual inflation and expected inflation for the professional forecasters have tracked quite well. The progress toward the anchoring of expectations is clouded by the absence of a significant effect of inflation on expected inflation, shown in Table 14, and of expected inflation on actual inflation for households, shown in Table 15. The positive results for professional forecasters are encouraging, but we do not understand how inflation expectations by households are formed. Nor can we yet learn how important this discrepancy might be in the presence of inflation shocks following expansive monetary policies in the near-term responses to the pandemic. A question left unanswered is which group's expectations matter more for the impact of expected inflation on current inflation. This has to do with who sets which prices and wages. I am not aware of an adequate analysis of the relative importance of professional forecaster expectations to help. I really appreciate that the authors present their analysis of whether expectations are becoming more anchored carefully and clearly, and forego reaching conclusions not yet ready to be made.

The fourth major contribution of the paper is the discussion of the monetary policy response to COVID-19 for India and escape clauses for inflation-targeting central banks in the face of *force majeure*. As noted by the authors, India, like other emerging market and middle-income countries, has acted quickly in its monetary policy response to the pandemic crisis by lowering policy rates four times since February. They argue that the RBI has some room to cut rates with inflation just at the upper bound of its target range of 6 percent. The paper nicely uses a standard textbook aggregate supply and aggregate demand model to explain how the timing of supply and demand shocks will determine qualitatively how inflationary policy rate cuts will be. I think this is the right explanation and the right way to communicate it. A central bank that enjoys anchored expectations under inflation targeting will have the credibility to use forward guidance to mitigate the inflationary consequences of an expansionary monetary response to a temporary supply shock. The authors close the paper with an insightful piece of empirical evidence in favor of inflation targeting. Table 17 shows that inflation-targeting central banks have been able to lower their policy rates more aggressively since the onset of the beginning of 2020 than non-inflation targeters.

The paper points out that if the disruptions to production and trade persist, then monetary policy in response to the supply shock should be contractionary. With a persistent pandemic, potential output will fall. Thus, the output gap rises, and the monetary policy rule instructs the central bank to raise policy rates. In such circumstances, as in the advanced economies in the 1970s, rising inflation is likely to lead to a loss of central bank credibility and a de-anchoring of expectations.

At the end, the paper raises the possibility that the theory of repeated games, albeit from a time long ago, may be useful for communicating departures from monetary policy rules under exceptional shocks. Several game theoretic analyses of the conflict between commitment and discretion in monetary policymaking have been published in recent years, showing that monetary policies can allow central bankers to use their private information about the state of the world. An implicit escape clause that allows the central bank to deviate from an inflation target in exigent circumstances observable by all will work in a basic reputational equilibrium. Rules that allow flexibility are possible and rely on reputations. This may be an exotic literature, but the difficulty for policymakers of any kind in the face of uncertainty, not risk, is a problem likely to be with macroeconomics for some time.

In summary, I found this to be a superb paper on monetary policy in the context of an emerging market economy containing a very large number of important results. The text is thoughtfully written so that it will reach policymakers and other observers without sacrificing sufficient empirical analysis, appropriate econometrics, and interpretations. I am hopeful that its main message will find a grateful audience.

References

Ball, Laurence, Anusha Chari, and Prachi Mishra. 2015–16. "Understanding Inflation in India." *India Policy Forum*, 12: 1–45. New Delhi: National Council of Applied Economic Research.

Mishra, Prachi, and Devesh Roy. 2011–12. "Explaining Inflation in India—The Role of Food Prices." *India Policy Forum*, 8: 139–224. New Delhi: National Council of Applied Economic Research.

Raj, Janak, Sangita Misra, Asish Thomas George, and Joice John. 2020. "Core Inflation Measures in India: An Empirical Evaluation using CPI Data" (RBI Working Paper No. 05). Mumbai: Reserve Bank of India, May 12.

Rath, Deba Prasad, Deepak Mohanty, and M. Ramaiah. 2000. "Measures of Core Inflation for India." *Economic & Political Weekly*, 35 (5): 273–275, January 29.

Rajeswari Sengupta
IGIDR

Using detailed empirical analysis, the paper comments on the effectiveness of the inflation targeting (IT) regime in India adopted in 2016. It finds that the Reserve Bank of India (RBI) has been a flexible inflation targeter since 2016 and has not neglected changes in output gap when setting policy rates. Specifically, it has not been an "inflation nutter" and has adjusted policy rates by less in response to inflation. The paper interprets this finding as a sign of enhanced credibility for the RBI as a monetary policy authority. This implies that smaller changes are needed to signal the RBI's intent. The paper also argues that inflation expectations have become better anchored with the advent of the IT regime, and other inflation-related outcomes, such as the exchange rate, are also more stable than before.

The essence of the paper is that the RBI has established its credibility as an inflation targeting central bank and the consequence of this, in the context of the ongoing COVID-19 pandemic, is that the central bank is now in a position to disregard the inflation target and ease monetary policy to help revive growth. This is a very detailed and well-written paper with a comprehensive assessment of the IT framework, which is also relevant from a policy perspective, given that the inflation target is about to be reviewed by the government in 2021 as per the law.

Our main comment centers around the key question: Has the RBI achieved credibility as an inflation targeting central bank in the last four years?

A good way to assess performance is by looking at inputs rather than outcomes. Outcomes can be affected by exogenous factors. Two important inputs that play a critical role in developing policy credibility are: (a) the technical ability to deliver, and (b) the commitment towards the objective. Significant questions remain on both.

In order to help understand whether the RBI has demonstrated the technical ability to achieve the inflation target, we analyze its forecasts, the macroeconomic data used to prepare these forecasts, and the state of monetary policy transmission in India.

The ability to forecast well is an integral element of successful inflation targeting because, in effect, the policy rate is supposed to target forecasted inflation in the medium term. In other words, the policy rate is based on the central bank's forecasts of future GDP growth and inflation. A comparison of RBI's forecasts and the actual data shows that since the advent of IT, the central bank has systematically overpredicted both the output gap and the inflation gap. Its projections on GDP growth have almost always been higher than the actual data, often prompting frequent revisions in the forecasts. The same applies to its inflation forecasts, resulting in arguably a more hawkish monetary policy stance than what could have been the case had the forecasts been more accurate.

Second, the RBI has been operating and making its statistical projections based on the new 2011–12 base year GDP series, and there has been ample evidence in the academic as well as policy domains that this series may not have conveyed the true picture of the economy, especially during the 2015–2018 period, which also coincided with the implementation of IT. The net result was that RBI's forecasts of closing the output gap, and hence risks to inflation, led to an excessively tight monetary policy (Bhoi et al. 2019). For instance, during the period September 2016 to March 2019, while CPI inflation averaged 3.7 percent, the policy repo rate was 6.3 percent and the real rate of interest was 3.2 percent.

Finally, it is well established in empirical research that monetary policy transmission in India is weak (Mishra et al. 2016). The effectiveness of transmission channels has not improved with the advent of IT. In the absence of well-functioning policy transmission, achieving the inflation target through changes in the policy rate becomes difficult. This, in turn, raises questions about the RBI's ability to deliver on the objective.

We next turn to the second input to assess the RBI's demonstrated commitment to its inflation target. Here, we focus on the liquidity actions taken by the central bank during the IT period as well as its official monetary policy communication. It is worth noting that the RBI's liquidity management has often contradicted the interest rate decision taken by the Monetary Policy Committee (MPC). For instance, in August 2017, the MPC lowered the repo rate from 6.25 percent to 6 percent, signaling an easing of monetary policy, but the RBI conducted an open market sale in the bond market, which is akin to a monetary policy contraction. Such policy contradictions hamper the transmission of rate actions to lending rates.

How strong was the RBI's commitment to the newly established inflation target as understood from its official communication? The RBI Amended Act (2016) explicitly mentions, "...the primary objective of the monetary policy is to maintain price stability while keeping in mind the objective of growth;..."

However, when Shaktikanta Das took over as the RBI Governor in January 2019, in his maiden speech he said the following:

At the RBI, we are committed to playing our role as the monetary authority for maintaining mandated price stability objective while keeping in mind the objective of growth; and as the regulator and supervisor of the banking sector and payment systems. We will take necessary steps to maintain financial stability and to facilitate enabling conditions for sustainable and robust growth.

This indicated that the RBI under his leadership would be flexible enough to assume multiple responsibilities, instead of the one-point agenda of remaining fixated on inflation, not quite a message that should be sent out by an inflation targeting central bank committed to achieving the target.

In terms of analytical specifics, the paper estimates a Taylor Rule equation to find out the kinds of weights assigned by the RBI to different macroeconomic variables such as inflation and output gap, and other variables. If the RBI was focusing on controlling inflation, as claimed by the paper, we should see an inflation coefficient greater than 1 in the Taylor Rule, and we should see the size of the estimated coefficient go up post adoption of IT. However, this is not what the paper finds. Instead, it finds that the relationship between inflation and the policy rate becomes weaker post IT.

What does this imply about: (a) RBI's pursuit of IT and (b) RBI establishing its credibility as an inflation targeting central bank? The main claim of the paper is that because the RBI has achieved credibility, it has changed interest rates by less since the introduction of IT. But there is no evidence of this credibility.

The paper finds that in the IT period, the effect of inflation on the policy rate is negative. This result contradicts actual data as well as existing research.

Some of the other quibbles with the paper are that the objective of the paper needs to be described more clearly, the metrics used for assessing the IT framework also need to be outlined, and a discussion of relevant factors such as low oil prices and record levels of food grain production, that is, factors that could have also kept CPI inflation low during the IT period, must be included.

In addition, in the Taylor Rule estimation, the 91-day treasury bill rate may be used as the dependent variable, as it is a comprehensive proxy for the overall monetary policy stance, the exchange rate needs to be included in the baseline model, given the occasional attempts by the RBI to manage exchange rate fluctuations using the policy rate, and the same inflation measure must be used everywhere for the sake of consistency.

The paper also claims that the exchange rate has been stable during the IT period, which is a sign of RBI's enhanced credibility, but that does not appear to be correct. The rate has been stable because the RBI has intervened regularly in the foreign exchange market. If anything, this calls into question the RBI's commitment to IT, given the trade-offs involved in the Impossible Trilemma framework.

Finally, the paper uses its assertion of increased credibility to recommend that the RBI can ignore the IT framework during the COVID-19 pandemic period and lower rates to boost growth. In this context, the post-2008 experience with inflation in the aftermath of the Global Financial Crisis might be worth revisiting.

There was a certain amount of complacency regarding inflation back then. The RBI lowered the policy rate (the repo rate came down from 9 percent in September 2008 to 4.75 percent in December 2009) and did a massive amount of liquidity infusion. Uncharted territory was cited, and hence erring on the side of caution was justified, quite similar to the current circumstances. CPI inflation went up from 6.2 percent in 2007–08 to 12.4 percent in 2009–10. The economy had to bear the cost of bringing inflation down and the RBI had to raise the policy rate from 4.75 percent to more than 8 percent in a series of consecutive monetary policy meetings. We should avoid making the same mistake again. The paper needs to take cognizance of this risk.

References

Bhoi, Barendra Kumar, Abhishek Kumar, and Prashant Mehul Parab. 2019. "Aggregate Demand Management, Policy Errors and Optimal Monetary Policy in India" (IGIDR Working Paper No. 2019-029). Mumbai: Indira Gandhi Institute of Developmental Research.

Mishra, Prachi, Peter Montiel, and Rajeswari Sengupta. 2016. "Monetary Transmission in Developing Countries: Evidence from India" (IMF Working Paper No. 16/167). Washington, DC: International Monetary Fund.

General Discussion

Participants in the General Discussion included **Raghuram Rajan, Sajjid Chinoy, Vijay Joshi, Ajay Chhibber**, and of course, the Chair, **Rakesh Mohan**.

To get a sense of the richness of this discussion, we invite you to view the video of the General Discussion segment of this IPF session. Please use the appropriate hyperlink on the IPF 2020 Program available at the links below.

The session video and all slide presentations for this IPF session are hyperlinked on the IPF Program available by scanning this QR code or going to
https://www.ncaer.org/IPF2020/Agenda/Agenda_IPF_2020.pdf

A N I R B A N S A N Y A L*
RBI and University of California, Santa Cruz

N I R V I K A R S I N G H†
University of California, Santa Cruz

Structural Change and Economic Growth: Patterns and Heterogeneity among Indian States and Implications for a Post-COVID Recovery§

ABSTRACT   This paper empirically examines the relationship between economic growth and structural change in India over recent decades. It first estimates panel regressions with state-level data to examine the impact of structural change on growth and vice versa. Bidirectional causality is found, which holds across different specifications and estimation methods: each variable positively impacts the other in a positive feedback loop. The second part of the analysis relaxes assumptions of constant impacts across states and over time, estimating time-varying autoregressive models for each state and each pair of variables. The impacts of structural change and growth on each other seem to vary across different states, as well as over time, and are differentially affected by state per capita income levels and national growth rates. Similar variability across states and over time is found in an alternative method: labor productivity decompositions using employment data. Some possible reasons for these differences are discussed. The analysis suggests that national economic policy formulation may benefit from closer consideration of the structural differences across states, and the resulting differences in growth responses. The paper concludes with some possible implications for India's post-pandemic recovery.

Keywords: India, Economic Growth, Structural Change, Panel Regression, Time Varying Parameters

JEL Classification: C11, C2, C3, O1, O5

* *ansanyal@ucsc.edu*
† *boxjenk@ucsc.edu*
§ The views expressed in this paper are those of the authors and not necessarily of the organizations to which they belong. The data used in this paper are sourced from the public domain. This is a revised version of the paper presented at the India Policy Forum, July 17, 2020. We are grateful to Barry Bosworth and Neelkanth Mishra for formal discussant comments at the conference, and to comments from the session chair, N. K. Singh, as well as from the audience, especially Rajnish Mehra.

143

1. Introduction

India's Independence in 1947 marked the beginning of the post-colonial era. It was followed two years later by China's Communist Revolution, and the two giants have stood out since then because of their population sizes, though they have differed in their political and economic trajectories, as well as in their heterogeneity. Arguably, India's more heterogeneous composition in terms of languages and cultures has compounded the challenges of democratic governance in the period in which both countries have pursued economic transformation. Heterogeneity in the economic dimension is a major theme of our analysis, along with that of structural change.

In the last three decades, economic reforms helped the Indian economy accelerate (see Joshi 2016; Panagariya 2008), becoming one of the fastest growing in the world, though still lagging behind China over this period. However, India's pattern of growth has been quite unusual, not conforming well to traditional models of economic development, which envisage a major shift in employment from lower productivity agriculture to higher productivity, labor-intensive, manufacturing. In India's case, manufacturing has not increased much as a share of GDP. Agriculture's share in GDP has declined, though agricultural employment has been slower to change. On the other hand, services, including new sectors such as software and information technology-enabled services, have contributed to accelerated growth. Most recently, India had again been experiencing slower growth, and before the nature of that deceleration could be fully understood, the negative shock of the Coronavirus pandemic and the resulting lockdowns have added a major wrinkle to the economy's trajectory.

States are a natural and commonly used unit of analysis when the performance of the Indian economy is disaggregated: they have significant responsibilities in terms of governance and economic policymaking within India's federal structure. Their population sizes are comparable to typical countries in Europe or Latin America. One of the most popular sets of state-level studies has explored convergence or divergence of per capita outputs across states.[1] These studies control for initial conditions, such as baseline economic level or structure, in predicting subsequent economic performance, but typically do not tackle the ongoing drivers of economic growth.

---

1. There are several dozen such studies: among the recent ones for India are Bandyopadhyay (2012), Chakraborty and Chakraborty (2018), Cherodian and Thirlwall (2015), Das (2012), Ghosh et al. (2013), and Mishra and Mishra (2018).

In contrast, relatively few studies for India have examined the connection between structural change and growth at the state level.[2] However, as briefly noted earlier, according to classical development theory, a specific kind of structural change of the economy is a major feature of growth. In these models, industrialization that involves reallocation of labor from low productivity to high productivity sectors drives economic growth (Chenery 1960; Kaldor 1957; Lewis 1954; Verdoorn 1949; Young 1928). Recent empirical work has identified this process as important in explaining varying growth performances across countries and regions. Specifically, McMillan and Rodrik (2011) conclude that

The bulk of the difference between Asia's recent growth, on the one hand, and Latin America's and Africa's, on the other, can be explained by the variation in the contribution of structural change to overall labor productivity.

For India, using the framework introduced by McMillan and Rodrik, Hasan et al. (2013) found that labor allocation toward high productivity sectors reduced poverty across Indian states. Cortuk and Singh (2011, 2015) implemented a different approach to measuring structural change and examined the connection between structural change and economic growth in India at the national and the state levels, respectively.

This paper provides a more detailed and updated examination of the role of structural change in affecting India's economic growth, using state-level data and multiple empirical approaches. One approach uses a Structural Change Index. In addition to panel regressions, which assume that states are subject to the same magnitudes of effects, the paper also includes state-by-state time series analyses. For the latter, the paper innovates by using a flexible empirical framework based on time-varying parameters. Finally, an empirical analysis that employs a decomposition of productivity growth into within-sector changes and structural change is also implemented. While the analysis was conceived before the pandemic and data limitations prevent inclusion of the country's most recent experience, the analysis may still have some possible implications for thinking about India's economic recovery from the pandemic.

The remainder of the paper is organized as follows: Section 2 provides a discussion of some relevant examples in the existing literature on structural change and its linkage with growth. Data description is provided in Section 3 along with some stylized facts distilled from the data. Section 4 lays out

---

2. Two exceptions are Cortuk and Singh (2015) and Hasan et al. (2013): these are discussed in detail later in the paper.

the empirical strategy with the estimation methodology, including panel regressions, time-varying parameter regressions, and productivity decompositions. This is followed in Section 5 by the empirical findings for the three approaches. Concluding remarks are presented in Section 6. In addition to summarizing our results, the conclusion offers some possible implications of our approach for thinking about the post-pandemic economic recovery.

2. Structural Change and Growth

Our specific focus on structural change and growth can be seen as a contribution to a broader literature that analyzes India's growth story in the last 50 years and its unusual pattern of development. Attention has been paid to the role of private and public investment (Sen 2014), services intensity (Eichengreen and Gupta 2011; Singh 2006), and skill intensity (Kochhar et al. 2006) to explain the country's growth trajectory. Stepping back from proximate causes, policy reforms have been credited as a major driver of growth that arguably accelerated from 1988 onward (Panagariya 2008). Ghate and Wright (2012) provided formal empirical evidence for a structural break in India's economic growth path in the 1980s at the time of the initial reforms.

Beyond aggregate growth, several studies have tried to explore the patterns of growth across subsectors of the economy. Wallack (2003), Virmani (2006), and Balakrishnan and Parameswaran (2007) analyzed the growth path of the manufacturing and services sectors. Mazumdar (2010) linked policy reforms and sectoral contributions to growth. Some of these studies identified a shift from slow-growing or low-productivity sectors to fast-growing or higher productivity sectors as part of India's growth experience. This is the point formalized by McMillan and Rodrik (2011), quoted earlier. Empirically, intersectoral reallocation of labor from low-productivity to high-productivity sectors is a measure of structural change. Working within this framework, Hasan et al. (2013) observed that structural change, measured in terms of a transition towards high-productivity sectors, reduced poverty across several of India's states. On similar lines, Ahsan and Mitra (2014) found that structural change contributed to significant shifts in labor productivity for various Indian states, especially after the 1991 policy reforms. In line with other studies of India's pattern of development, they found that most of the gains came in the services sector rather than in manufacturing.[3]

3. Sen (2014) provides an overview of the patterns of growth and structural change in the Indian economy, including work based on the McMillan–Rodrik approach. He documents and emphasizes the atypical nature of India's structural transformation.

An alternative approach to measuring structural change avoids incorporating productivity changes into the measure.[4] This method directly aggregates changes in sectoral shares. Since these changes are both positive and negative, and have to add up to zero, the signs are removed by using absolute values (Michaely 1962; Stoikov 1966) or squares (Lilien 1982).[5] This approach measures structural change independently of productivity or growth, typically using national accounting data for sectoral shares. Hence, it enables a regression analysis of the link between structural change and growth, instead of accounting decompositions of productivity. In this manner, Cortuk and Singh (2011) conducted the first empirical study of the effect of structural change on India's growth. Using annual data from 1951 to 2007, they found unidirectional Granger causality from structural change to growth. Using panel data for 16 states over the period 2000–06, Cortuk and Singh (2015) found the same unidirectional causality. Thind and Singh (2018) appears to be the only other study of Indian data that calculates structural change indices, but the authors of this study did not perform any regression analysis.[6]

3. Data and Stylized Facts

The analysis uses state-level GDP data (SGDP) at annual frequency across 20 states and union territories (UTs). In some cases, states were split during this period, and we use data for the new states, where the series have been adjusted, to take account of the splits. The SGDP data has been obtained from the States of India database of the Centre for Monitoring Indian Economy (CMIE).[7] The states and UTs considered for the paper are

4. We should note that the two approaches presented here are not the only possibilities for examining structural change and development. A well-known and important example is Bosworth and Collins (2008): they compare India and China for the period 1978–2004. Using growth accounting methods, they calculate aggregate growth in output per worker as well as for three sectors, namely, agriculture, industry, and services. The residual from this decomposition is interpreted as a reallocation effect, that is, due to structural shifts in employment. In other examples, Fan et al. (2003) and Chen et al. (2011) use production function estimates combined with decompositions of sources of productivity growth for China. Valli and Saccone (2009) use a decomposition method due to Syrquin (1986), which differs from that popularized by McMillan and Rodrik, to compare China and India's structural change. Mallick (2017) makes the same comparison of the two countries using an input–output approach. None of these studies disaggregates to the subnational level.

5. The formulas for both types of measures are described in the next section.

6. They also performed McMillan–Rodrik type structural change calculations, making theirs one of the few papers to consider both approaches to measuring structural change.

7. https://statesofindia.cmie.com

T A B L E 1 .   Indian States and Unions Territories used in this Paper

Assam (AS)	Bihar (BR)	Chandigarh UT (CH)	Chhattisgarh (CG)
Delhi-NCR (DL)	Gujarat (GJ)	Haryana (HR)	Himachal Pradesh (HP)
Jharkhand (JH)	Karnataka (KA)	Kerala (KL)	Madhya Pradesh (MP)
Maharashtra (MH)	Odisha (OD)	Punjab (PB)	Rajasthan (RJ)
Tamil Nadu (TN)	Uttar Pradesh (UP)	Uttarakhand (UK)	West Bengal (WB)

Note: UT = union territory, NCR = National Capital Region. State name abbreviations shown here are used frequently in the paper below.

listed in Table 1. We have included the UT of Chandigarh and the National Capital Region of Delhi (Delhi-NCR, which is not a state, but not strictly a UT either) because of their geographic position, but we have excluded other UTs, small states in the Northeast, and Jammu and Kashmir, which is a special case in several dimensions. Where major states have been excluded, the reason was lack of consistent data for the period of analysis.[8]

The time period of the analysis is mostly from 1994–95 to 2014–15, with some analysis using a later starting year due to data limitations. The SGDP data for Kerala, Gujarat, and Himachal Pradesh are not available after 2013–14. As an organizing principle, we sometimes order the states with respect to their average real per capita income levels over the 1997–2015 period. To do this, we deflated reported nominal data with state-specific deflators constructed from another source. The average deflated values, scaled across the 20 sample regions, are displayed in Figure 1, where the states are arranged alphabetically on the horizontal axis.

Along with aggregate SGDP data, we use sectoral and subsectoral level output data for the states to derive structural change indices. Sector and subsector shares of SGDP for the 20 states are in Table 2, ordered from poorest to richest by the criterion described in the last paragraph. We calculated average shares separately across two subperiods, 1995–2001 and 2001–15.[9] The period beginning with the new millennium appears to represent one where the growth accelerates, as compared to the 1990s.[10] The changes in average shares vary across the states. The share of agriculture declined during 2001–15, with the drop particularly apparent for Tamil Nadu, Gujarat, Uttarakhand, Odisha, and Kerala. Punjab, on the other hand, remained more

8. In our subsequent presentations of results, we use two-letter abbreviations for the states and UTs as shown in Table 1.

9. Or 2001–14, depending on data availability for individual states.

10. As noted earlier, our data do not cover the period of the recent slowdown.

FIGURE 1.   Average per capita Income across States during 1997–2015 (scaled)

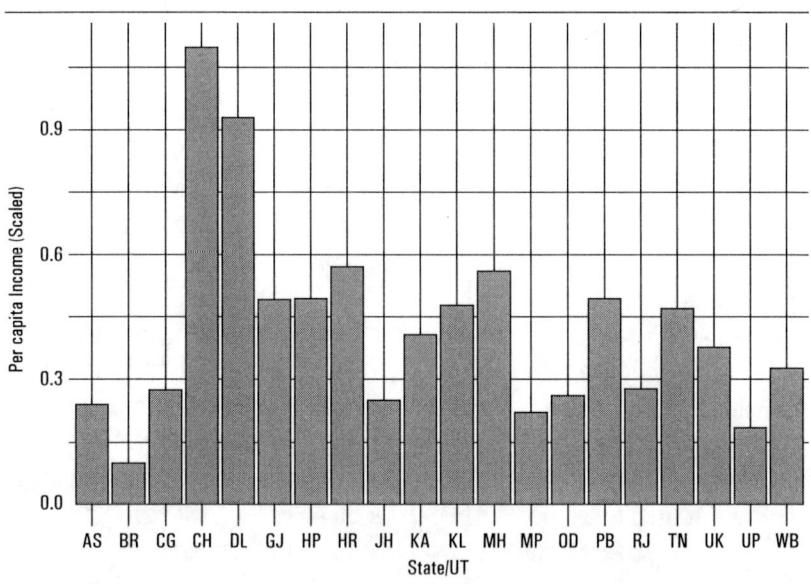

Sources: CMIE; Authors' calculations.

Note: Average state per capita income over 1997–2015 is scaled for the 20 states/UT and a scalar added in each case to show all scaled values as nonzero. The resulting ranking of states is used as a presentation device for showing state-wise results. See text for details.

TABLE 2.   Sector and Subsector Shares of State GDP (in %)

State */Years		Agriculture & Allied Activities	Agriculture	Forestry	Fishing	Industry Subgroups	Mining	Manufacturing	Electricity	Construction	Services	Trade & Transport	Financial Services	Public Administration & Others
Bihar	1995–01	35.9	30.8	3.7	1.2	12.5	0.1	7.0	2.0	3.6	51.6	10.2	12.1	29.3
	2001–15	26.7	22.9	2.5	1.3	16.6	0.1	5.3	1.4	9.8	56.7	28.5	9.9	18.2
Uttar Pradesh	1995–01	33.7	31.2	1.7	0.3	21.7	1.0	14.6	1.5	4.3	44.6	9.7	17.4	17.5
	2001–15	26.4	23.9	2.1	0.4	23.0	0.9	13.4	1.3	7.3	50.6	21.6	15.2	13.8
Madhya Pradesh	1995–01	32.4	28.6	3.5	0.2	24.6	4.5	12.8	2.5	5.0	43.0	8.9	15.2	18.9
	2001–15	25.9	23.2	2.6	0.2	28.2	4.4	12.1	2.7	9.1	45.9	19.7	12.8	13.3
Assam	1995–01	33.0	28.3	3.0	1.7	23.1	10.1	7.6	1.0	5.9	43.9	8.8	8.4	26.7
	2001–15	24.1	20.2	2.4	1.5	24.3	7.2	8.5	1.4	7.3	51.6	22.2	7.1	22.2
Jhar-khand	1995–01	15.1	11.2	3.0	0.8	55.3	13.2	34.6	1.9	6.0	29.6	5.9	5.7	18.0
	2001–15	16.5	12.9	3.2	0.3	43.8	11.6	23.9	1.3	7.0	39.7	18.6	7.8	13.1

(Table 2 Contd.)

(Table 2 Contd.)

State */Years		Agriculture & Allied Activities	Agriculture	Forestry	Fishing	Industry Subgroups	Mining	Manufacturing	Electricity	Construction	Services	Trade & Transport	Financial Services	Public Administration & Others
Odisha	1995–01	30.8	24.8	4.3	1.7	29.4	5.2	8.9	4.1	14.5	39.8	6.5	13.4	19.9
Odisha	2001–15	20.6	16.5	2.8	1.3	33.4	7.1	12.7	3.2	10.8	46.0	20.6	11.1	14.1
Chhattis-garh	1995–01	30.2	22.2	6.5	0.9	37.7	8.4	17.6	6.5	5.2	54.7	9.4	19.6	25.8
Chhattis-garh	2001–15	21.2	15.4	4.6	1.1	42.9	10.5	17.8	4.8	9.8	63.7	14.2	9.7	12.0
Rajas-than	1995–01	29.3	25.2	3.5	0.1	27.6	1.9	12.7	4.4	8.6	43.1	8.3	15.5	19.3
Rajas-than	2001–15	22.7	19.7	2.9	0.1	31.1	3.1	14.0	3.4	10.6	46.2	20.2	12.8	13.2
West Bengal	1995–01	29.9	24.5	1.1	4.1	19.4	1.4	10.5	1.8	5.6	50.7	10.9	16.6	23.2
West Bengal	2001–15	20.9	16.6	1.0	3.3	20.1	1.1	10.6	1.9	6.5	59.0	25.7	16.0	17.3
Uttara-khand	1995–01	30.4	22.5	8.3	0.0	20.6	0.9	12.4	1.0	7.0	49.0	10.8	16.4	21.8
Uttara-khand	2001–15	16.0	11.8	4.1	0.0	33.0	0.9	20.9	1.5	9.7	51.0	28.3	9.4	13.4
Karna-taka	1995–01	28.3	24.0	3.6	0.6	27.7	0.7	16.9	2.3	7.6	44.0	7.8	20.8	15.4
Karna-taka	2001–15	17.1	14.5	2.2	0.4	29.8	0.9	17.8	2.0	9.1	53.1	21.0	21.0	11.1
Tamil Nadu	1995–01	15.8	13.6	1.0	1.2	32.1	0.6	21.7	3.1	6.6	52.1	10.8	22.0	19.3
Tamil Nadu	2001–15	9.9	8.5	0.6	0.8	30.6	0.6	19.9	1.3	8.8	59.5	26.6	20.0	12.9
Kerala	1995–01	23.8	19.3	2.4	2.1	21.6	0.4	10.6	1.4	9.7	54.6	14.3	20.1	20.2
Kerala	2001–14	14.1	11.3	1.6	1.3	21.7	0.4	8.2	1.6	11.6	64.2	32.2	18.0	13.9
Gujarat	1995–01	20.5	16.5	2.4	1.2	39.7	4.6	27.7	3.1	4.7	39.8	9.5	17.4	12.9
Gujarat	2001–15	14.8	12.4	1.7	0.7	39.9	2.7	27.2	3.2	6.8	45.3	25.4	12.0	7.8
Himachal Pradesh	1995–01	27.6	20.4	8.0	0.2	39.0	0.3	11.3	6.2	21.4	33.4	5.4	9.2	18.9
Himachal Pradesh	2001–15	22.0	16.4	5.5	0.1	39.8	0.3	13.9	7.3	18.3	38.2	15.0	8.0	15.3
Punjab	1995–01	37.2	35.6	1.4	0.2	24.0	0.0	15.8	3.2	5.0	38.8	7.1	13.1	18.7
Punjab	2001–15	28.0	26.7	1.1	0.3	27.6	0.0	17.8	3.0	6.8	44.4	18.3	11.8	14.3
Maha-rashtra	1995–01	13.6	10.1	4.2	0.5	33.5	0.8	22.9	2.2	7.7	52.9	9.8	27.1	15.9
Maha-rashtra	2001–15	10.0	7.8	2.0	0.3	30.1	0.7	21.1	1.8	6.6	59.9	23.6	25.7	10.6
Haryana	1995–01	31.9	30.2	1.6	0.1	31.3	0.3	22.0	1.7	7.3	36.8	10.3	13.2	13.2
Haryana	2001–15	19.7	18.7	0.9	0.1	30.5	0.2	19.8	1.7	8.8	49.8	27.6	13.8	8.4
Delhi	1995–01	1.5	1.4	0.1	0.0	18.5	0.0	9.1	1.4	7.4	80.0	12.9	45.4	21.7
Delhi	2001–15	0.9	0.8	0.1	0.0	14.5	0.0	6.4	1.3	6.7	84.6	27.8	42.1	14.7
Chandi-garh	1995–01	1.7	1.5	0.3	0.0	15.1	0.0	9.2	2.0	4.8	84.1	9.7	35.9	21.4
Chandi-garh	2001–15	0.7	0.7	0.1	0.0	15.1	0.0	6.1	1.3	7.8	84.4	34.0	35.4	15.0

Source: CMIE; Authors' calculations.

dependent on agriculture, which contributed about 28 percent to state GDP, on average, in 2001–15.

The shares of industry and services increased during this period, so there was a gradual shift towards a more services- and manufacturing-oriented economy, and away from agriculture. This process was more rapid in states such as Kerala, Tamil Nadu, Karnataka, and Uttarakhand. In other states, the change was more gradual. Furthermore, states shifted towards trading activity (trade and transport being the first subcategory in services) more than other types of services, possibly suggestive of national or subnational economic integration, perhaps driven by better road connectivity and infrastructure development. Somewhat atypically, Jharkhand had a gradual increase in agriculture and services sector shares, while manufacturing and mining activity declined in relative importance.

The change in sector-wise shares provides initial evidence of the real-location of economic activity towards potentially more productive sectors in the 2000s. These changes in sectoral contribution underline the structural change in the Indian economy. Accordingly, the level of structural change has been quantified using the Norm of Absolute Value (NAV), proposed by Michaely (1962) and Stoikov (1966), and the Modified Lilien Index, introduced by Lilien (1982) and revised by Stamer (1999). The first measure, NAV, is defined by

$$NAV = \frac{1}{2} \sum_{i=1}^{n} | x_{it} - x_{is} | \qquad (1)$$

where x_{it} is the share of GDP of sector i at time t, and x_{is} is the share of GDP in the base period, time s. The NAV index measures the average of the absolute distance between the output shares of all sectors across two different time periods. The sum of the absolute amounts of the differences is divided by two since each change is counted twice: this ensures that the range of the index is from 0 (no structural change) to 1 (maximum structural change). The logic of this index is that it summarizes the overall change in the distribution of economic activity across different sectors, but it does not make any prejudgments about whether this shift is from low-productivity to high-productivity sectors.

In a departure from Cortuk and Singh (2011, 2015), in this paper the index is calculated with respect to a fixed base year. So, in the following empirical analysis it is a cumulative measure rather than an annual change. We make this modification to facilitate comparison with the structural change calculations based on the McMillan–Rodrik approach, which is typically also based on cumulative changes. In our initial data analysis, we have used 1994–95 as the starting year, owing to the fact that the progression of structural change and opening up of the Indian economy, which is typically associated with policy reforms in 1991, started stabilizing in 1994–95.[11] The NAV is calculated at two different levels: (a) Level 1 at the sector level, that is, for Agriculture, Industry and Services, and (b) Level 2 at the subsector level, that is, for Agriculture, Fisheries, Forestry, Mining, Manufacturing, Electricity, Construction, Trade, Finance, and Community Services. The empirical analysis was conducted at both levels to check robustness, but we report only the results based on the more disaggregated measure, since they are qualitatively similar.

The Modified Lilien Index (MLI), on the other hand, was first proposed by Lilien (1982) for measuring the variation in sectoral growth rates of employment and was modified by Stamer (1999). The MLI is defined as follows[12]:

$$MLI = \sum_{i=1}^{n} \sqrt{x_{it} x_{is} \left(ln \frac{x_{it}}{x_{is}} \right)^2}$$
(2)

FIGURE 2. Heat Map of Structural Change Index (rescaled)[13]

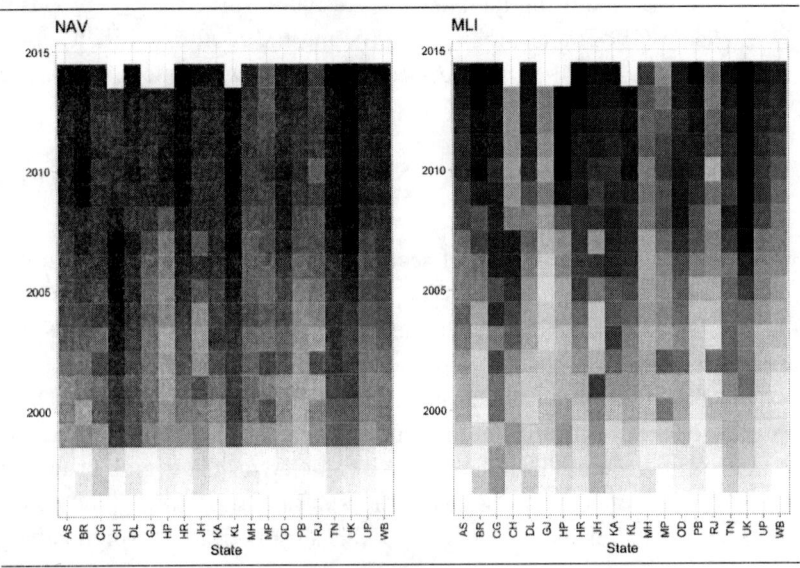

Source: CMIE; Authors' calculations. Darker shades show higher values of the Index.

11. As noted earlier, in some portions of our analysis, our starting year is later, due to data limitations.

12. The MLI also varies theoretically from 0 to 1.

13. While the NAV and MLI are theoretically between 0 and 1, the actual range is much more compressed. Accordingly, for the heatmap, the actual values have been mapped to the full interval from 0 to 1, by subtracting the minimum value and standardizing by the actual range.

State-level structural change is found to vary across the states. The heat-map of NAV and MLI values (see Figure 2) displays the time progression of the different Indian states in our sample through the stages of structural change. A significant amount of structural change occurred immediately before 2000, when the services sector came into greater prominence. Within our sample, Kerala and Tamil Nadu were among those states that were frontrunners in adapting to the new patterns of economic activity. Other states were more gradual in shifting their economic makeup, as seen in Figure 2.[14]

Juxtaposing structural change with the pattern of growth across states, a positive relationship between structural change and state-level growth emerges from a scatter plot of the two variables. Figure 3 displays the scatter plot between average growth and average structural change for the sample. Note that the structural change indices are converted to a percentage scale for this figure.[15] The size of the circles represents scaled per capita income.

FIGURE 3.   **Average Structural Change and Growth across States**

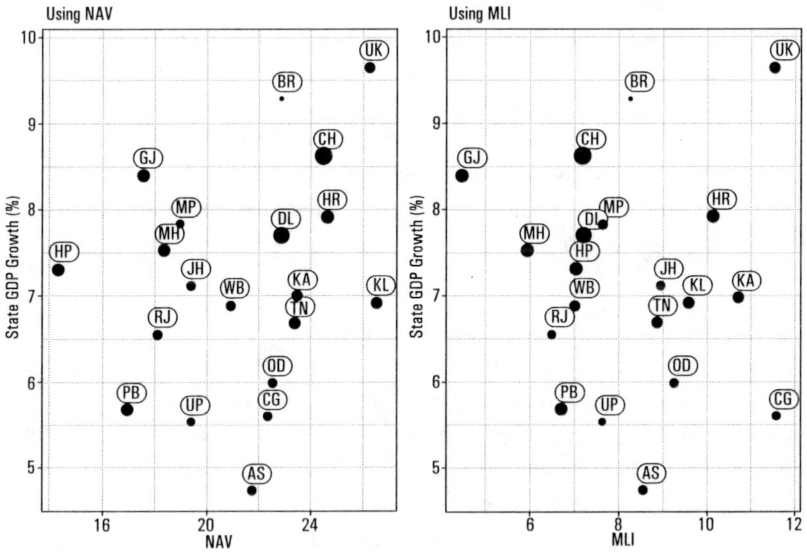

Source: CMIE; Authors' calculations.
Note: Circle size represents scaled per capita income.

14. Our discussant, Neelkanth Mishra, suggested that the heatmaps for NAV and MLI are quite different, but we would argue that the similarities are greater than the differences. For the purpose of this paper, they are meant to be an illustrative prelude to our econometric analysis.

15. In Cortuk and Singh (2015), the magnitudes of NAV and MLI were roughly compara-ble, but here the MLI figures tend to be lower than the NAV numbers: this will happen with more unequal shares. Because of data availability, the classification of subsectors used here is somewhat different than in the earlier paper.

A larger circle size, therefore, represents a higher per capita income. It seems that, on the whole, average state-level growth is higher for states that had higher structural change, though there are outliers in all four directions. It is clear from the scatter plot that there is no simple story connecting structural change and growth. For example, two very different states, Bihar and Uttarakhand, display high structural change and high growth. Similarly, the states with low structural change and low growth, namely Assam, Punjab, and Uttar Pradesh, are all different in their characteristics. There are also outliers such as Gujarat and Himachal Pradesh, which have had relatively high growth but low structural change.[16]

When structural change is considered, there is also significant variation among the states in the time dimension, whereas growth rates vary less over time within and across states. These patterns can be seen in Figure 4, which plots kernel densities of each variable for each state: the densities are reflected across vertical axes to obtain "violin plots." Structural change was relatively low during the initial time period of these data, and this fact is reflected in the lower tails of the kernel density estimates of structural changeover during the sample period. Except for a few states, the structural change levels were concentrated around the average over time. As seen in the scatter plots, the kernel densities also show that states such as Uttarakhand, Kerala, and Haryana experienced higher structural change as compared to other states. The time pattern of growth rates, on the other hand, was highly concentrated around the average growth across states. On the other hand, a few states such as Jharkhand and Rajasthan did experience greater variation in state-level growth over time.

3.1. Control Variables

While our focus is on the interaction between structural change and growth, there are clearly other factors at work that help drive both processes. For example, neoclassical growth theory suggests that poorer states would grow faster as they would be less subject to diminishing returns, thereby catching up with richer states. This is the often-examined convergence hypothesis. Typically, this is qualified as "absolute" convergence, since a variety of other economic conditions can matter aside from per capita income levels—analyses that account for these other conditions examine

---

16. One can conjecture that the growth in these states has been driven by productivity increases within sectors: in this case, the McMillan–Rodrik type of measure of structural change might pick up that phenomenon.

FIGURE 4. Time Variation in Structural Change and Growth across States

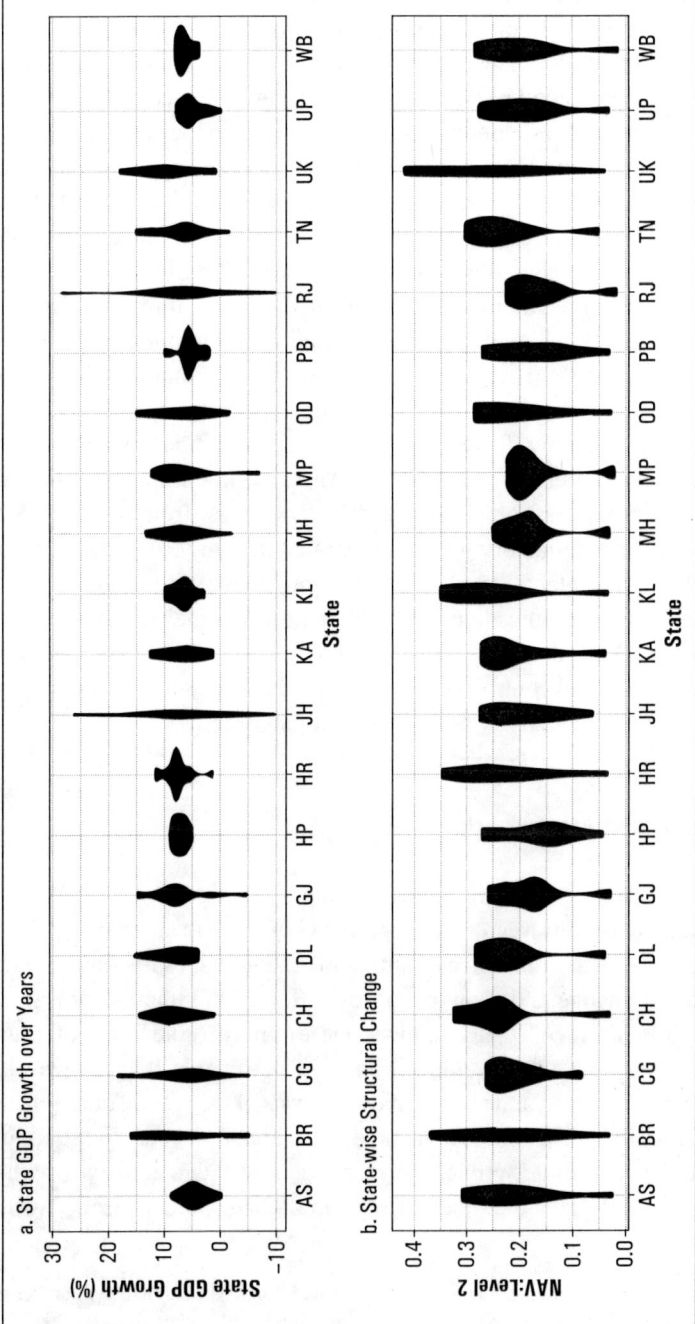

a. State GDP Growth over Years

b. State-wise Structural Change

Source: CMIE; Authors' calculations.

"conditional" convergence. Following this latter method, we incorporate several control variables to allow for differences in state conditions that might affect the processes of growth and of structural change. As noted, state-level per capita income is included to reflect growth theory. Other important aspects of state-level conditions are infrastructure, the state-specific invest-ment environment, human capital, and the national economic environment.

The availability of suitable data was the determining factor for some of the control variable choices. The impact of initial income levels is captured by including the lagged value of per capita SGDP. State-level variation in infrastructure development has been incorporated through a measure of railway density. Human capital is proxied by a variable measuring enroll-ment in primary and secondary education. State variation in the investment environment is proxied through two indicators, namely (a) investment ratio and (b) factory growth. The investment ratio is defined as new investment intentions as a percentage of SGDP. The investment intention data is col-lected by CMIE, at the project level across states, from major investment announcements. Factory growth is estimated from year-on-year growth of manufacturing plants covered in the Annual Survey of Industries. Finally, the national economic environment is captured by the lagged growth rate of national GDP. India's GDP data are sourced from the St Louis Fed database. All the state-level control variables are available at annual frequency for our sample from the CMIE States of India database.[17]

4. Empirical Framework

The empirical framework revolves around two questions: (a) What is the causality between structural change and GDP growth at the state-level?; and (b) If there is any influence of structural change, does the linkage between structural change and growth vary over time? Only the use of a structural change index (NAV/MLI) allows one to analyze the issue of causality; productivity growth decomposition does not enable that. However, both approaches to structural change allow analysis of the second question, though with very different conceptual and empirical approaches. In the following, our empirical strategy has, therefore, been divided into two parts—the first part highlights the index of structural change and causality, while the

17. We also explored a few alternative variables such as road density, number of bank branches, and literacy rates. None of these controls improved or altered our results. We further investigated the possibility of other controls suggested during the general discussion at the IPF, but a combination of time and data limitations restricted us from modifying our regressions.

second part focuses on variation of impacts over time, using the two different approaches to measuring structural change.

4.1. Causality between Structural Change and Economic Growth

Directional causality can be tested in a familiar manner using Granger causality in the time domain. The time domain analysis of causality relies on a regression framework in which the lags of dependent and independent variables are included together to check the impact of one variable on the other. In a panel framework, causality between structural change and GDP growth has been studied by factoring in state-specific heterogeneity and time effects.[18] In all cases, to allow for likely heteroskedasticity associated with size differences among states and other heterogeneities, we use robust standard errors. For each regression, the lagged value of the dependent variable has been used to estimate the persistent feature of each data generating process. In other words, the lagged value of structural change is included in the regression of structural change on state GDP growth, and lagged growth is included in the regression of growth on structural change. The various controls discussed earlier are also included in both regressions.

Following the above discussion, the panel regressions used for testing causality are specified as follows:

$$g_{it} = \alpha_i + \beta_t + \gamma_{10}s_{it-1} + \gamma_{11}g_{it-1} + \gamma_{12}PCGSDP_{it-1} + \gamma_{13}X_{it-1} + \epsilon_{it}^1$$
$$s_{it} = \alpha_i + \beta_t + \gamma_{20}s_{it-1} + \gamma_{21}g_{it-1} + \gamma_{22}PCGSDP_{it-1} + \gamma_{23}X_{it-1} + \epsilon_{it}^1 \quad (3)$$

where s_{it} is the structural change index in state i at time t, g_{it} is real SGDP growth. *PCGSDP* is per capita SGDP, included in level form with a lag, to capture initial conditions. A significant value for coefficient γ_{10} in the first equation and a significant value for γ_{21} in the second equation are evidence for causality between s_{it} and g_{it}, in the respective directions of the regression specification. As noted, s_{it} can be measured as NAV as well as MLI at the sector and subsector levels of aggregation. Since the results were similar for the different levels of disaggregation, we use the more disaggregated measure in this paper. Lastly, the vector of control variables is represented in X_{it-1}.

The panel regressions are estimated using both generalized least squares (GLS, i.e., fixed effects with robust standard errors) and the generalized method of moments (GMM). GLS estimates can suffer from consistency problems in such dynamic panel models, as the regressors are not strictly exogenous. The bias, sometimes known as Nickell's bias (Nickell 1981),

---

18. Dietrich (2009) performed a panel analysis of this kind of causality for seven OECD countries and provided a detailed discussion of methodological issues.

causes problems in typical two-stage methods for implementing fixed effects estimation in a dynamic panel. Hence the GMM approach developed by Arellano and Bond (1991) is often used to estimate these dynamic panel models. The attractiveness of the Arellano–Bond estimator (or its variants) relies on asymptotic properties, and it may not perform well in some types of finite samples. Therefore, in this paper, both approaches have been used and reported. The time period used for estimation ranges from 2000–01 to 2014–15. Lack of data availability of control variables for the newly formed states restricted the time span of estimation to begin in 2000–01.

4.2. Time-varying Impacts of Structural Change

To relax the panel regression assumption that the impacts of structural change and growth on each other are the same across the states, we examine time-varying impacts with two different approaches. The first uses the structural change indices, as is the case for the panel regressions. The second uses the productivity-based decomposition of growth into within-sector change and structural change. In addition to relaxing the assumption of constant impacts over time, both these latter methods also relax the assumption of homogeneity of impacts across states.

Using the structural change index, we estimate a time-varying regression model to allow for more general causal impacts. The model is benchmarked by estimating the standard linear model for each state (rather than as a panel) before the time variation in parameter space is incorporated in the estimation. Furthermore, a stochastic volatility assumption has been built into the model. The time-varying regression model for estimating the impact of structural change on growth can be written as

$$g_{it} = \beta_{0t} + \beta_{1t}g_{it-1} + \beta_{2t}s_{it-1} + \beta_{3t}PCGSDP_{it-1} + \beta_{4t}GGDP_{t-1} + \epsilon_{it}$$
$$g_{it} = \beta_t Y_{it-1} + \epsilon_{it} \tag{4}$$

where β_{it} (i = 0,1,2,3,4) are the time-varying coefficients, GGDP is the national GDP growth rate, and ε_{it} is the error term, with mean zero and variance σ^2. σ_t varies over time and thereby helps to capture the stochastic volatility component. The state equations for capturing the dynamics of the time-varying parameters are expressed in the following manner:

$$\beta_t = \beta_{t-1} + \eta_t^1$$
$$h_t = \log\left(\sigma_t^2\right) \tag{5}$$
$$h_t = \alpha h_{t-1} + \eta_t^2$$

The state equation for the parameters β_t is assumed to be a random walk to capture any structural change in the data (Bernanke et al. 2004). Further, the stochastic volatility component is modeled as AR(1), with persistence of impact captured by the AR(1) coefficient. The model is estimated using the multimode Gibbs Sampling technique, suggested by Carter and Kohn (1994) and extended to time-varying autoregressive models by Nakajima (2011). The time-varying regression model has been estimated using 20,000 MCMC draws, with initial 10,000 draws as the burn-in period. The time span of estimation is from 1997–98 till 2014–15. Unlike the panel regression, the time span of estimation of the time-varying model is kept longer (excluding some potential control variables) for two reasons. First, the controls used in this model are available from 1997–98 onward. Furthermore, the longer time span provides better precision in time-varying estimates where the estimation state-by-state makes the issue of degrees of freedom more central.

The time-varying regression for estimating the impact of growth on structural change is illustrated as follows:

$$
\begin{aligned}
s_{it} &= \alpha_{0t} + \alpha_{1t}g_{it-1} + \alpha_{2t}s_{it-1} + \alpha_{3t}PCGSDP_{it-1} + \alpha_{4t}GGDP_{t-1} + \epsilon_{it} \\
s_{it} &= \alpha_t Y_{it-1} + \epsilon_{it}
\end{aligned}
\tag{6}
$$

The time-varying coefficient α_t is assumed to follow a random walk and a stochastic volatility component has been included in the model following Equation (5).

Alternatively, the McMillan and Rodrick (2011) approach also allows the impact of structural change to vary over time. Instead of using an index, it estimates the contribution of structural change to productivity change by decomposing productivity changes into within-sector changes and those associated with factor movements across sectors (typically from low- to high-productivity sectors).[19]

Total productivity is defined as:

$$
P_t = \sum_i \theta_{it} p_{it}
\tag{7}
$$

where θ_{it} is the employment share of the ith sector at time t and p_{it} is the productivity of sector i during the same time.

Taking differences and separating sectoral changes in productivity from changes in employment shares, the total change of productivity is

---

19. This analysis was added to the paper after the IPF, based on the comments of our discussant, Barry Bosworth, echoed by many of those participating in the general discussion. We are grateful to all of them, though more work can, of course, be done in this direction.

decomposed into the sum of within-sector changes and aggregate structural change, as follows:

$$\Delta P_t = \underbrace{\sum_i \theta_{i,t-k}\Delta p_{i,t}}_{\text{Within sector}} + \underbrace{\sum_i p_{i,t}\Delta \theta_{i,t}}_{\text{Structural change}} \tag{8}$$

The first component is calculated using base-period sectoral employment shares. The second component weighs changes in employment shares by the respective productivity contributions and thereby captures the change in productivity associated with movement of economic activity across sectors. Intuitively, workers from low-productivity sectors migrate to high-productivity sectors as the economy develops and grows. Our analysis uses employment survey data from the NSSO for the requisite calculations. The base year for calculating within-sector changes is 1993–94, while the final year varies depending on the relevant NSSO sample year (1999–2000, 2004–05, and 2011–12). Since the NSSO data is collected at intervals of several years, this data is not well-suited for time series analysis. More importantly, this method of estimating structural change does not conceptually or empirically separate growth and structural change in a manner that allows for regression analysis.[20]

5. Empirical Findings

In this section, we first detail the panel regression results, which provide a familiar baseline and relatively straightforward conclusions. Then we present the time-varying regression results, which are more novel, and require more nuanced consideration, since they reveal various patterns of change over time, and are also state-specific, adding further heterogeneity. This is followed by the productivity-decomposition results, which also allow for differences of impacts over time and across states.

5.1. Panel Regressions and Causality

The results for the panel estimations are presented in Tables 3 through 6. We focus on results for the NAV measure of structural change since the results for the MLI measure are qualitatively similar: the latter are in an Appendix

---

20. Erumban et al. (2019) use a variant of the productivity decomposition method, analyzing structural change based on input–output data for 27 sectors, covering the period 1981–2011. Again, this is only a national-level analysis. This paper also has numerous additional references to empirical studies using this approach. See also de Vries et al. (2015) for a review of variations on the decomposition approach.

TABLE 3.   Fixed Effects Model: Growth of SGDP

	(1) GSGDP	(2) GSGDP	(3) GSGDP
GSGDP (−1)	−0.348**	−0.351**	−0.349**
	(0.127)	(0.126)	(0.126)
NAV (−1)	0.395***	0.381***	0.398***
	−0.087	−0.084	−0.081
Per Capita SGDP (−1)	−1.215***	−1.128***	−1.119***
	−0.375	−0.373	−0.375
Enrollment Ratio	113.880*	117.638*	123.752*
	(57.149)	(57.261)	(59.413)
Rail Density (−1)	−0.071		
	(0.061)		
Investment Ratio (−1)	0.419	0.431	
	(0.270)	(0.271)	
Factory Growth	0.093**	0.092**	0.095**
	(0.037)	(0.037)	(0.036)
GGDP (−1)	0.334**	0.339**	0.369**
	(0.141)	(0.140)	(0.136)
Constant	10.991*	9.264*	11.190*
	(5.259)	(4.918)	(5.392)
State FE	Yes	Yes	Yes
Time FE	Yes	Yes	Yes
Robust SE	Yes	Yes	Yes
Observations	244	244	244
Adjusted R-square	0.246	0.249	0.248

Source: Authors' calculations.
Notes: Standard errors in parentheses. * $p < 0.10$, ** $p < 0.05$, *** $p < 0.01$.

available from the authors. To assist in interpreting the estimated impacts from one variable to another, growth rates as well as structural change are measured on the same percentage scale, that is, NAV is scaled from 0 to 100 for the regressions. As noted earlier, there are two relationships that are of interest: the impact of state-level structural change on growth, and the impact of state-level growth on structural change. We consider two estimation methods, as discussed earlier. The results are quite robust across the two estimation methods. There is a statistically significant positive effect of lagged structural change on growth, and lagged growth on structural change. We would argue that the positive effect of structural change on growth is particularly striking because this kind of measure of structural change does not build in any assumption of shifts from low-productivity

TABLE 4. Fixed Effects Model: NAV

	(1) NAV	(2) NAV	(3) NAV
GSGDP (–1)	0.123*** (0.023)	0.132*** (0.022)	0.131*** (0.022)
NAV(–1)	0.751*** (0.082)	0.789*** (0.072)	0.784*** (0.069)
Per Capita SGDP (–1)	0.856** (0.349)	0.624* (0.308)	0.622* (0.308)
Enrollment Ratio	44.788 (27.828)	34.748 (25.702)	33.164 (26.893)
Rail Density (–1)	0.189* (0.099)		
Investment Ratio (–1)	–0.079 (0.188)	–0.112 (0.194)	
Factory Growth	0.030*** (0.008)	0.032*** (0.008)	0.031*** (0.007)
GGDP (–1)	0.019 (0.028)	0.004 (0.028)	–0.003 (0.032)
Constant	–4.392 (3.649)	0.221 (2.051)	–0.278 (1.481)
State FE	Yes	Yes	Yes
Time FE	Yes	Yes	Yes
Robust SE	Yes	Yes	Yes
Observations	244	244	244
Adjusted R-square	0.896	0.892	0.892

Source: Authors' calculations.
Notes: Standard errors in parentheses. $* \ p < 0.10$, $** \ p < 0.05$, $*** \ p < 0.01$.

to high-productivity sectors—though that is presumably the mechanism by which structural change positively affects growth. The two positive coefficients together imply a positive feedback loop between growth and structural change. These results are stronger than the earlier results of Cortuk and Singh (2015), since here we find a significant effect of growth on structural change. Intuitively, this difference is likely due to the fact that the current analysis uses a cumulative index of structural change rather than year-to-year changes. Recall that this was chosen to facilitate comparison with the productivity decomposition method.

Each specification controls for the lagged value of the dependent variable. Here, there are differences across the two directions of impact. While high growth in one year is followed by relatively lower growth in the next year (indicated by the negative and statistically significant coefficient of the lagged dependent variable), high structural change in one year is followed by relatively high structural change in the next year (the coefficient of the lagged dependent variable is positive and statistically significant). This persistence of structural change is to be expected, given the cumulative nature of the measure. For example, the fixed effects results for growth of SGDP (GSGDP) in Table 3 indicate that 1 percentage point higher growth would result in growth the next year being lower by about 0.35 percentage point, but if structural change was also higher by a percentage point, this would fully offset the subsequent negative growth impact. In the case of the GMM method (Table 5), the structural change effect on the next year's growth is estimated to be much greater in magnitude, so that structural change more easily sustains the growth momentum.

T A B L E 5 .   GMM Estimation: Growth of SGDP

	(1) GSGDP	(2) GSGDP	(3) GSGDP
GSGDP (−1)	−0.432*** (0.062)	−0.430*** (0.062)	−0.424*** (0.062)
NAV(−1)	1.027*** (0.161)	1.031*** (0.160)	0.995*** (0.155)
Per Capita SGDP (−1)	−3.565*** (0.626)	−3.600*** (0.619)	−3.611*** (0.616)
Enrollment Ratio	107.097 (90.119)	109.277 (89.880)	112.076 (89.804)
Rail Density (−1)	0.086 (0.170)		
Investment Ratio (−1)	−0.511 (0.476)	−0.523 (0.473)	
Factory Growth	0.094*** (0.034)	0.094*** (0.034)	0.091*** (0.033)
GGDP (−1)	0.449*** (0.110)	0.445*** (0.110)	0.400*** (0.102)
State FE	Yes	Yes	Yes
Time FE	Yes	Yes	Yes
Robust SE	Yes	Yes	Yes
Observations	244	244	244

Source: Authors' calculations.
Notes: Standard errors in parentheses. * $p < 0.10$, ** $p < 0.05$, *** $p < 0.01$.

TABLE 6. GMM Estimation: NAV

	(1) NAV	(2) NAV	(3) NAV
NAV(−1)	0.701***	0.711***	0.699***
	(0.071)	(0.071)	(0.069)
GSGDP (−1)	0.135***	0.138***	0.140***
	(0.025)	(0.025)	(0.025)
Per Capita SGDP (−1)	1.198***	1.138***	1.118***
	(0.273)	(0.269)	(0.267)
Enrollment Ratio	57.168	60.755	62.610
	(41.431)	(41.529)	(41.191)
Rail Density (−1)	0.092		
	(0.071)		
Investment Ratio (−1)	−0.217	−0.245	
	(0.207)	(0.207)	
Factory Growth	0.029**	0.029**	0.028**
	(0.014)	(0.014)	(0.014)
GGDP (−1)	0.022	0.017	−0.002
	(0.045)	(0.045)	(0.042)
State FE	Yes	Yes	Yes
Time FE	Yes	Yes	Yes
Robust SE	Yes	Yes	Yes
Observations	244	244	244

Source: Authors' calculations.
Notes: Standard errors in parentheses. * $p < 0.10$, ** $p < 0.05$, *** $p < 0.01$.

The results presented here are somewhat more decisive than earlier results on the relationship between structural change and growth (Cortuk and Singh 2015), partly because of the use of a cumulative index of structural change. Another reason may be that here we cover a longer and more recent time period and include a more robust estimation method (GMM) than the earlier analysis. A further important difference is in the control variables used. As in earlier papers, we include per capita SGDP, which is a standard control variable from models that consider questions of convergence or divergence across countries or regions (Indian states in this case). Those analyses typically focus on long-run growth, and use initial-year income levels, so our estimation approach here is different. In our results, we find very clear and strong evidence of conditional convergence in the two growth regressions, as evidenced by the negative coefficients of lagged per capita SGDP. However, this effect is somewhat offset by the strong positive coefficients of lagged per capita SGDP in the two structural change regressions. Hence, richer states will tend to have greater structural change, and this will translate into higher growth in the future, somewhat offsetting the tendency of richer states to grow more slowly (according to the growth regressions). Although it is not our focus, our empirical results may provide some additional insights for the large literature on India's regional growth patterns and the question of growth convergence or divergence.

A novel feature of our paper is the inclusion of several additional controls, which were not used in the previous analyses of structural change and growth.[21] We considered a range of possible control variables: in some cases there were data issues, and in others there was a lack of any statistically significant effect on state-level growth and structural change. The estimations presented in the paper are relatively parsimonious and provide some useful subsidiary information on the overall growth process. We summarize the results, which are mostly consistent across estimation methods and measures of structural change. Education enrollment has a statistically significant positive effect on growth but not on structural change. Rail density has a positive impact on structural change in the fixed effects estimation, but not in the GMM estimation or in either of the growth regressions. The investment ratio is never statistically significant in any of the estimation results. Both the growth of factories and the national growth rate have positive and statistically significant impacts on state-level growth for both estimation methods. On the other hand, the national growth rate does not have a significant effect on structural change, as opposed to the state-level growth rate, which does: this is consistent with structural change in a state being a function of the state's growth, and not of overall national growth. Of course, there is still an indirect effect of national growth on state-level structural change through the effect on state-level growth. Finally, factory growth has a positive and significant impact on structural change in all four regressions, for growth and structural change, and for each estimation method.

5.2. Time-Varying Parameter Model Results

The panel regression results are plausible and relatively robust across estimation methods, but the panel approach places strong restrictions on the relationship between structural change and growth across states and over time. In order to explore what we can learn from relaxing these restrictions, we estimate time-varying autoregressive (TVAR) models (see Equations (4) and (6)) for each of the 20 states and UTs in our sample. Ideally, we would want to allow for the possibility that different control variables are relevant for different states. However, some exploratory regression estimates and considerations of

---

21. We are indebted to Barry Bosworth for stressing the importance of accounting for additional possible explanatory or control variables.

degrees of freedom led us to estimate the same specification for each state, with the level of per capita SGDP and the national growth rate as the only controls (in addition to lagged values of the structural change and state-level growth). Also, since the results do not vary much for the two measures of structural change, we again only report the results for the NAV measure.

Table 7 summarizes the results of the TVAR model's estimation for the impact of structural change on state-level growth. For reference, the coefficient estimates from the two panel methods are included in the table.

TABLE 7. **Impact of Structural Change on Growth**

Equation: $g_{it} = \beta_{0t} + \beta_{1t}\, g_{it-1} + \beta_{2t}\, s_{it-1} + \beta_{3t}\, PCGSDP_{it-1} + \beta_{4t}\, GGDP_{t-1} + \epsilon_{it}$

	Median	Interquartile Range	Range
Fixed effects panel	0.39		
Dynamic panel	1.03		
State Heterogeneity			
BR	0.46	0.07	0.74
UP	0.10	0.03	0.16
AS	0.25	0.03	0.16
MP	0.77	0.23	0.97
JH	1.01	0.23	3.95
OD	0.30	0.16	0.70
CG	0.37	0.17	0.74
RJ	0.74	0.19	1.12
WB	0.16	0.06	0.33
KA	0.90	0.13	0.77
KL	0.19	0.08	0.47
UK	0.81	0.11	0.66
HP	0.28	0.05	0.46
GJ	0.17	0.14	0.77
PB	0.08	0.04	0.25
TN	0.29	0.11	0.55
MH	0.48	0.14	0.74
HR	0.16	0.07	0.26
DL	0.62	0.18	0.83
CH	0.20	0.06	0.59

Source: Authors' calculations.
Note: Table shows results for β_{2t}.

The first column in the table reports the median value (across the sample years) of the coefficient for each state. It is immediately apparent that there is considerable heterogeneity across states, with median impacts ranging from 0.08 (Punjab) to as high as 1.01 (Jharkhand). Of the 20 median impacts, 12 are below the estimated impact from the fixed effects panel estimates, but all are below the GMM estimate of the impact of structural change on growth. There is also considerable heterogeneity in estimated impacts across the sample years. The interquartile ranges are relatively small, ranging from 0.03 to 0.23, but the ranges are much greater, varying from 0.16 to as high as 3.95. In other words, the impact of structural change on growth may not be stable over time. At this stage, we can merely note this phenomenon: either it can be taken to imply that structural change is not a useful guide for predicting future growth, or it can suggest that further investigation into the relationship is needed. The heterogeneity of impacts across states, however, is a reminder of the differences across Indian states in their economic structures as well as their growth processes. The magnitudes of the coefficients from these time-varying regressions do not necessarily line up with the simple scatter plots of structural change and growth (Figure 3): one striking example where they do is the case of Punjab, which is near the bottom in terms of structural change (Figure 3) and the effect of structural change on growth (Table 7).

Table 8 complements Table 7, showing the TVAR results for the effect of lagged SGDP growth on state-level growth (i.e., this is a different coefficient for the same equation). In concordance with the panel results, most of the median values for the time-varying coefficients are negative, but there are three positive median values, with the value for Himachal Pradesh being as high as 1.48. This suggests that persistence in growth rates is possible and that the negative panel regression coefficients that indicate mean reversion in growth are not an iron law. Turning to the time variation of this effect, as in Table 7, the interquartile ranges are again not very large, going from 0.01 to 0.44 across the different states, while the ranges are again mostly much greater in magnitude than the interquartile ranges, varying from 0.10 to 3.75 across the states. At a minimum, one can conclude from Tables 7 and 8 that there is a great deal of heterogeneity in growth processes across the states and over time.

Further representation of the time pattern of impacts of structural change on growth can be seen from the time series plots in Figure 5. In the figure, the 20 states are grouped in five groups of four states each, preserving the ordering of states by per capita SGDP. Hence, the first panel of Figure 5

TABLE 8.   Impact of Lagged SGDP Growth on State-level Growth

Equation: $g_{it} = \beta_{0t} + \beta_{1t} g_{it-1} + \beta_{2t} s_{it-1} + \beta_{3t} PCGSDP_{it-1} + \beta_{4t} GGDP_{t-1} + \epsilon_{it}$

	Median	Interquartile Range	Range
Fixed effects panel	−0.35		
Dynamic panel	−0.43		
State Heterogeneity			
BR	−0.65	0.06	0.5
UP	−0.12	0.07	0.58
AS	−0.26	0.01	0.10
MP	−0.27	0.32	3.75
JH	−0.32	0.19	1.85
OD	−0.86	0.21	1.12
CG	−0.54	0.02	0.27
RJ	−0.22	0.27	3.39
WB	−0.46	0.09	1.34
KA	−0.09	0.41	3.69
KL	−0.17	0.13	0.99
UK	−0.42	0.07	0.48
HP	1.48	0.04	1.76
GJ	−0.53	0.11	0.80
PB	−0.02	0.09	0.46
TN	0.17	0.07	0.34
MH	−0.58	0.24	0.97
HR	−0.20	0.13	0.91
DL	0.30	0.44	2.26
CH	−0.46	0.08	0.58

Source: Authors' calculations.
Note: Table shows results for β_{1t}.

compares the four poorest states in our sample, Uttar Pradesh, Assam, Bihar, and Madhya Pradesh. In each cluster of states, there are some similarities in how the impact of structural change on growth varies over time, but there does not appear to be a high degree of synchronicity within the clusters.

The results for the other direction of causality, from growth to structural change, are displayed in Table 9. Interestingly, the median estimated impacts of state-level growth on structural change are higher than both the panel estimates for 18 of the 20 states, varying from 0.10 to 1.17. Again, Himachal Pradesh is a positive outlier in terms of magnitude of impact. On the other

FIGURE 5. Time Variation in Structural Change Impact

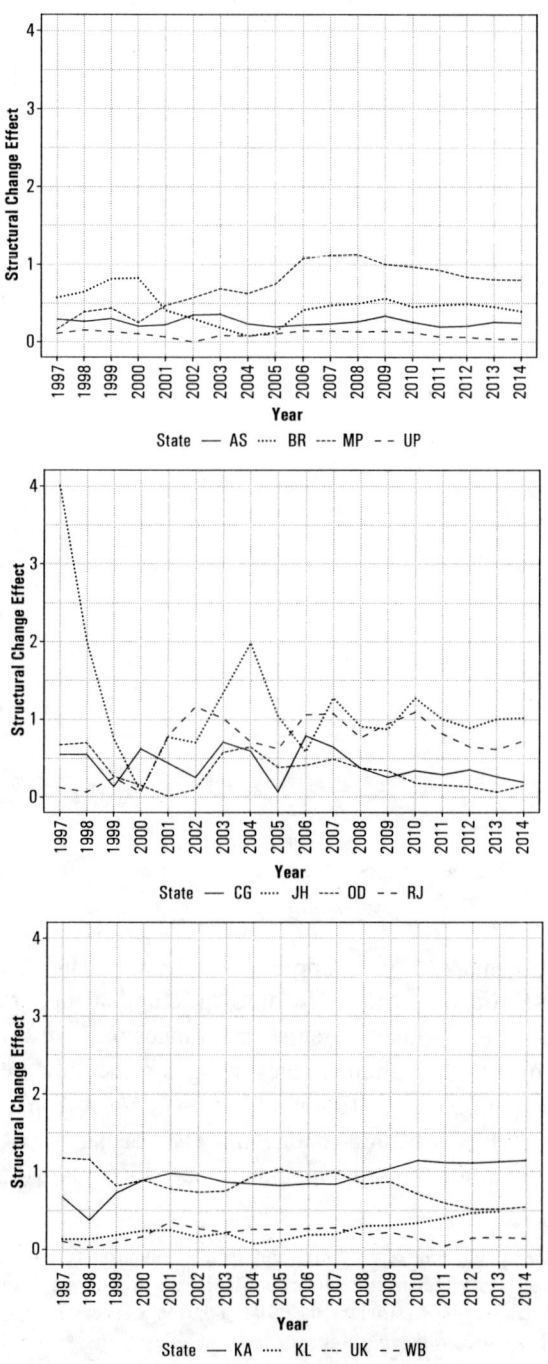

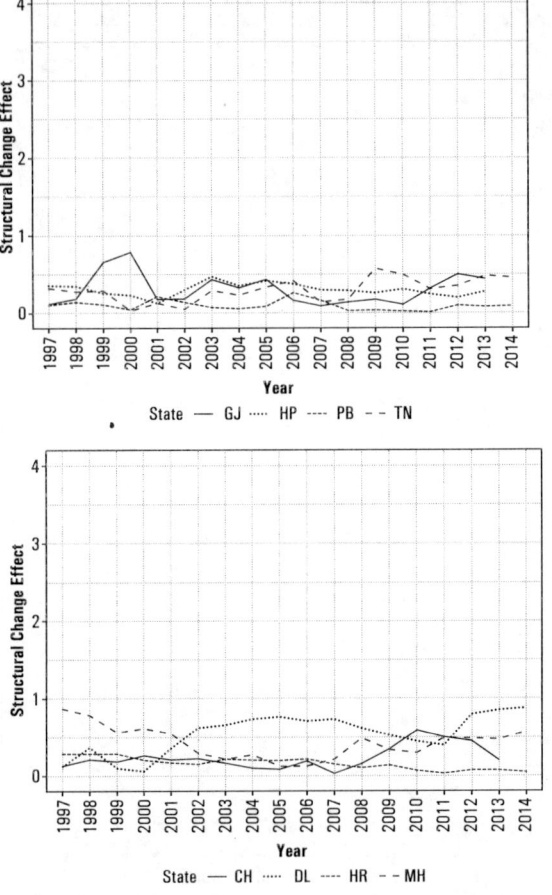

Source: Authors' calculations.

hand, Punjab remains as an example of a state with relatively low impact in this reverse direction, from growth to structural change, reinforcing its outlier status. The interquartile ranges and ranges indicate similar patterns of variation over time, with the ranges being considerably greater than the interquartile ranges.[22] Table 10 complements Table 9, displaying the estimated persistence of structural change impacts. The panel coefficients were both almost equal to 1, and the median impacts in Table 10 are mostly of

22. To provide a point of reference, for the uniform distribution on [0,1], the range is twice the interquartile range. For a symmetric triangular distribution on [0,1], the range is almost four times the interquartile range. In our estimates, the ratios of the ranges of coefficients over time to the interquartile ranges are considerably higher.

TABLE 9.   **Impact of Lagged SGDP Growth on Structural Change**

Equation: $s_{it} = \beta_{0t} + \alpha_{1t} g_{it-1} + \alpha_{2t} s_{it-1} + \alpha_{3t} PCGSDP_{it-1} + \alpha_{4t} GGDP_{t-1} + \epsilon_{it}$

	Median	Interquartile Range	Range
Fixed effects panel	0.12		
Dynamic panel	0.14		
State Heterogeneity			
BR	0.20	0.18	1.39
UP	0.33	0.24	3.68
AS	0.65	0.52	4.19
MP	0.29	0.08	1.41
JH	0.17	0.12	0.58
OD	0.10	0.03	0.22
CG	0.16	0.03	0.22
RJ	0.32	0.28	1.07
WB	0.29	0.15	1.80
KA	0.34	0.11	0.55
KL	0.13	0.13	2.74
UK	0.17	0.10	0.72
HP	1.17	0.27	1.84
GJ	0.15	0.09	1.74
PB	0.15	0.11	1.50
TN	0.18	0.05	0.55
MH	0.45	0.07	0.58
HR	0.22	0.19	2.26
DL	0.68	0.27	1.24
CH	0.59	0.34	1.80

Source: Authors' calculations.
Note: Table shows results for α_{1t}.

similar magnitudes or higher. Interestingly, Punjab has the highest median value for this coefficient in the sample of states.

The time series plots in Figure 6 indicate that the largest impacts of growth on structural change occur toward the beginning of our sample period. This may reflect a period when cumulative reforms in the late 1990s, or possibly exogenous changes in technology or trade, were starting to have an impact on economic structures. Certainly, the time pattern of the magnitudes of these coefficients is different than those for the impact of structural change on growth. Finally, there is no indication of any positive correlation

TABLE 10. Impact of Lagged Structural Change

Equation: $s_{it} = \beta_{0t} + \alpha_{1t} g_{it-1} + \alpha_{2t} s_{it-1} + \alpha_{3t} PCGSDP_{it-1} + \alpha_{4t} GGDP_{t-1} + \epsilon_{it}$

	Median	Interquartile Range	Range
Fixed effects panel	0.88		
Dynamic panel	0.94		
State Heterogeneity			
BR	0.88	0.07	0.67
UP	0.80	0.01	0.36
AS	0.88	0.05	0.87
MP	1.17	0.04	0.62
JH	0.31	0.06	0.77
OD	0.46	0.04	0.29
CG	0.75	0.07	0.36
RJ	0.12	0.09	0.44
WB	1.21	0.06	0.90
KA	1.48	0.10	0.44
KL	1.28	0.12	1.34
UK	0.77	0.03	0.15
HP	0.64	0.08	0.80
GJ	1.17	0.03	1.27
PB	1.66	0.05	0.84
TN	0.25	0.12	0.58
MH	0.29	0.04	0.90
HR	0.96	0.08	0.63
DL	1.55	0.12	1.74
CH	0.86	0.09	1.28

Source: Authors' calculations.
Note: Table shows results for α_{2t}.

in the median coefficients for the two different directions of impact—a state with a higher estimated impact of structural change on growth does not necessarily have a high impact of growth on structural change.

5.3. Impact of Controls in Time-Varying Parameter Regressions

In this subsection, we briefly consider the impacts of the two control variables in the time-varying parameter regressions of SGDP growth and structural change: the interactions of those two focus variables were considered in Tables 7 through 10 and the accompanying discussion. Recall that the

FIGURE 6.   **Time Variation in Growth Impact**

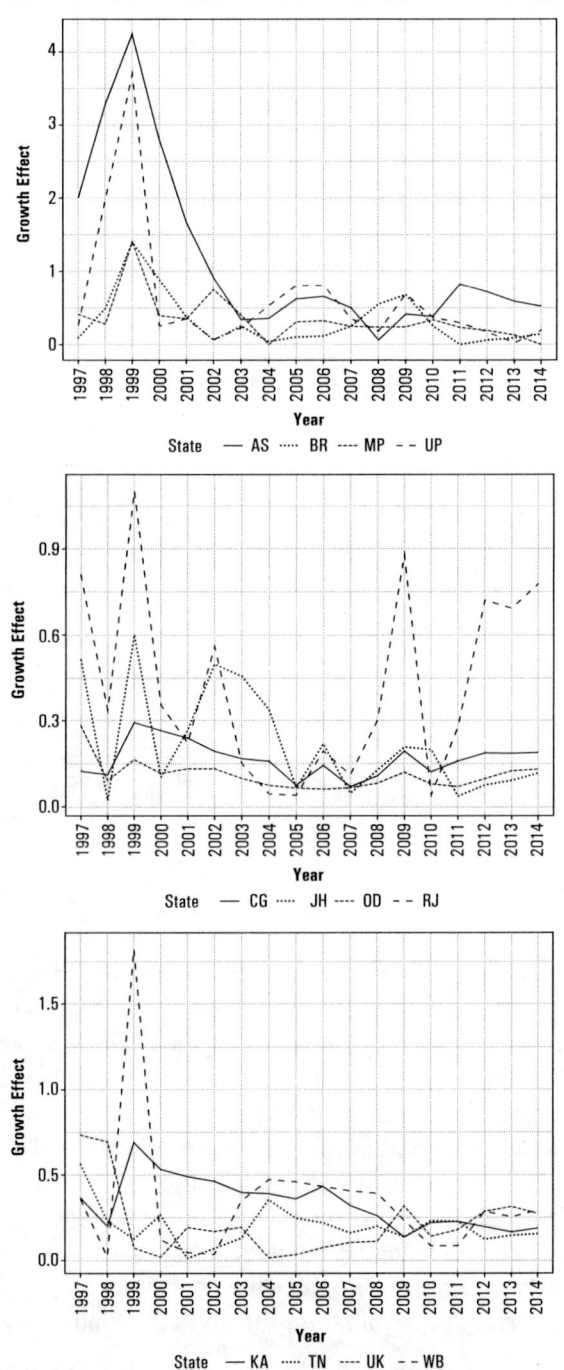

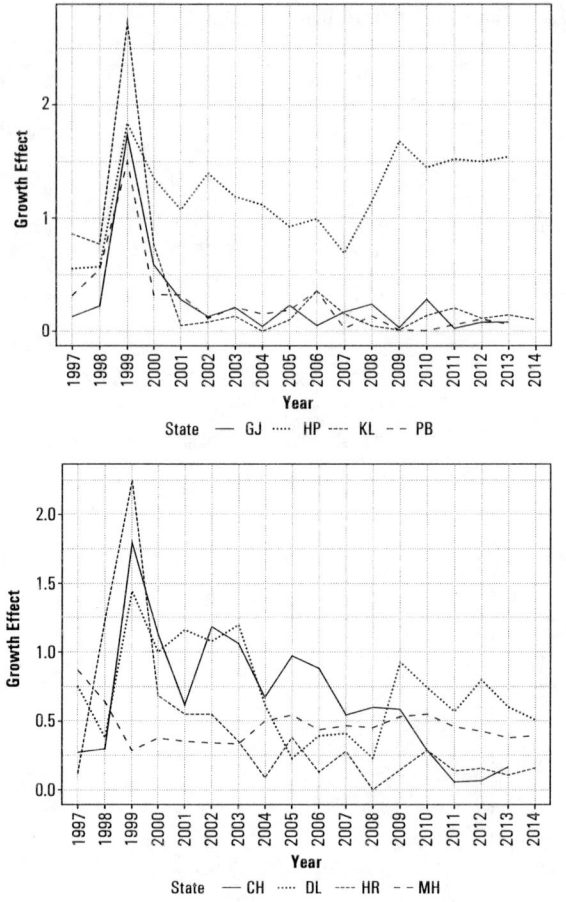

Source: Authors' calculations.

panel regression results indicated a negative impact of per capita SGDP on state-level growth, and a positive impact of national growth on state-level growth (Tables 3 and 5). In addition, per capita SGDP was found to have a positive impact on structural change, but national growth had no significant impact on structural change (Tables 4 and 6).

The results for the TVAR estimations are presented in Tables 11 through 14: the first two tables report the impacts of the two controls on state-level growth, while the next two report the impacts of the two controls on structural change. While the main interactions (Tables 7 through 10) were consistent in the directions of impact when comparing the panel regressions and the time-varying regressions, the effects of the controls are less so. For

T A B L E 1 1 .   **Impact of per Capita SGDP on SGDP Growth**

Equation: $g_{it} = \beta_{0t} + \beta_{1t}g_{it-1} + \beta_{2t}s_{it-1} + \beta_{3t}PCGSDP_{it-1} + \beta_{4t}GGDP_{t-1} + \epsilon_{it}$

State	Median	Interquartile Range	Minimum	Maximum
BR	−3.50	2.03	−6.05	0.41
UP	2.00	1.27	−0.89	3.92
AS	−1.27	3.19	−7.68	3.32
MP	0.21	1.75	−1.59	3.56
JH	−3.36	3.09	−7.26	1.06
OD	−2.96	1.23	−4.49	−0.36
CG	−1.58	1.01	−2.93	0.35
RJ	−1.15	1.08	−2.48	1.24
WB	−0.21	0.84	−1.20	1.56
KA	−1.12	0.84	−1.97	0.6
KL	3.61	1.09	1.62	5.31
UK	−2.00	1.19	−3.76	0.54
HP	0.88	0.32	0.37	1.49
GJ	1.16	0.92	−0.92	2.61
PB	1.30	0.81	−0.38	2.33
TN	−1.14	0.65	−1.81	0.27
MH	1.38	0.37	0.70	1.99
HR	0.32	0.81	−1.46	1.11
DL	−0.47	0.48	−1.02	0.59
CH	0.74	0.43	0.08	1.56

Source: Authors' calculations.
Note: Table shows results for β_{3t}.

example, in the case of Table 11, the panel regressions would have suggested that negative coefficients would be estimated. However, only 11 of the 20 median coefficients are negative. Furthermore, in only one case (Odisha) is the set of estimated coefficients negative over the entire time period; on the other hand, all the estimated coefficients for Kerala, Maharashtra, and Chandigarh are positive, in contrast to the results of the panel regressions. It is the case that the time-varying parameter results for the other impacts are less in conflict: the patterns in Tables 12 and 13 are mostly consistent with the panel regressions in terms of direction of impacts, and the panel results corresponding to Table 14 were inconclusive in any case. Since the time-varying parameter estimation method does not allow for calculating

TABLE 12. Impact of Lagged GDP Growth on SGDP Growth

Equation: $g_{it} = \beta_{0t} + \beta_{1t}g_{it-1} + \beta_{2t}s_{it-1} + \beta_{3t}PCGSDP_{it-1} + \beta_{4t}GGDP_{t-1} + \epsilon_{it}$

State	Median	Interquartile Range	Minimum	Maximum
BR	1.00	0.15	0.69	1.33
UP	0.29	0.18	−0.03	0.68
AS	0.32	0.52	−0.37	1.32
MP	−0.01	0.22	−0.45	0.37
JH	1.23	0.85	−0.08	2.52
OD	1.45	0.16	1.14	1.76
CG	0.79	0.16	0.48	1.08
RJ	0.58	0.13	0.35	0.83
WB	0.04	0.35	−0.51	0.75
KA	0.82	0.20	0.35	1.15
KL	−0.09	0.25	−0.57	0.39
UK	0.03	0.24	−0.47	0.46
HP	−0.21	0.16	−0.51	0.14
GJ	0.66	0.56	−0.81	1.38
PB	0.05	0.26	−0.44	0.49
TN	1.23	0.11	1.02	1.45
MH	1.33	0.22	0.98	1.69
HR	0.59	0.21	0.23	1.03
DL	0.86	0.27	0.45	1.37
CH	0.12	0.30	−0.39	0.80

Source: Authors' calculations.
Note: Table shows results for β_{4t}.

TABLE 13. Impact of per Capita SGDP on Structural Change

Equation: $s_{it} = \alpha_{0t} + \alpha_{1t}g_{it-1} + \alpha_{2t}s_{it-1} + \alpha_{3t}PCGSDP_{it-1} + \alpha_{4t}GGDP_{t-1} + \epsilon_{it}$

State	Median	Interquartile Range	Minimum	Maximum
BR	5.48	1.92	2.90	9.12
UP	1.89	2.07	−2.28	5.87
AS	1.98	2.10	−2.19	6.34
MP	1.38	1.71	−0.39	4.82
JH	4.57	1.54	1.10	6.56
OD	2.00	1.88	−1.64	4.95
CG	0.80	1.80	−1.19	4.14
RJ	2.85	0.63	1.25	3.71
WB	2.42	1.00	1.18	4.60
KA	1.56	1.34	0.15	4.12

(Table 13 Contd.)

(Table 13 Contd.)

State	Median	Interquartile Range	Minimum	Maximum
KL	3.33	0.38	2.61	4.02
UK	0.73	1.32	−1.98	3.30
HP	2.41	0.34	1.71	3.07
GJ	−0.26	1.13	−1.78	2.37
PB	−0.49	0.73	−1.43	1.19
TN	2.41	0.39	1.65	2.84
MH	1.42	0.33	0.77	2.10
HR	0.48	0.33	−0.17	1.00
DL	1.79	0.33	1.09	2.26
CH	1.35	0.29	0.63	1.89

Source: Authors' calculations.
Note: Table shows results for α_{3t}.

T A B L E   1 4 .   Impact of Lagged GDP Growth on Structural Change

Equation: $s_{it} = \alpha_{0t} + \alpha_{1t}g_{it-1} + \alpha_{2t}s_{it-1} + \alpha_{3t}PCGSDP_{it-1} + \alpha_{4t}GGDP_{t-1} + \epsilon_{it}$

State	Median	Interquartile Range	Minimum	Maximum
BR	0.75	0.48	0.07	1.68
UP	0.48	0.26	−0.02	0.99
AS	0.41	0.24	−0.06	0.86
MP	0.59	0.20	0.21	0.97
JH	0.43	0.49	−0.39	1.22
OD	0.48	0.33	−0.10	1.03
CG	0.85	0.22	0.43	1.40
RJ	0.90	0.17	0.60	1.24
WB	0.36	0.26	−0.10	0.92
KA	−0.15	0.27	−0.62	0.50
KL	0.25	0.33	−0.21	1.11
UK	0.40	0.27	−0.14	0.94
HP	0.04	0.22	−0.36	0.40
GJ	0.23	0.29	−0.20	0.90
PB	−0.14	0.15	−0.40	0.17
TN	0.77	0.32	0.32	1.37
MH	1.53	0.25	1.15	1.99
HR	−0.09	0.15	−0.33	0.31
DL	1.13	0.30	0.61	1.67
CH	0.91	0.30	0.38	1.56

Source: Authors' calculations.
Note: Table shows results for α_{4t}.

conventional standard errors or conducting traditional significance tests of coefficients, we also do not want to overstate the inconsistencies: this point is made more explicitly in discussing the time patterns of impacts in the next subsection. What we can repeat, however, is that the processes of growth and structural change appear to be different across states in a manner that deserves further empirical analysis.

5.4. Time-Varying Impact of Structural Change on Growth

Before turning to productivity decompositions as an alternative way of capturing heterogeneity over time and across states, we briefly discuss time plots of the impact of structural change on state-level growth for each state for four different specifications, and the impact of state-level growth on structural change, also for four specifications. These plots are displayed in the Appendix (see Figures A1 and A2).[23] For each state, the four specifications are: no controls, per capita state GDP as a control, the national GDP growth rate as a control, and both controls. To broadly summarize the implications of these graphs, there are differences across states in how inclusion of controls affects the measured impacts of structural change on growth, reflecting the different signs of the coefficients of the controls across states. There are also differences in the variability of the impacts over time. However, the overall conclusion from visual inspection of the graphs seems to support a considerable degree of stability of impacts over time, and, to some extent, across states. Hence, the panel regression results and time-varying parameter estimates do seem to provide some consistent information about the interaction of growth and structural change in India's economic trajectory.

5.5. Productivity Decompositions

To round out our quantitative analysis, the results of the productivity decompositions are presented in Tables 15 and 16. Table 15 reports cumulative figures, while Table 16 has the corresponding annualized numbers. In each case, the base year is always 1993–94. Overall, the productivity gains are not very large, with several states showing negative productivity changes. The decompositions suggest that productivity gains within sectors have been larger than those associated with structural change. There is also considerable variation across states and over time periods. It is difficult to discern any clear patterns in the numbers, perhaps reflective of the subnational heterogeneity of the Indian growth experience.

---

23. The plots can also be downloaded in color for better legibility from: https://people.ucsc.edu/~boxjenk/IPFPaperSanyalSinghFiguresA1andA2.pdf.

TABLE 15. Productivity Changes: Within-sector Changes and Structural Changes (cumulative % change)

	1999-2000		2004-05		2011-12	
	Within	*Structural*	*Within*	*Structural*	*Within*	*Structural*
HR	7.49	2.91	0.31	2.96	-3.59	5.87
DL	5.80	2.13	1.41	-16.53	20.02	15.37
RJ	-0.38	-4.21	-2.42	0.68	0.89	-2.19
UP	4.68	-18.25	5.77	-2.15	2.83	-9.00
UK	2.00	-18.45	-2.28	1.51	-8.90	-7.86
AS	29.82	-15.49	17.14	-1.75	16.01	3.20
WB	1.70	0.95	-1.22	-1.03	-3.22	-2.60
JH	-5.29	1.04	1.61	4.75	26.82	6.06
BR	5.10	0.30	36.95	-5.37	57.62	-5.53
OD	4.71	-1.37	-0.32	0.91	-2.87	1.70
KL	5.34	3.52	-7.38	2.93	-12.25	5.47
TN	0.15	2.58	-9.01	2.52	-10.28	4.97
KA	4.52	-1.78	1.63	0.72	-8.14	-0.53
MP	1.61	-5.82	-4.89	-2.29	-4.62	-1.20
MH	3.18	-8.95	-7.68	1.60	-15.45	-1.10
GJ	4.28	0.94	-1.90	2.80	-8.35	4.49
HP	5.34	7.91	25.90	1.71	16.46	4.17
PB	6.40	1.69	2.97	1.91	6.13	2.52
CH	45.94	-2.61	16.79	-15.49	45.82	7.94
CG	-1.35	-2.99	2.80	-14.52	-3.78	-4.63

Source: Authors' calculations.

Focusing on the cumulative results up to 2011–12, Delhi, Chandigarh, and Haryana have three of the four highest productivity gains associated with structural change, which might be suggestive of a regional development pattern, though the fourth state in this group is Jharkhand, which is very different in economic structure.[24] The worst performers in terms of structural change-related productivity gains are Uttar Pradesh,

---

24. In his discussant's comments at the IPF, Neelkanth Mishra provided several illustrations of how very state-specific institutional changes can have an impact on growth. For most of his examples, it would be impossible to perform the kind of quantitative analysis that we have undertaken here, so we merely acknowledge that qualitative institutional knowledge can be important in understanding gaps or puzzles in the econometric results.

TABLE 16. Productivity Changes: Within-Sector Changes and Structural Changes (annual % change)

	1999–2000		2004–05		2011–12	
	Within	Structural	Within	Structural	Within	Structural
HR	1.25	0.49	0.03	0.27	−0.20	0.33
DL	0.97	0.35	0.13	−1.50	1.11	0.85
RJ	−0.06	−0.70	−0.22	0.06	0.05	−0.12
UP	0.78	−3.04	0.52	−0.20	0.16	−0.50
UK	0.33	−3.08	−0.21	0.14	−0.49	−0.44
AS	4.97	−2.58	1.56	−0.16	0.89	0.18
WB	0.28	0.16	−0.11	−0.09	−0.18	−0.14
JH	−0.88	0.17	0.15	0.43	1.49	0.34
BR	0.85	0.05	3.36	−0.49	3.20	−0.31
OD	0.79	−0.23	−0.03	0.08	−0.16	0.09
KL	0.89	0.59	−0.67	0.27	−0.68	0.30
TN	0.02	0.43	−0.82	0.23	−0.57	0.28
KA	0.75	−0.30	0.15	0.07	−0.45	−0.03
MP	0.27	−0.97	−0.44	−0.21	−0.26	−0.07
MH	0.53	−1.49	−0.70	0.15	−0.86	−0.06
GJ	0.71	0.16	−0.17	0.25	−0.46	0.25
HP	0.89	1.32	2.35	0.16	0.91	0.23
PB	1.07	0.28	0.27	0.17	0.34	0.14
CH	7.66	−0.43	1.53	−1.41	2.55	0.44
CG	−0.23	−0.50	0.25	−1.32	−0.21	−0.26

Source: Authors' calculations.

Uttarakhand, Bihar, and Chhattisgarh, which also can be thought of as representing a regional clustering.

However, one should be cautious about reading too much into these numbers. First, they are based on somewhat less-than-comprehensive surveys of employment. Second, they calculate labor productivity only rather than total factor productivity. For example, in Figure 3, Uttarakhand appears to be a stellar performer in terms of SGDP growth, and this is associated with relatively high structural change, measured as shifts in the composition of economic activity, without regard to employment or productivity, of course. The causal results from the TVAR models (Tables 7 through 10) suggest that Uttarakhand is not as much of an outlier as Figure 3 would suggest, but it displays strong impacts of structural change on SGDP growth. Since

Tables 15 and 16 employ a significantly different methodology, the results are not technically inconsistent, but they raise the question of how one can explain the differences.

To take another example, Punjab does quite respectably in labor productivity calculations of Tables 15 and 16, both overall and in the contribution of structural change. This is in stark contrast to its position in Figure 3. Similarly, the TVAR results in Table 7 indicate a relatively weak impact of structural change on SGDP growth in Punjab, though Table 10 suggests that structural change has more cumulative power for that state. These two observations suggest, again, that arrested structural change in Punjab is a cause of its anemic growth—this also fits in with the declining growth of the agricultural sector in that state.[25] In any case, the two methodologies provide very different pictures of economic activity and development that require further analysis. Potentially, one can look at each state in detail and compare the results for the two approaches to try and construct a more rounded perspective on the economic performance of that state.

6. Conclusion

In this paper, we have empirically examined the relationship between economic growth and structural change in India over recent decades. We first generalized previous work with panel regressions using state-level data to estimate the impact of structural change on growth and growth on structural change. Panel regressions using fixed effects estimation as well as GMM for a dynamic panel found two-way causality: each variable positively impacts the other, suggesting a positive feedback mechanism between structural change and growth. We allowed for various control variables (also improving on previous work in that respect) and obtained results consistent with conditional convergence in the direct impacts of per capita income levels on subsequent growth. On the other hand, the indirect impacts could work in the opposite direction, since higher per capita income levels are followed by greater structural change, which affects subsequent growth positively. Perhaps the strongest and most obvious result of the panel estimations was that growth in the number of plants or factories positively impacts both growth and structural change, reflecting a very traditional perspective on

---

25. One can note once more that the level of aggregation matters. A shift from wheat and rice to higher value added crops could boost Punjab's agricultural sector performance without showing up as structural change.

the nature of economic development and reminding us of a dimension in which India continues to struggle.

The second part of our empirical analysis relaxed the assumptions of constant impacts across states and over time by estimating time-varying auto-regressive models for each state and each pair of variables. The impacts of structural change on growth and growth on structural change turned out to vary across different states, as well as over time, and were seen to be differentially affected by state per capita income levels and by national growth rates. In some cases, such as Punjab, one can guess the reasons for the differences: Punjab has been locked into a particular pattern of agriculture. In other cases, the results are less obvious and require further investigation; for example, Himachal Pradesh appears to be a positive outlier in its performance.

The analysis of the paper has several implications for economic policy-making in India at both the national and state levels. First, by systematically exploring the interaction between structural change and growth, it provides policymakers with a better sense of what the growth process might be in their state or for the nation as a whole. In particular, even though the empirical results are not conclusive by any means, they go beyond league tables of per capita SGDP, and they also add a dimension to analyses of convergence and divergence across the states of India.

Second, our analysis and results suggest that national economic policy formulation may benefit from a better understanding of the structural differences across states, and the resulting differences in growth responses. Our analysis does not provide definitive reasons for differences in growth processes and performance across states, but it may have pointers toward where more detailed empirical investigation is needed. For state-level policymakers, our results provide some summary information on how other states are doing in terms of economic performance, not just from the perspective of per capita SGDP levels, or other indicators such as education or infrastructure, but also in how such variables affect the growth process at the state level.

A final aspect of our formal results, the positive impact of factory growth on both SGDP growth and structural change, is a reminder of the most obvious example of India's failure to achieve consistently rapid economic growth—its industrial sector has remained stunted.[26] Of course, one cannot

---

26. Certainly, the panel regression results with respect to the positive impacts of school enrollments and rail density on growth and structural change, respectively, while statistically weak, are consistent with what we might expect in terms of theoretical economic reasoning.

necessarily extrapolate too much from the coefficients of our panel regressions, and there is no guidance from our results in terms of exact policy measures that would change the current situation, whether with respect to land and labor laws, trade policy, infrastructure, or other areas for improving the environment for industrial development. But at least our results are another reminder of where policymakers might beneficially focus their attention.

With these caveats, we conclude the paper by offering some thoughts on possible implications of our analysis for a post-pandemic economic recovery. The pandemic has disrupted production and consumption in many ways, restricting movements of people and goods, preventing gatherings of people for production (factories and offices) and consumption (shopping, sports, and other mass entertainment), and disrupting education, especially at the vital foundational level. The pandemic has also made visible the importance and the vulnerability of migrant labor, both within the country and internationally in places like the Middle East.[27] Recovery will require attention to specifics of each of these situations in restoring confidence and trust and overcoming suspicions born of the fear of contagion. Using our conceptual framework, we can offer some complementary perspectives.

Our discussion focuses on some of the apparent differences in growth processes across the states, and what they might imply for post-pandemic policy responses in those cases. We will keep time variation in the background since even our approach does not account for the impact of a major shock such as the pandemic.[28] In this vein, consider the two states of Himachal Pradesh and Uttarakhand. Their patterns of feedback between growth and structural change are somewhat different, but both display strong feedback effects and good economic performance. One can possibly associate this with food processing or the production of high value added crops. In either case, their access to outside markets is crucial for their success. One could argue, therefore, that economic policies for recovery must focus on protecting that access or even strengthening it for other states. From this perspective, the national government's proposed reforms in agricultural marketing, long

27. For states such as Kerala and Punjab, the reduction in remittances and the choking off of labor migration may have post-pandemic implications that are not captured in our empirical analysis, even when time-varying parameters are estimated.

28. In this context, the role of information technology and digital infrastructure is also potentially important. The pandemic and lockdown accelerated some features of digitization of the economy, but overall, the digital infrastructure may not be robust enough for sustaining that change in the short run. Depending on policy decisions and implementation in this area, that situation could change, affecting the location of some kinds of work or the organization of supply chains.

discussed but accelerated by the crisis, may be extremely important, if well implemented, for economic recovery in these states.[29]

A very different example is presented by the state of Punjab. Its anemic growth performance is reflected in the weak interactions between structural change and growth that show up in our empirical analysis, as well as the low average levels of both variables for Punjab in the sample. If one believes that part of the reason for Punjab's economic record is the particular political economy of its premier position in providing wheat and rice for national food grains procurement, then the crisis may disrupt that equilibrium and spur policies that promote structural change and lead to higher growth.[30] In this case, the disruption of migration from states such as Bihar may also be a factor in reshaping Punjab's economy after the pandemic.

Another interesting comparison is among the three relatively poor states of Bihar, Madhya Pradesh, and Uttar Pradesh. Despite similarities in per capita income levels, they have had very different experiences in terms of average structural change and growth over the sample period (Figure 3). These differences are paralleled by differences in the estimated impacts of structural change on growth (Table 7), but not of the impact in the reverse direction (Table 9). It may be that their post-pandemic recoveries will be tied to state-specific factors such as patterns of internal migration for Bihar or new frictions in the movement of people and goods (for UP in relation to Delhi), and our analysis merely reminds us that, even prior to such pandemic/lockdown effects, the growth process has differed across these roughly equally poor states.[31]

A final consideration in thinking about the economic recovery of the different states after the pandemic is that they display very different sensitivities to national growth performance. Of course, national growth is the aggregate of individual state growth rates, but no state dominates completely. Both rich and poor states are among those most sensitive to national growth: these include Maharashtra, Tamil Nadu, Odisha, Jharkhand, and Bihar (Table 12). Other states such as Kerala, Punjab, Uttarakhand, and West Bengal are more insulated from national growth fluctuations. The implication is that states

---

29. Initial political events have been discouraging, but one can hope for long-run success.

30. This perspective is consistent with the recent creation of an "Expert Group" charged with making recommendations to improve growth, but framed in terms of a response to the pandemic-induced crisis.

31. As noted before, the detailed qualitative institutional insights of experts such as Neelkanth Mishra and N. K. Singh offered in the IPF session can be important in understanding the specifics of the growth process in each state.

may suffer differentially as a result of the pandemic, and their recoveries may also be different as the national economy picks up.[32] On the other hand, it may be that the lockdown's shock to national growth is completely different in nature than previous cyclical fluctuations, and these past connections will not hold up in the future.

We conclude this somewhat speculative discussion with a reminder of its basis. Our empirical work established possible patterns of joint evolution of growth and simple indicators of structural change and showed how these have differed over time and across states, albeit with possible commonalities. This empirical analysis provides a quantitative backdrop for thinking about what might be different in the economic structures of the different states and possible implications these may have for post-pandemic economic recovery. This is a framework for envisioning patterns of recovery rather than predictions or specific policy recommendations. We can also note that while the nature of national accounting limits the currency of our data, other, more immediate, and high-frequency data such as night light intensity or agricultural market arrivals may provide signals for the patterns and prospects of economic recovery.

Appendix

This appendix contains the figures described in Section 5.4. They may also be downloaded in colour for better legibility from https://people.ucsc.edu/~boxjenk/IPFPaperSanyalSinghFiguresA1andA2.pdf.

---

32. One other possibility that may be important is the nature of regional linkages if adjacent states are more or less economically tied to each other. We have not explored this here. If post-pandemic restrictions on movement disrupt flows of goods or people between adjacent geographies, recovery patterns could be affected.

FIGURE A.1. Time-Varying Impact of Structural Change on Growth

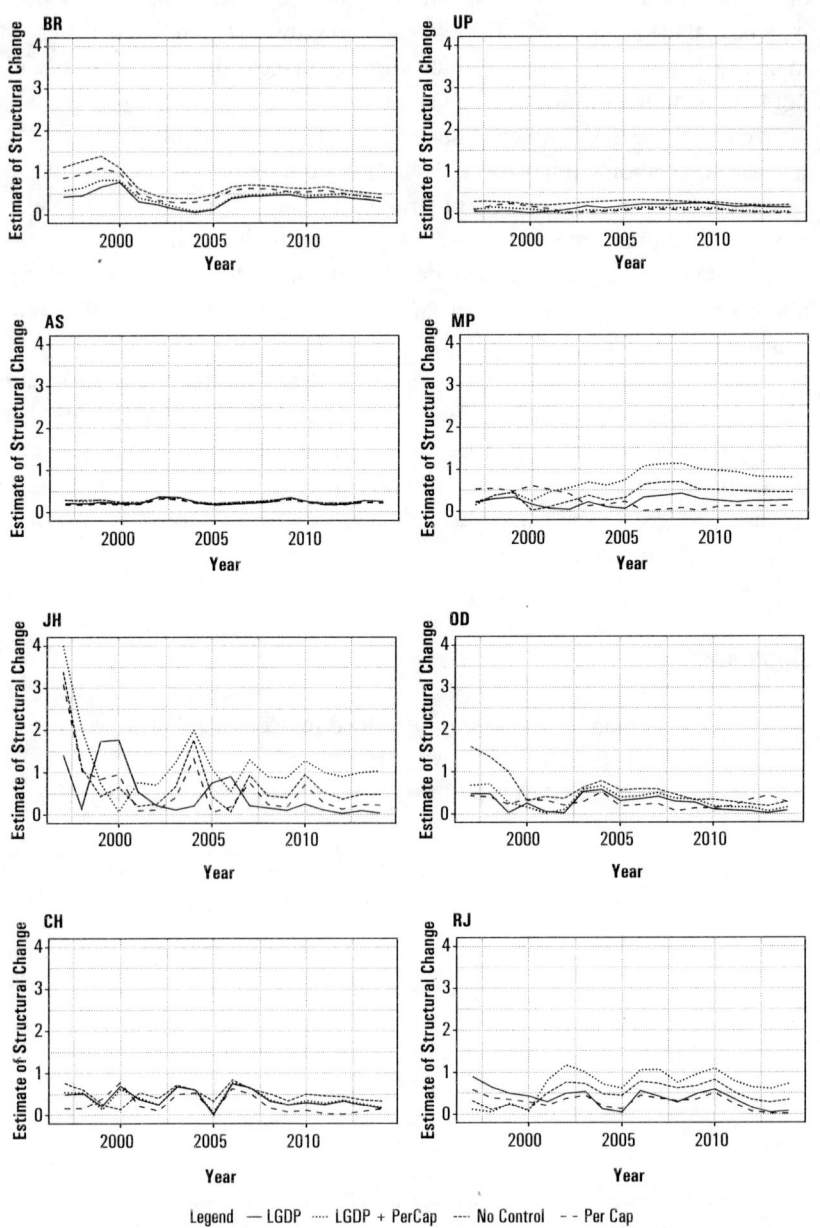

Legend — LGDP ⋯⋯ LGDP + PerCap --- No Control - - Per Cap

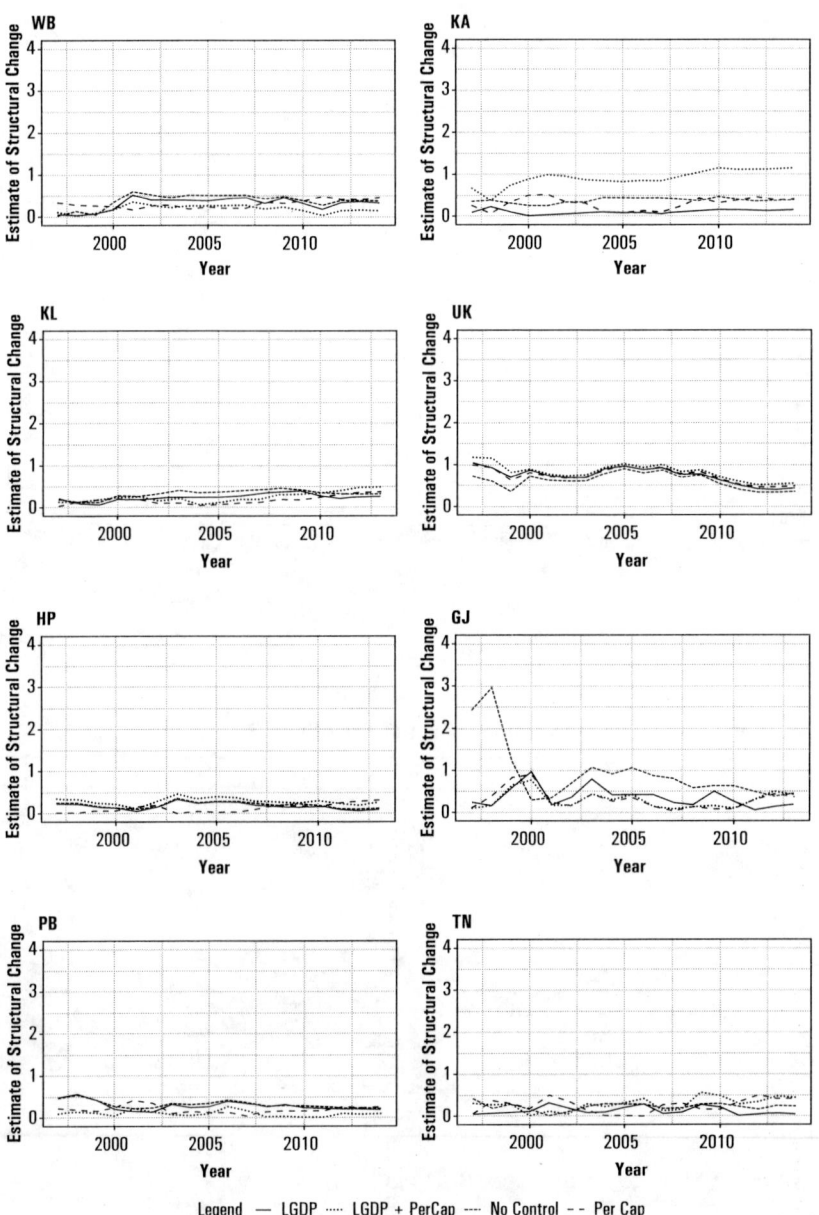

Legend — LGDP ····· LGDP + PerCap --- No Control – – Per Cap

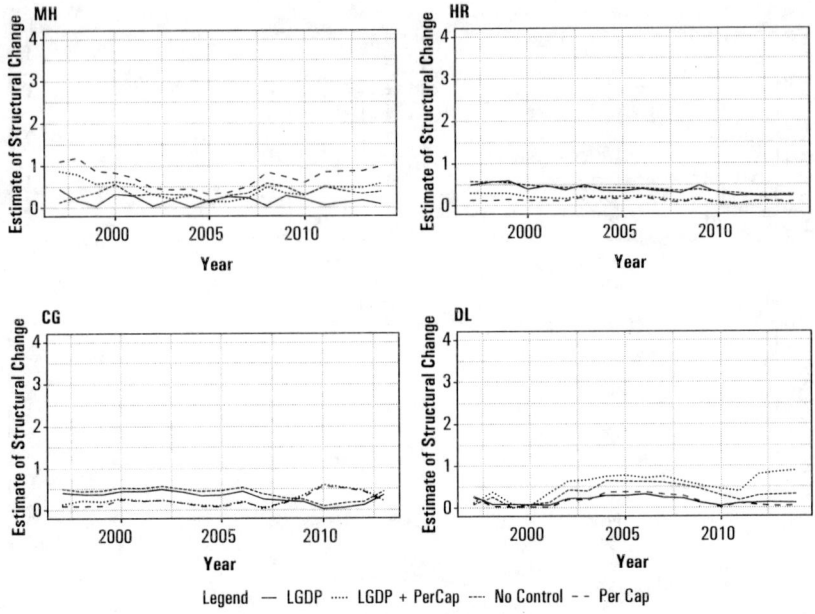

Source: Authors' calculations.

FIGURE A.2. Time-Varying Impact of Growth on Structural Change

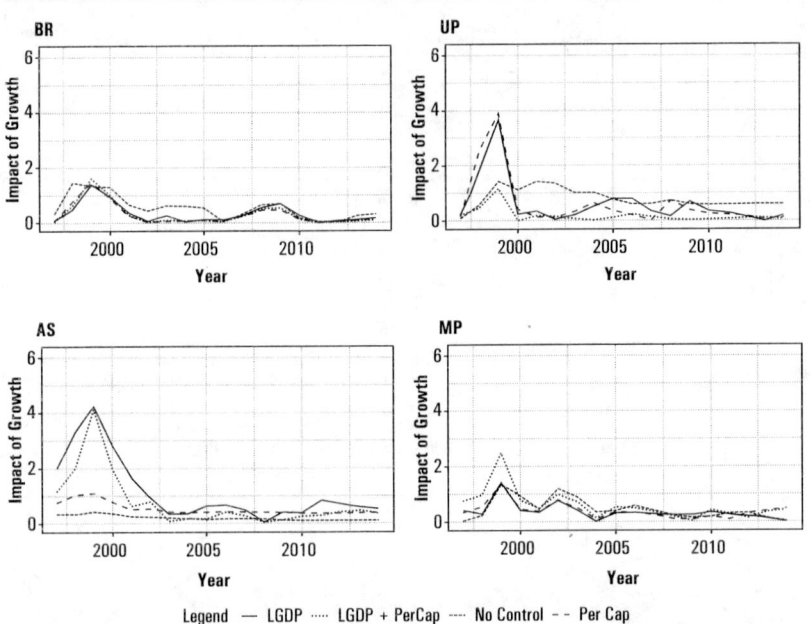

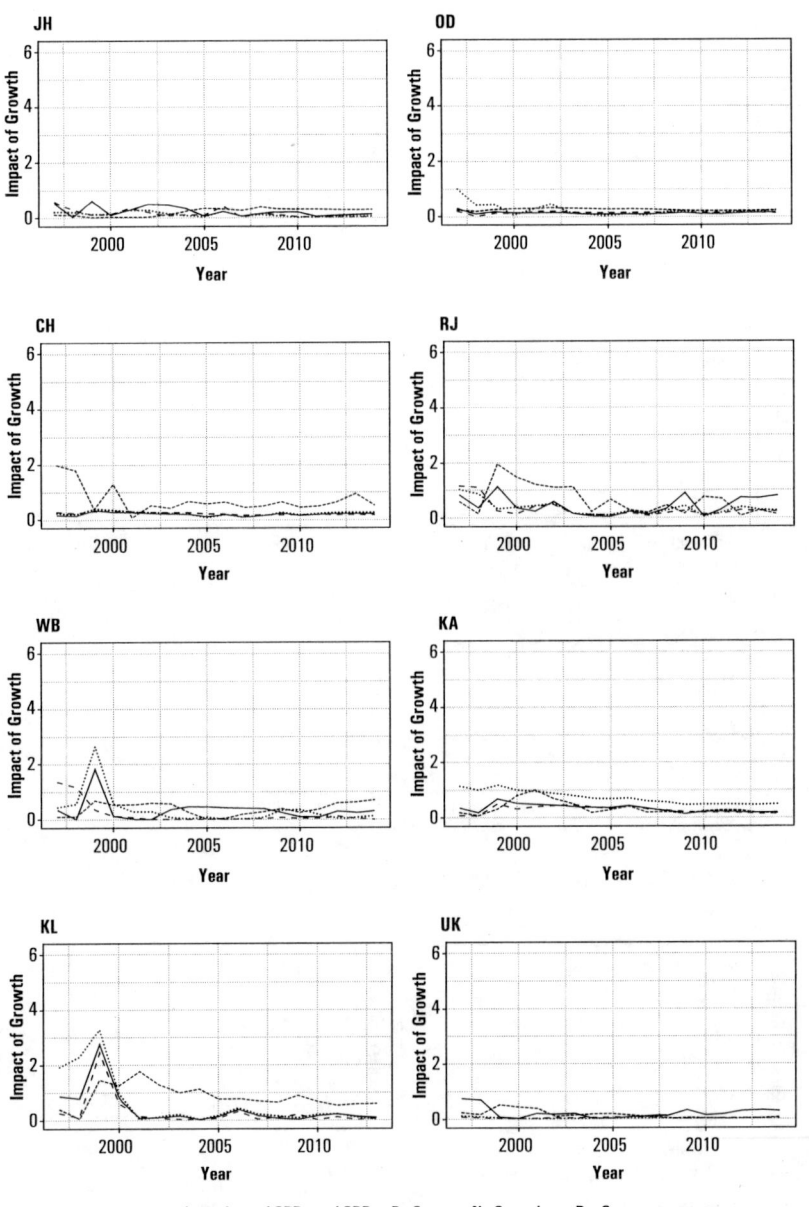

Legend — LGDP ····· LGDP + PerCap --- No Control -- Per Cap

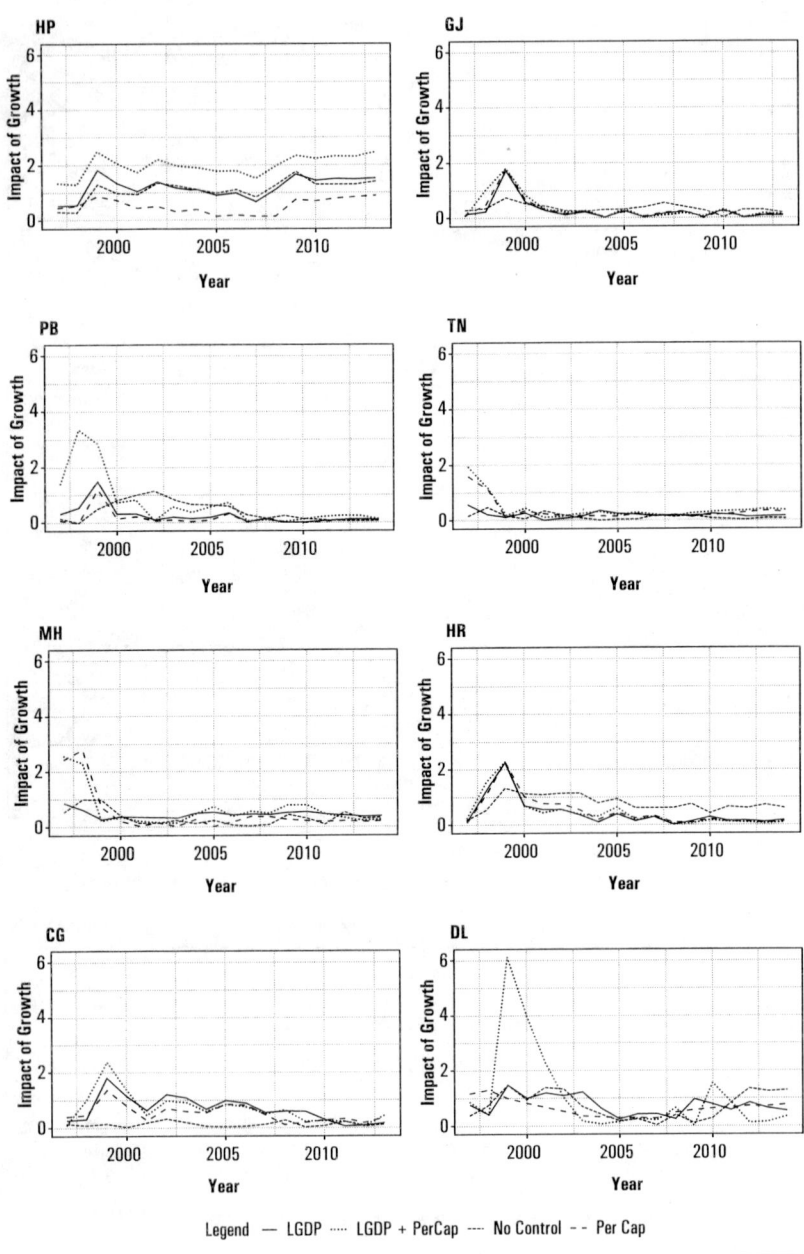

Source: Authors' calculations.

References

Ahsan, R. N., and Devashish Mitra. 2014. "Trade Liberalization and Labor's Slice of the Pie: Evidence from Indian Firms." *Journal of Development Economics,* 108 (c): 1–16.

Arellano, Manuel, and Stephen Bond. 1991. "Some Tests of Specification for Panel Data: Monte Carlo Evidence and an Application to Employment Equations." *Review of Economic Studies,* 58 (2): 277–97.

Balakrishnan, Pulapre, and M. Parameswaran. 2007. "Understanding Economic Growth in India: A Pre-requisite." *Economic & Political Weekly,* 42 (27–28), July 14.

Bandyopadhyay, S. 2012. "Convergence Clubs in Incomes across Indian States: Is There Evidence of a Neighbours' Effect?" *Economics Letters,* 116 (3): 565–70.

Bernanke, Ben S., Jean Boivin, and Piotr Eliasz. 2004. "Measuring the Effects of Monetary Policy: A Factor-augmented Vector Autoregressive (FAVAR) Approach." *Quarterly Journal of Economics,* v120 (1): 387–422.

Bosworth, Barry, and Susan M. Collins. 2008. "Accounting for Growth: Comparing China and India." *Journal of Economic Perspectives,* 22 (1): 45–66.

Carter, C. K., and R. Kohn. 1994. "On Gibbs Sampling for State Space Model." *Biometrika,* 81 (3): 541–53.

Chakraborty, L., and P. Chakraborty. 2018. "Federalism, Fiscal Asymmetries and Economic Convergence: Evidence from Indian States." *Asia-Pacific Journal of Regional Science,* 2 (1): 83–113.

Chen, Shiyi, Gary H. Jefferson, and Jun Zhang. 2011. "Structural Change, Productivity Growth and Industrial Transformation in China." *China Economic Review,* 22 (1): 133–50.

Chenery, H. 1960. "Patterns of Industrial Growth." *American Economic Review,* 50: 624–54.

Cherodian, R., and A. P. Thirlwall. 2015. "Regional Disparities in per Capita Income in India: Convergence or Divergence?" *Journal of Post Keynesian Economics,* 37 (3): 384–407.

Cortuk, Orcan, and Nirvikar Singh. 2011. "Structural Change and Growth in India." *Economic Letters,* 110 (3): 178–81.

———.2015, June. "Analyzing the Structural Change and Growth Relationship in India: State-level Evidence." *Economic & Political Weekly,* 50 (24).

Das, S. 2012. "The Convergence Debate and Econometric Approaches: Evidence from India." In *The Oxford Handbook of the Indian Economy,* edited by C. Ghate, 766–84. New York: Oxford University Press.

de Vries, G., M. P. Timmer, and K. de Vries. 2015. "Structural Transformation in Africa: Static Gains, Dynamic Losses." *Journal of Development Studies,* 51 (6): 674–88.

Dietrich, A. 2009. "Does Growth Cause Structural Change, or Is It the Other Way Round? A Dynamic Panel Data Analysis for Seven OECD Countries" (Jena

Research Papers in Economics). Available at http://econpapers.repec.org/paper/jrpjrpwrp/2009-034.htm (accessed 24 April 2021).

Eichengreen, Barry, and Poonam Gupta. 2011. "The Service Sector as India's Road to Economic Growth" (Working Paper No. 16757). Cambridge: National Bureau of Economic Research.

Erumban, Abdul Azeez, Deb Kusum Das, Suresh Aggarwal, and Pilu Chandra Das. 2019. "Structural Change and Economic Growth in India." *Structural Change and Economic Dynamics,* 51 (C): 186–202.

Fan, Shenggen, Xiaobo Zhang, and Sherman Robinson. 2003. "Structural Change and Economic Growth in China." *Review of Development Economics* 7 (3): 360–77.

Ghate, Chetan, and Stephen Wright. 2012. "The 'V-factor': Distribution, Timing, and Correlates of the Great Indian Growth Turnaround." *Journal of Development Economics,* 99 (1): 58–67.

Ghosh, M., A. Ghoshray, and I. Malki. 2013. "Regional Divergence and Club Convergence in India." *Economic Modelling,* 30 (1): 733–42.

Hasan, Rana, Sneha Lamba, and Abhijit Sen Gupta. 2013, November. "Growth, Structural Change, and Poverty Reduction: Evidence from India" (ADB South Asia Working Paper Series No. 22). Manila: Asian Development Bank.

Joshi, Vijay. 2016. *India's Long Road: The Search for Prosperity.* Noida: Penguin Random House India.

Kaldor, Nicholas. 1957. "A Model of Economic Growth." *Economic Journal,* 67 (268): 591–624.

Kochhar, K., U. Kumar, R. Rajan, A. Subramanian, and I. Tokatlidis. 2006. "India's Pattern of Development: What Happened, What Follows?" *Journal of Monetary Economics,* 53 (5): 981–1019.

Lilien, D. M. 1982. "Sectoral Shifts and Cyclical Unemployment." *Journal of Political Economy,* 90: 777–93.

Mallick, Jagannath. 2017. "Structural Change and Productivity Growth in India and the People's Republic of China" (ADBI Working Paper No. 656). Tokyo: Asian Development Bank Institute.

Mazumdar, S. 2010. "Industry and Services in Growth and Structural Change in India: Some Unexplored Features" (Working Paper No. 2010/02). New Delhi: Institute for Studies in Industrial Development.

McMillan, Margaret S., and Dani Rodrik. 2011. "Globalization, Structural Change and Productivity Growth" (NBER Working Paper No. 17143). Cambridge: National Bureau of Economic Research.

Michaely, M. 1962. *Concentration in International Trade.* Amsterdam: North Holland.

Mishra, A., and V. Mishra. 2018. "Re-examination of Convergence Hypothesis among Indian States in Panel Stationarity Testing Framework with Structural Breaks." *Applied Economics,* 50 (3): 268–86.

Nakajima, J. 2011. "Time-varying Parameter VAR Model with Stochastic Volatility: An Overview of Methodology and Empirical Applications." *Monetary and Economic Studies,* 29: 107–42.

Nickell, S. 1981. "Biases in Dynamic Models with Fixed Effects." *Econometrica,* 49 (6): 1417–426.

Panagariya, Arvind. 2008. *India: The Emerging Giant.* New York: Oxford University Press.

Sen, Kunal 2014. "The Indian Economy in the Post-Reform Period: Growth without Structural Transformation." In *China–India: Pathways of Economic and Social Development,* edited by Delia Davin and Barbara Harriss-White, 27–63. Oxford: Oxford University Press.

Singh, Nirvikar. 2006. "Services-led industrialization in India: Assessment and lessons." In *Industrial Development for the 21st Century: Sustainable Development Perspectives,* edited by David O'Connor, 235–91. New York: UN-DESA.

Stamer, M. 1999. "Strukturwandel und wirtschaftliche Entwicklung in Deutschland, den USA und Japan." Aachen: Shaker.

Stoikov, V. 1966. "Some Determinants of the Level of Frictional Unemployment: A Comparative Study." *International Labour Review,* 93: 530–49.

Syrquin, M. 1986. "Productivity Growth and Factor Reallocation." In *Industrialization and Growth,* edited by H. B. Chenery, 228–62. Oxford: Oxford University Press.

Thind, Monica, and Lakhwinder Singh. 2018. "Structural Change and Economic Growth across Major States of India." *Millennial Asia,* 9 (2): 162–82.

Valli, Vittorio, and Donatella Saccone. 2009. "Structural Change and Economic Development in China and India." *The European Journal of Comparative Economics,* 6 (1): 101–29.

Verdoorn, P. J. 1949. "Fattori che regolano lo sviluppo della produttivita del lavoro." *L'Industria,* 1: 3–10.

Virmani, Arvind. 2006. "India's Economic Growth History: Fluctuations, Tends, Break Points, and Phases." *Indian Economic Review,* 41 (July): 81–103.

Wallack, Jessica. 2003. "Structural Breaks in Indian Macroeconomic Data." *Economic & Political Weekly,* 38 (41): 4312–315.

Young, Allyn A. 1928. "Increasing Returns and Economic Progress." *The Economic Journal,* 38 (152): 527–42.

Comments and Discussion[*]

Chair: N. K. Singh

Chairman, 15th Finance Commission

Barry Bosworth
Brookings Institution

I will start by noting that this issue of structural change is one of the oldest subjects of economic growth. In some of the earliest growth literature, the sector composition of output and employment was related to the stages of growth (by Kuznets, Chenery, and many others). In effect, low-income states focused on primary materials production. Middle-income states were thought to emphasize manufacturing, and high-income states would be devoted to service production. Economic growth was thus coupled with structural changes through both demand-side and supply-side linkages. On the demand side, most of the analysis relied on varying income elasticities. The income elasticity was thought to be low for agricultural products, in the middle for goods, and higher for services, so that rising incomes would induce a shift towards industry, and then towards services. The supply-side effects were motivated by noting that sectors differ in levels of productivity, largely due to differences in technology, and the more advanced sectors can produce products at a lower price or higher level of wages implying that over time, their structure would shift towards the higher productivity industries.

This paper explores the link between structural change and growth by focusing on growth at the level of individual Indian states over the past two decades—the reallocation of workers from agriculture to higher productivity industry and services. It is an extension of prior work by Nirvikar and his coauthors, other researchers in India, and related studies in other countries. It explores alternative measures of structural change and the direction of causation—is structural change a driver of economic growth or a result (or outcome) of that process? It differs from other studies that emphasize regulatory liberalization and institutional reforms as primary drivers of growth. The time period is very extensive, encompassing the years from 1994–95 up to 2014–15.

---

[*] To preserve the sense of the discussions at the India Policy Forum, these discussants' comments reflect the views expressed at the IPF and do not necessarily take into account revisions to the conference version of the paper in response to these and other comments in preparing the final, revised version published in this volume. The original conference version of the paper is available on NCAER's website at the links provided at the end of this section.

194

The study finds strong evidence of bi-directional Granger causality effects. Those effects, though, are highly heterogeneous across Indian states; but I did not really understand why that would be true, or whether there was some underlying third factor that accounted for the differences. Prior state-level GDP per capita has a negative effect on growth in the panel regressions, implying convergence of income over time. But the effect was highly variable in those regressions that allowed for time-varying results.

I would note that the index of structural change is a very simple summation of annual *absolute* changes in shares. As a result, it does not capture any notion of a shift toward higher productivity industries. The paper emphasizes a bi-directional link between its measure of structural change and economic growth, but I do not understand the underlying causal model that would give rise to such a correlation. I am also concerned about the endogeneity of growth and structural change. Both are occurring at the same time, but they may well be driven by a third set of factors. There is no underlying model that explains the relationship.

I gave some thought to what could be done to extend this analysis. First, I would like to have seen a relative contribution of within-sector growth for each state, compared to sectoral change. Is resource reallocation a big part of the story? One way to examine that would be to measure structural change in terms of the distribution of employment instead of the distribution of output. We would be interested to know the industries that people are moving to and from. Further, I do not understand the reliance on absolute changes in shares for the index of structural change, which ignores the issue of whether or not the structural change involves the movement of workers to higher productivity jobs. Finally, I would be interested to know the relative importance of the broad-based accumulation of human capital versus institutional capabilities (governance, rule of law, the business environment).

More work could be done to identify the drivers behind the growth process, but I really do want to compliment the authors for having developed this state-level analysis with impressive amounts of detail.

Neelkanth Mishra
Credit Suisse and Member, Economic Advisory Council to the Prime Minister

I commend the authors for their ambition. It is not an easy problem: after all, it is very challenging to summarize the collective economic performance of a sixth of humanity over 20 years into a conference paper. Another reason why this is not attempted is that the Delhi-centric view of the Indian economy persists: drilling down to state-level data is just too daunting. If you are looking at not 30–32 provinces but even 20, as the authors have done, there are just too many variables, and to then streamline and come up with something that is tangible and can be easily explained in a short amount of time is very challenging.

Even as economists in many developed nations are analyzing why some cities thrive, whereas others do not, we have seen a complete lack of analysis on subnational growth patterns. To their credit, as the authors also say, at least they are trying to go beyond simple per capita GDP growth analysis. I believe that India disappoints the optimists due to a persistence of a Delhi-centric view of governance, and the reason it disappoints the pessimists is that states and individuals within them continue bringing about change that few keep track of.

The problem in the economics of what drives growth is an age-old one. That the authors focused on looking at only structural change as a driver makes the bite-size more manageable. Within the limits that they have defined, I think they have been quite thorough and objective, and the analysis is made without any biases or preconceived notions.

The finding on growth convergence is very interesting, and it should be an important consideration for the 15th Finance Commission on how the horizontal devolution of funds should be taken up.

It is also good to see confirmation of the persistence of structural change, and that some change keeps happening even if growth is volatile. However, as they have rightly concluded, the analysis did not turn up any surprising conclusions other than possibly some evidence of bidirectionality between growth and structural change.

Some suggestions on what could have been or can be changed.

The first is the choice of structural change as a variable, as defined by the changing mix of state GDP. While this has made the analysis more doable, I wonder if it could have been looked at with a slightly wider prism so that the conclusions could have been more useful. The change in the mix of GDP is an important indicator of growth as they found, but is it a driver of growth? Are we losing out on some drivers of absolute growth? If say, law and order, or administrative quality, is to change, would not everything rebound? I am quite biased by my home state of Bihar, where a simple change in law and order—and I will speak some more on it—actually had a meaningful impact on growth. Or take Madhya Pradesh. It has been an absolutely stellar performer, an outlier in terms of agricultural growth. Irrigation, procurement, rural infrastructure improvement—including rural roads, electrification of households, access to computerized service centers where farmers can go and register, land record computerization, and crop procurement—all these changes have driven growth in Madhya Pradesh. Thus, Madhya Pradesh has grown despite the sectoral share of agriculture staying constant. The authors' framework misses out on these changes.

In Jharkhand, the authors observe the increase in the share of agriculture. This deserved more analysis. For example, earlier in Jharkhand all fish came from Andhra Pradesh, and all eggs came from Tamil Nadu, but now you can find local eggs and local fish. The same is true in Bihar. These are important changes. Even as the drop in the value of iron ore, or steel, or even, say, coal—which Jharkhand has an abundance of and whose supply it used to dominate—have hurt, other changes are driving growth in the state.

Or take Rajasthan. In the paper's violin charts, the sharp divergence could reflect big changes in the development of Cairn's oil fields, or changes in the price of zinc and lead, because Hindustan Zinc has ramped up from nothing to nearly 1.5 million tons of zinc and lead production in Rajasthan.

There are other variables, like infrastructure, where more exploration may have helped. While railways has been tested, I think it is one of the sectors that has moved the least. On the other hand, whereas the paper says the authors looked at road density, I am not sure if this included rural roads. Rural roads have, as per our research, completely transformed the economy—not just the agrarian economy but also labor mobility, health care, and educational outcomes. Household electrification per capita, electricity consumption, and irrigation are also important indicators of infrastructure. I would include law and order as well. In the extreme case of Bihar, the improvement in law and order increased the number of hours that people can work, and I think that has meant a lot of growth in economic output.

There is also the issue of migration. Take Bihar again: an extreme case, but similar trends exist in West Bengal and Odisha. Why is services growth in Bihar so high? Telecom penetration is growing rapidly, but then how are people able to pay for telecom services if they are not occupied and earning? I think domestic remittances are a very big factor. There could be nearly 1 percent of GDP of income transfers that goes to just two or three states. So remittances can also be important.

There is also a fiscal perspective. Maybe I am biased because I have worked with the FRBM Act Review Committee, and now with the 15th Finance Commission, but fiscal issues are very important for growth. Therefore, in any such study that is intended to look at government action, or to influence it, fiscal issues must be considered. In practice, state deficits are capped by the Central Government, but it does not prevent states from tapping into new revenue sources, or improving their tax compliance, which can then be deployed to drive growth.

Some variables like education enrolment have been included. However, if it is primary education, other than the economic impact of the education itself, or the employment of teachers, I do not think it is something that can be expected to affect economic outcomes immediately. It will show up with a long lag. However, if it was tertiary education or college education or even ITIs, these may have a more immediate impact.

Similarly, investment intentions data can be quite misleading, not just due to the lag with which investment impacts activity on the ground. I found it surprising that the authors did not find much of a correlation there.

If the outcome of this paper were to be some prescriptions that policymakers could chew over, I think expanding the list of variables may actually have helped.

I will end with some data issues. Data are a limitation, particularly in a largely informal economy, where the GDP base is reset every 5–6 years. This can change the mix of industry and services, as it did in 2012: a lot of manufacturing services were really a part of services that moved back to manufacturing. In the authors' violin plots and other splits, one must factor in such changes, as these can have a meaningful impact on structural change that the authors are trying to map.

Lastly, a suggestion for a minor addition. The heat maps in Figure 2 show that the differences between the two measures, the Norm of Absolute Value and Modified Lilien Index, have clearly been reported very differently. They show very different levels of structural change, so some more exploration of that would help.

General Discussion

Participants in the General Discussion included **Rajnish Mehra, Suman Bery, Rajeswari Sengupta, Anupam Khanna, Rakesh Mohan, C. N. Raghupati Cavale**, and **Manoj Panda**.

To get a sense of the richness of this discussion, we invite you to view the video of the General Discussion segment of this IPF session. Please use the appropriate hyperlink on the IPF 2020 Program available at the links below.

The session video and all slide presentations for this IPF session are hyperlinked on the IPF Program available by scanning this QR code or going to https://www.ncaer.org/IPF2020/Agenda/Agenda_IPF_2020.pdf

Moderator

ASHOK LAHIRI
15th Finance Commission

Panelists

ABHIJIT BANERJEE
MIT and J-PAL

KARTHIK MURALIDHARAN
University of California, San Diego and NCAER

RENANA JHABVALA
SEWA

T. V. SOMANATHAN
Ministry of Finance

IPF 2020 POLICY ROUNDTABLE 1

What Do the Pandemic and India's Shutdowns Teach Us about Meeting India's Safety Net Challenges?*

Introduction

In the first of the two IPF 2020 Roundtables, four eminent panelists from a mix of policy, practice, and research came together to explore the lessons for policymakers and researchers on India's safety nets from the first four months of the Coronavirus pandemic. After detailed remarks from the panelists, participants engaged in a lively discussion moderated by Ashok Lahiri. This is a short summary of the roundtable. For a more complete rendition, please view the session video hyperlinked at the end of this summary.

* The Editors are grateful to Mousumi Das at NCAER for her notes on this IPF Roundtable.

Abhijit Banerjee
Three critical policy omissions have come to hurt us

Abhijit Banerjee, whose prerecorded contribution was played first, noted that this roundtable is the topic of the day, perhaps the most important issue confronting India. There are three critical omissions or mistakes that India has made that have hurt us in this pandemic. *First*, despite internal migration being an enormous part of India's growth story—Bihar and Uttar Pradesh have reduced poverty because of out-migration—we have no official data or policy basis for understanding migration. Our surveys are domicile based. They simply do not capture the migrant living on a construction site. We could have continued, pre-pandemic, believing for a while that this is a small number of people who do not matter. We now know that this is a huge number, and we have some idea of their origin and job location, but we have no easy way of systematically extending help to them. We do not know where they live and who they are.

The *second,* related mistake is not providing urban housing, which has been our classic *jugaad* strategy for low-wage labor. Getting migrants is a low-cost method of manning low-cost industries and construction sites because they can sleep on the site. The pandemic has exposed the pitfalls of such *jugaad*. In the early days of Indian urbanization, there may have been land to grab, but no more, and now we have urban slums. The demand and supply of urban low-cost housing are both now hurting India's cities, governments, and urban policymakers. And for migrants, there is no place to stay because what is available is too expensive. If all this deters internal migration, and industries have to hire locally, that will become a major drag on growth post pandemic.

Third, our welfare system has been largely domicile based. This needs to change. One-Nation-One-Ration Card is an excellent idea, but it must be implemented liberally, especially now, otherwise it will lead to a lot of exclusion errors. Trust in the system is really important at this juncture, and we should not get into the politics of who is entitled to what. We should support the idea of the Inclusive Growth Dividend (IGD) that Ghatak and Muralidharan had proposed in their 2019 IPF paper, which is similar to the Universal Ultra Basic Income proposed in the Banerjee–Duflo book, *Poor Economics*. The amounts may be small, but it is worth having an efficient, open channel connecting to each citizen. And we need to deal with urban housing: Dharavi required an extraordinary effort to manage the pandemic, but other densely populated urban areas may not be as lucky. On MGNREGS, we cannot depend on it as an emergency safety net because it is cumbersome and not designed for that. And we have to think of an urban counterpart. So there is much to be done on improving our welfare system.

Ashok Lahiri
Moderator

Ashok Lahiri posed several questions for the panelists. In spending more on social protection in the pandemic, would we be shortchanging health and education over the longer run, repeating the mistakes of the central planning years? Responding to the shortage of ICUs and ventilators, would we be taking away resources from primary and public health? Providing reasonable urban housing and making ration cards portable is a must, but are there ways of making the resulting urbanization more orderly?

Karthik Muralidharan
It is time to introduce an inclusive growth dividend for all

Karthik Muralidharan *first* pushed back on the notion that social protection is charity and distorts incentives to work. There is much empirical evidence to support the finding that *well-designed* social protection schemes create no conflict between efficiency and equity, particularly at low or subsistence levels. Instead, they can be the foundations of a broad-based recovery, for which they not only provide protection but can also enhance productivity. *Second*, Muralidharan responded to Lahiri's question on portability by noting that he thought it was actually a good thing, and that the government had done well to emphasize it during the pandemic. The idea of creating rural jobs to prevent migration may be well-intentioned, but it is misguided. Almost every development experience in history shows that urbanization is one of the strongest drivers of development through agglomeration externalities and more productive urban jobs. Building a nationally portable benefits architecture could be one of the greatest benefits coming out of the pandemic.

Third, Muralidharan discussed at some length the Inclusive Growth Dividend proposal, pegged at 1 percent of GDP per capita, presented in his 2019 IPF paper with Maitreesh Ghatak. Traditional Universal Basic Income proposals designed to eliminate poverty have gone nowhere because they are just too expensive fiscally, possibly requiring 3.5–10 percent of GDP. Winding down existing programs is difficult politically and ethically. The IGD is about less is more, pegged in their IPF paper as a supplement and not a substitute at ₹120 per month, which is about ₹500 for a household of four. The key design features include universality, payments to individuals, and payments to children below 16 years of age into their mother's account.

The IGD has much to recommend itself: as a dividend, it would be part of a *portfolio* of anti-poverty measures, but, like any dividend, not in itself enough to live on; it is inclusive since it is universal, though we could exclude people at the top; it is progressive because the amount would mean much more to the poor; it addresses spatial redistribution of concern to Finance Commissions because poorer states have more poor people; for the bottom 10 percent of the income distribution, it can raise monthly consumption by almost 20 percent; it brings in growth, so it is the sharing of national prosperity by all as the economy grows; it is rank preserving and hence socially more acceptable; it is too small to impact work incentives; it would empower females and improve intrahousehold targeting; and its regularity would encourage saving, crowd in credit, mitigate risk, and provide modest insurance. There is overwhelming evidence from microstudies that all this would alleviate poverty.

The IGD would also enhance state capacity by helping clean up the country's social protection plumbing and ensuring that *Jan Dhan* accounts were operational. As importantly, when the state is assuredly able to transfer a benefit every month to every citizen, it would enhance state credibility. Credible state capacity can be used not only in future crises but also for other kinds of policy reforms requiring compensation or transient protection. Financing an IGD through some combination of revenue, expenditure reduction, borrowing, or printing money would not spook bond markets if we could show that an IGD's high social return would actually support a broad-based recovery in a time of depressed demand. Most importantly, an IGD would create a sense of social solidarity in these pandemic times and give true meaning to the government's slogan of *Sabka Saath, Sabka Vikas, Sabka Vishwas.* Just as MGNREGS remains the signal achievement of the UPA government, so could an IGD become the signal contribution of the NDA government.

Renana Jhabvala

Basic income transfers work, convert MGNREGS into a pure cash transfer, and redesign safety nets to ensure better performance

Renana Jhabvala noted that had a basic income transfer mechanism been in place prior to the pandemic, we might have avoided some of the worst problems that the returning migrants faced. She reported on SEWA's large, successful basic income pilot in Madhya Pradesh, involving about 12,000 persons who were given ₹300 each, with children receiving ₹150 each. The results showed that nutrition, health, and education improved, there was no increase in alcoholism, and there was an increase in incomes as people started saving and investing a part of their basic income in income-generating assets. Almost 50 percent of the recipients were better off after five years. So, the Muralidharan-Ghatak proposal for an IGD should be fully endorsed. On MGNREGS, Jhabvala was convinced that it should be transformed into a pure cash transfer program since its beneficial effects did not come from the output of the work done by participants, but from the income they earned.

Jhabvala noted that the pandemic had revealed many fault lines in our safety nets. On ration cards, the problem she saw was not just portability, but, for example, an urban migrant trying to use her ration card when the card was already in use by her family in the village. Could she keep one part of the card and the other remain with her family? On *Jan Dhan*, the problem was that many people in rural areas, particularly the very poor, did not have them, or they were not being used, or they were non-operational. She also flagged the issue of unorganized informal sector workers who are not registered with anyone, making it difficult to cover them through any protection scheme. A glaring example was urban construction workers, many of whom are migrants. Although each state has a construction or building workers fund with crores in it, the funds typically lie unused since the workers are not registered or their registrations are allowed to expire.

T. V. Somanathan

Government quickly deployed multiple safety nets focusing on food and some cash transfers to good effect

T. V. Somanathan began by listing the safety nets that the government launched early on. These included free food grains and pulses to cover some 800 million people, initially for three months and then extended for another five; cash transfers into *Jan Dhan* accounts for some 200 million women; cash for three LPG cylinders per household transferred to 8 million women; cash transferred into the provident fund accounts of 7.8 million enterprises for workers with wages below ₹15,000; an advance release to registered farmers of the quarterly payments under the *PM Kisan Yojana*; ₹4,000 crore disbursed by liberalizing the use of the Building Workers' Funds; and a big increase in the MGNREGS budget provision. Concerning food for migrants, starting March 15, 2020, states were given three months of unlimited access to food grains on credit and, in May, state food quotas were further increased by 10 percent, equivalent to the entitlement for an additional 80 million people.

Somanathan reported on an April–June 2020, 15-state telephone survey by the consulting firm Dalberg on the efficacy of government entitlements for low-income, BPL households. Some 91 percent of the households surveyed had received PDS food grains, and of the 9 percent not covered, some 48 percent had received free or subsidized grain from the state government. Some 84 percent of the households surveyed had received cash from at least one scheme. For *Jan Dhan*, while there were inoperative accounts, some 72 percent of those surveyed had received a transfer in the account of a woman in the family. Somanathan also reported superior results for *Jan Dhan* and *Ujjwala* transfers and PDS coverage for Scheduled Castes and Scheduled Tribes. He noted that PDS and India's food stocks, with all their inefficiencies, had turned out to be a lifeline in the crisis so far.

Responding to Abhijit Banerjee's point about migrants, Somanathan reiterated the liberal access to food grain stocks given to states. Banerjee's point about urban housing for migrant workers had been recognized. Pilots were being launched to convert available public housing into rental housing tenements operated by the private sector, and to get new government or private land approved by municipalities for such construction. He noted that the One-Nation-One-Ration Card scheme provided for a simple *Aadhaar*-based way of splitting ration cards digitally. MGNREGS did not actually require domicile, just a job card. Somanathan found Jhabvala's suggestion of converting MGNREGS into a cash transfer scheme very interesting and thought that it deserved greater study. But doing so would lose the self-targeting of MGNREGS.

On IGD and a universal basic income, Somanathan noted that however you term it, it is in the end a *subsidy*, and we already have a universal basic subsidy in the form of food, which a large portion of the population is entitled to. He noted that Muralidharan was not advocating winding down PDS before deploying an IGD, so a UBI or IGD would be quite expensive. On the political economy of a UBI/IGD, he felt that had such a system been in place say on March 22, 2020, it would simply not have been acceptable politically for the government to tell people to go ahead and use the ongoing UBI to cope with the crisis as it unfolded. Governments are expected to respond with something more than what is already in place. So the case for an IGD or UBI should not be linked to calamities, but must stand on its own merits. And the higher are existing transfers, the less fiscal room there would be in an emergency.

On a bigger fiscal stimulus and how bond markets and credit rating agencies might view it, Somanathan agreed that in principle they should look at both the stimulus funding in the numerator and the potential GDP impact in the denominator, but the latter is probabilistic and uncertain, whereas the numerator is fully known and public. In dealing with hard-nosed analysts, it is not obvious that they factor in potential GDP impacts as readily. If they did, of course, the job of government would be easier.

Finally, on the question of whether the fiscal response was adequate so far, he noted that fiscal authorities have a choice of announcing a big package upfront without knowing how long the crisis may last or what resources may be needed, or calibrating their response gradually as the situation evolves. The government had clearly chosen the latter approach and not the former. There were so many unknowns in this situation, and it was important to take in more information to ensure that limited resources were being used optimally. In the short run, as of July 2020, there appears to be a substantial increase in the precautionary demand for money as households remain apprehensive about the future, so they may not necessarily spend more if more was transferred into their accounts.

Open Discussion with the Roundtable Panelists

The remarks by the four panelists were followed by a rich discussion led by **Ashok Lahiri** with opening questions on subsidies versus transfers and PDS reforms; **Pranab Bardhan** on labor laws for migrants, the urbanization of poverty, and the undesirability of converting MGNREGS into a cash transfer program; **Raghuram Rajan** on keeping relief, repair, and stimulus separate in what is not a standard recession-like situation, and why precautionary household savings may be going up because the government had not committed to longer term support; **Raghavan Srinivasan** on Tamil Nadu's experience with the PDS during the crisis; **Manoj Panda** on the possibility of a self-targeting scheme for urban India similar to MGNREGS; **Santanu Pramanik** on results from the NCAER Delhi Coronavirus Telephone Survey showing urban income losses as more severe than rural, and the BPL-focused sample of the Dalberg survey, which needed to be kept in mind in interpreting their results; **Raghupati Cavale** on the sociology of migrant labor and how this crisis may lead to more job automation; **Vijay Joshi** on not drawing too sharp a contrast between relief, repair, and stimulus, and the role of helicopter money in coming out of the pandemic; and finally, closing comebacks from **Karthik Muralidharan**, **Renana Jhabvala**, and **T. V. Somanathan**.

For the full flavor of the richness of this roundtable discussion, we invite you to view the video of this session using the links mentioned in the box below.

To view the video of this IPF Roundtable, please scan this QR code or use the following URL: https://www.youtube.com/watch?v=PBFW2W382GM

Moderator

SHEKHAR SHAH
NCAER

Panelists

B. J. PANDA
Bhartiya Janata Party

JAHANGIR AZIZ
JPMorgan Chase

ROHINI SOMANATHAN
Delhi School of Economics

ANANTH NARAYAN
SP Jain Institute of Management & Research

JUNAID AHMAD
World Bank

IPF 2020 POLICY ROUNDTABLE 2

What Do the Pandemic and India's Shutdowns Teach Us about Meeting India's Economic Growth and Jobs Challenges?*

Introduction

The second of two IPF Roundtables, and the final, closing session of the IPF 2020, brought together five eminent panelists for nearly two hours to explore the lessons from the first four months of the Coronavirus pandemic. Their focus was on what the pandemic had taught us so far on

* The Editors are grateful to Madhura Dasgupta at NCAER for her notes on this IPF Roundtable.

how to address India's twin challenges of creating more and better jobs and faster economic growth against the immediate priorities of relief, recovery, and rebuilding. After their initial remarks, the panelists were joined in a lively discussion by other roundtable participants. This is a short summary of the roundtable. For a more complete rendition, please view the session video hyperlinked at the end of this summary.

Shekhar Shah
Moderator

Shekhar Shah kicked off the Policy Roundtable by posing several key questions to the panel: What do we already know about how to deal with the impact of this unprecedented economic and health crisis India was going through and the fault lines it has exposed? How will this deeper understanding of the workings of the economy in crisis help us meet these challenges when we return back to more normal times? How will it help us build back better?

B. J. Panda
In this unprecedented crisis, we first prioritized lives over jobs

Baijayant Panda emphasized that no one in living memory had dealt with a pandemic of these proportions. Early actions had to be quick even when information and knowledge were scarce. The government initially prioritized lives over jobs in shutting down quickly, combining it with many exhortations from the Prime Minister on down about the behavior change needed so that the lockdowns could be ended sooner rather than later. Everyone knew that the lockdowns would cause a lot of disruption. Early on, the government announced the first tranche of ₹1.75 lakh crores of support aimed at the bottom of the pyramid. The JAM trilogy made it possible to transfer money into *Jan Dhan* accounts for some 22 million migrant workers, and eventually to some 80 million rural women. Free rations were made available, initially for three months, and then extended to November 2020. These measures staved off the immediate consequences of job losses due to the lockdowns.

The policy gears shifted within five to six weeks to a focus on economic recovery. We were already seeing signs of revival in many areas. On the initial plight of returning rural migrants that media attention highlighted, there was a lot that was done on food and cash transfers by the government and others, and eventually on special trains, and all of this averted a much bigger calamity arising out of urban job losses. MGNREGS support helped in rural areas. We still have a long haul ahead given the depth of the disruption that India, and every other country in the world, had faced up until July 2020. But there was evidence to show that we will have a V-shaped economic recovery with a rapid rebound, and we are all hopeful that it would happen sooner rather than later.

Jahangir Aziz
A very different emerging markets crisis and its impact

Jahangir Aziz spoke of the growth outlook for emerging market economies (EMEs) and the policy framework needed for recovery, and how these might relate to India's prospects. He also spoke about India's fiscal response against the backdrop of what other countries were doing. He shared his growth projections for developed countries and EMEs, and highlighted the role of China's positive growth in 2020 in bringing up the EME numbers, the only country doing so. He spoke of a production-led recovery in China and a consumption-led recovery in the US and the Eurozone. Although he too predicted a V-shaped fiscal 2021 recovery, the concern was about nominal GDP *levels*. The world is likely to have lost about $3.3 trillion in nominal GDP by the end of fiscal 2021, roughly the size of the Indian economy. India will suffer its own loss of GDP, and the policy response will have to be commensurate with the size of this shock.

Policymakers in emerging markets have hesitated in responding. This was because the current crisis was different from almost all previous EME crises, including the 2013 taper tantrum. He drew the contrast with the past when economies had overheated and invited sudden stops. Policymakers then tightened monetary and fiscal policies in an attempt to repair damaged balance sheets for firms and households as a precondition for recovery, and they carried out structural reforms that had become politically more acceptable. In contrast, the current crisis almost everywhere had been preceded by slowdowns, certainly the case for India in January 2020, and rather than damaged balance sheets leading to an economic crisis, the sequence had been reversed. EME policymakers needed to reverse course on their policy responses to address this different crisis, something they were not used to. Central banks almost everywhere had stepped forward by loosening monetary policy and lowering interest rates, even in the face of sharply depreciating currencies, but the fiscal response had been much more hesitant. India faced a challenging fiscal situation. It needed to balance its fiscal response to the pandemic between doing too little too late and doing too much. The nature of the fiscal policy response also had to be calibrated carefully to be meaningful in repairing household and enterprise balance sheets. This Aziz saw as the major challenge facing policymakers in India during the rest of 2020 and into 2021.

Rohini Somanathan
COVID-19 notes from the field and their lessons for policymakers

Rohini Somanathan brought the discussion down to the ground-level realities of how the pandemic had impacted poor people. While attention gets focused on the big macroeconomic variables and measurable metrics of economic performance, what is also important in crises are institutions of the state, society, and community that promote or hinder economic and social interactions. That was the motivation for the work she was reporting on based on the COVID-19 vignettes she and her team had been assembling of ordinary people impacted by the crisis. She spoke of three distinct lessons, which she hoped would help meet the challenges on policy and program design in the coming months and then into the medium and longer term.

First, the economy-level trade-offs that we talk about between lives and livelihoods in a pandemic do not quite translate that way for many who become vulnerable in a crisis. They suffer heightened risks both on their lives and livelihoods, having already possibly lost their jobs or informal occupations, and therefore their means of survival. There was no trade-off for these people, and not recognizing this and planning for it is a failure of policy. This was true particularly for migrants. *Second*, trust in state and local governments and community organizations really matters. Kerala stands out for this, with the extraordinary level of trust all the way from the Chief Minister, speaking to citizens every day, down to community organizations such as those serving free meals to migrants and supplying hospitals. This was all happening without any top-down guidance, there was no stigma attached to desperation, and people really trusted government. *Third*, safety nets were really not available in the early stages or were inappropriate. Supplying rice and wheat was fine, but what can you do when you have nowhere to cook and no food outlets that were open? Community kitchens were the only solutions.

Shortages of things like testing kits led to innovation among the better trained civil service officers, for example, deploying limited testing kits at points of entry at major bus depots to maximize the community value of testing. Unfortunately, the bureaucracy was also responsible for too many and too frequent changes of policy, making even simple activities subject to avoidable uncertainty, especially for people least able to deal with that uncertainty. Somanathan in closing came back to the importance of institutions that promote trust, pointing out that if we want to trust the state and each other, then the first thing is to be honest about data, both measuring accurately and sharing the data quickly, and she wished she saw more of that.

Ananth Narayan
Four priorities for reform that have been known well before the pandemic

Ananth Narayan noted that the lessons on jobs and growth were known well before the pandemic, and going back to them would be worth it. For starters, he fully agreed with Rohini Somanathan on the two high-level issues that needed attention: complete truth on data and promoting the empowerment of experts and those who had solutions. These were prior requirements for any serious progress on growth and a jobs strategy. He saw a lot of pain ahead: by some estimates, some 20 percent of India's 63 million MSMEs faced existential crisis, and Narayan saw non-performing assets at financial institutions rising to 18–20 percent of advances. In the short term, spending on MGNREGS and food security were good things, and the monsoon was likely to be good, so that rural demand would pick up. The problem areas were MSMEs and firms. Credit guarantees may not be enough; more relief for the top line and the bottom line was required.

Narayan pointed to four key areas that needed attention if we are to boost growth and jobs. *First*, the financial system needs urgent attention at every level, including on governance, balance sheets, and markets. Nonbank financial institutions have not gone through the needed asset quality review, the overhang of NPAs is too large for the bankruptcy system to handle, and we need a one-time solution of a bad bank or a Troubled Asset Relief Program. And we need to take steps to ensure that this does not repeat all over again. *Second*, important sectors of the economy such as power, shipping, telecom, real estate, and airlines are saddled with chronic stresses, and kicking the can down the road should stop. For both these priorities, the messes need to be cleared out, though that in itself will not create jobs and output growth.

Third, to actually create job growth, we simply have to improve the investment climate in India and the ease of doing business. Supply chains moving out to China should not have India low down on the list as possible destinations, but at the top. This involves all the lessons we know well already, including labor and land reforms, legal reforms, and better contract enforcement. *Fourth*, we simply do not know what jobs will look like in the next 5–15 years. One thing we can learn from the pandemic is that we need to equip our children with quality education, quality health care, and quality nutrition so that they can tackle the challenges that will be out there. In closing, Narayan reiterated the importance of two things: more transparency and accuracy in the data on the economy so that there is the evidence to take good decisions, and an empowerment of experts who can work with the political leadership and a competent bureaucracy to design, implement, monitor, and adapt the hard reforms that are needed to both come out of the pandemic and advance on the challenges of jobs and growth.

Junaid Ahmad
India's future lies in its cities and in fiscal federalism

Junaid Ahmad, speaking for himself as a professional development economist, said that the *first* and most important lesson he had learnt from the pandemic was that the state, as a generic term for government, had now become much more important, and it must change the way it works. For example, the principles of macroeconomics that applied in the past do not necessarily apply now, including when looking at measures like fiscal deficits, where governments need to be much bolder.

Second, it is a mistake to believe that the pandemic was over. Unless COVID-19 is stopped in the large urban metros of India, it will not be possible to unlock India safely. For this to happen, we need a modern, responsive, and accountable urban public health system. COVID-19 has revealed many fault lines, and urban is one of them. India is still seeking an urban political economy, something that many other large cities elsewhere possess in the persons of powerful mayors or city managers. City management needs to be integrated horizontally at the local level so that accountability can also be promoted. Instead, we have vertical silos that try to manage cities and make a well-functioning, integrated urban public health system difficult. And without such a system, we cannot have good health surveillance, good community responses, good isolation practices, and good health outcomes in pandemic or normal times.

Third, taking from the urban fault lines, India needs to accelerate its move to greater federalism, with states and local governments playing a much bigger role in economic growth and job creation. This requires greater decision-making powers at that level, and commensurately greater local accountability that changes the relationship between the citizen and the state. Linked to federalism is the rethinking of India's social protection system, which needs to become pan-India, also covering its urban areas. We need to protect the urban informal worker. Finally, turning to the Bretton Woods and other global institutions, Ahmad noted the need to rethink these institutions so that they can proactively anticipate global shocks, such as pandemics and climate change, and help plan for them, rather than retroactively respond to them country by country after the shocks have hit.

Open Discussion with the Roundtable Panelists

The remarks by the five panelists were followed by a rich discussion led by **Shekhar Shah** with the roundtable participants, with prominent questions and interventions by **Sudipto Mundle** on macroeconomic and growth forecasts; **Karthik Muralidharan** on protocols for fiscal spending that the Bretton Woods institutions might put out so that there is a unified understanding of what is acceptable in such situations and the need for providing additional fiscal resources to states that lack not only capacity but also resources; **Raghuram Rajan** on the size of the additional fiscal stimulus in India when comparing it with what other countries were doing; **Pranab Bardhan** on the dissonance between the images and vignettes from the ground and the data put out by public authorities; **Rajeswari Sengupta** on debt dynamics and fiscal pressures and how to avoid kicking the can down the road on key reforms; **Soumya Kanti Ghosh** on the prospects for a rural-led recovery; and **Anupam Khanna** on localized unlocking opportunities that are not being explored.

The session ended with closing remarks on the roundtable and the IPF 2020, deep appreciation for the team at NCAER that put together this virtual version of the IPF 2020 for the first time in 17 years, and farewells to all participants by the IPF Editors, **Shekhar Shah, Karthik Muralidharan,** and **Barry Bosworth.**

For the full flavor of the richness of this roundtable discussion, we invite you to view the video of this session using the links mentioned in the box below.

To view the video of this IPF Roundtable, please scan this QR code or use the following URL
https://www.youtube.com/watch?v=ESWtVIgymFQ

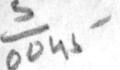